ON SIX ${C}$ONTINENTS

ON SIX CONTINENTS

A LIFE IN CANADA'S FOREIGN SERVICE

1966-2002

JAMES BARTLEMAN

A DOUGLAS GIBSON BOOK

M&S

National Library of Canada Cataloguing in Publication

Bartleman, James, 1939-
On six continents : a life in Canada's foreign service, 1966-2002 / James Bartleman.

Includes bibliographical references.
ISBN 0-7710-1090-7

1. Bartleman, James, 1939-   2. Lieutenant governors–Ontario–Biography.
3. Ambassadors–Canada–Biography. 4. Ojibwa Indians–Ontario–Biography. I. Title.

FC636.B37A3 2004   971.064'092   C2003-905346-6

We acknowledge the financial support of the Government of Canada through the
Book Publishing Industry Development Program and that of the Government of
Ontario through the Ontario Media Development Corporation's Ontario Book
Initiative. We further acknowledge the support of the Canada Council for the Arts
and the Ontario Arts Council for our publishing program.

Typeset in Bembo by M&S, Toronto
Printed and bound in Canada

This book is printed on acid-free paper that is
100% ancient forest friendly (100% post-consumer recycled)

A Douglas Gibson book

McClelland & Stewart Ltd.
The Canadian Publishers
481 University Avenue
Toronto, Ontario
M5G 2E9
www.mcclelland.com

1   2   3   4   5   08   07   06   05   04

For the members of Canada's Foreign Service
and their long-suffering families

Acknowledgements

Thank you to Marie-Jeanne and Alain, Sandra Black, Allan Bowker, Micheline Roche O'Neal, Thomas O'Neal, Arthur Menzies, Richard Gorham, and the late Arthur Blanchette. Thanks also to Lewis MacKenzie for reviewing the chapter on Bosnia.

Contents

Part Two: The Ambassador 1981-2002

ON SIX CONTINENTS

Prologue

I first saw Dhaka on a sweltering afternoon in June 1972. The two-hour flight from Bangkok over Burma and the Bay of Bengal gave me time to sit back in air-conditioned comfort and feel that everything was going my way. Here I was, from the wrong side of the tracks in small-town Ontario, setting out at the age of thirty-two to open up the first Canadian diplomatic mission in Bangladesh. Life was good. Around me elegant flight attendants served exotic foods and supplied ice-cold beer in the luxury of Thai International business class.

Approaching landfall, the aircraft descended through black monsoon clouds until we could see the lush green delta of the Meghna, Ganges, and Bramaputra Rivers. From that far up, there were no signs of the recent catastrophes that had hit the new country of Bangladesh: the cyclone of 1970 that killed half a million people; the just-ended civil war against West Pakistan in which hundreds of thousands died; the massive smallpox epidemic that was still ravaging the population.

The landing at Dhaka International Airport was rough – the tarmac was still pockmarked with crudely repaired craters left over from the heavy bombing by the Indian air force the previous December. Workers rolled the airport's only functioning set of stairs up to the aircraft door and the petite attendant smiled as she opened the door to . . . another world. A stench of humid, sweet-and-sour air poured in, smothering the sterile air-conditioned comfort of the cabin. A mob of half-clad beggars waited, clamouring piteously for baksheesh, or charity, as I descended the rickety staircase. Some with hands but no feet hobbled on their knees, grabbing at my clothes. Others, with feet but no hands, stuck damp stumps of their festering limbs in my face. Their eyes were wild and their skin pitted with smallpox scars. Within seconds I was drenched in sweat.

There was no protocol officer to greet me, even though I was Canada's new acting high commissioner. In fact there were no officials of any sort present to keep order as I fought my way through packs of mendicants to the immigration counter and then to the baggage reception area. Once again I was besieged, this time by porters fighting among themselves to carry my one bag. I grabbed it myself and joined a half-dozen other expatriates competing for transport into the city. A solitary taxi waited at the exit. Watching all those old American war movies then paid off. Like Milo Minderbinder of *Catch-22* in wartime Italy, I pulled out a carton of American cigarettes and held it aloft as our safari-suited band of brothers bore down on the driver. I was the chosen one. The driver flashed me a smile, opened the back door, and, leaving the others behind, drove me to the only modern hotel in the city, the Intercontinental.

Afterwards, curious to learn more about this city that was now my new home, I made my way, fascinated and appalled, through the crowds that choked the roads and sidewalks day and night in Bangladesh's capital. The streets were filled with bicycle rickshaws decorated with hand-painted scenes from the civil war, pushcarts manned by sweating labourers, buses with more passengers on the roof than inside, wandering cattle, and wagons and stagecoaches drawn by skeletal horses. Overhead, tangles of wire cluttered the telephone poles and the sky was black with crows and, yes, vultures. Cloying smoke from the burning dried cow dung used for cooking hung in the air, mixing with the acrid smell of black exhaust fumes spewing from ill-maintained bus, truck, and car motors and the odour of tens of thousands of unwashed bodies.

Women modestly enveloped from head to foot in burkas, black garments with openings for the eyes and nose, and men dressed in dhotis, a type of skirt, thronged the thoroughfares. Mentally disabled people, often naked and filthy, competed with stray dogs foraging for food among the garbage heaps. In the absence of sanitary facilities, men and women, their mouths crimson from the juice of betel nuts, squatted in the gutters with as much dignity as they could muster. Others exposed the corpses of their loved ones on the sidewalks, begging for money to accord them a decent burial. In this, my initial encounter with South Asia, the colour, vibrancy, and authenticity of local life that I was later to discover were overwhelmed by poverty and human misery.

Beggars surrounded me just as they had at the airport. About five hundred metres from the hotel, I gave a small coin to a half-blind man crawling along on the sidewalk. Another, more robust, individual snatched it from him and a crowd sprang up clamouring for more. I turned and headed back to the hotel with the wretched of the earth following behind, howling. The wronged recipient of my bounty wobbled after me, crab-like, wailing that he had been robbed and appealing for another handout. I did not want to run – after all, I was Canada's acting high commissioner.

I walked faster. Somehow the beggar kept up. The crowd followed, hoping I would weaken and offer another coin that they could steal. I went faster but the half-blind beggar kept coming. The crowd stopped at the hotel property line but the poor unfortunate continued through. The uniformed doorkeeper opened the heavy glass door to let me in and slammed it in his face. Literally. I looked back – his face and body were squashed against the glass, his tongue hung from his open mouth, and his protruding eyes met mine. I went up to my comfortable room but did not sleep well that night, and not for many more to come. I had not counted on this when I joined Canada's foreign service.

PART ONE

THE APPRENTICE
1966–1981

I

Canada and New York

I was supposed to prostrate myself on the ground and crawl forward, face downwards, when meeting the King of Thailand. Afraid of ruining my one good suit, I simply bowed my head slightly and shook his hand.

I was not predestined to be a diplomat, just lucky. In the central Ontario village of Port Carling, Muskoka, where I spent my boyhood and youth in the 1940s and 1950s, the Bartleman family was at the bottom of the social order. Our first home was a tent near the dump. My mother was a Native from the local reserve who had lost her legal status as a Treaty Indian and was denied the right to live on the territory of her ancestors when she married a white man. My brother, two sisters, and I fitted into neither world when we were growing up and were subject to the petty racism of the time. My father was an unconventional character who could have been taken from a Mark Twain novel. He rode the rails across Canada as a hobo during the Depression, worked as a lumberjack, miner, steelworker, and casual labourer in the years before he drifted to Port Carling in 1946, close to the home reserve of my mother. He made no secret of his preference for Indians over white people, engaged in out-of-season fishing, and revelled in telling outrageous tall tales. To make matters worse, he was a vegetarian in a world where such eating habits were regarded as bizarre, an atheist in a deeply religious community, and a maker of homebrew so conscientious about the quality of his product that he spent much of his time sampling it – for testing purposes, he said – to the chagrin of our teetotalling neighbours. He made no effort to fit in and the locals treated him and our family accordingly.

For reasons beyond their control, neither of my parents had completed elementary school. As a child, I assumed that I would follow my father's footsteps and become a manual labourer. My introduction to the village school was not auspicious: a teacher forced me to repeat the initial year but provided neither a report card nor an oral assessment of my abilities to justify her decision. Faced with coping with six classes of students in one room, she had little time to evaluate the abilities of her individual charges. To my bitter disappointment, I was found wanting, even though, unlike most of my classmates, I already knew how to read and write.

In time, largely due to the efforts of my mother, the Bartlemans were accepted. My mother used her family-allowance cheques to purchase a dilapidated old house that we fixed up into a comfortable home. She then started working as a cleaning lady for summer residents, supplementing my father's wages with her earnings. My father, an honest and hard worker despite his free-spirited ways, eventually found permanent employment. My own after-school and summer jobs quickly taught me that unskilled work was difficult, boring, and poorly paid. Discovery of the village library widened my horizons. I had the good luck to encounter understanding teachers who balanced out indifferent and brutal ones and I began to do reasonably well academically. My big break came when an American millionaire befriended me, providing funding to permit me to complete high school and attend university, graduating from the University of Western Ontario in Honours History in June 1963. After spending a year as a backpacker in Europe, I returned to Canada to accept a position as a teacher at a high school in southwestern Ontario for the 1965-66 academic year.

The Foreign Service

What I really wanted to do, however, was to become a foreign-service officer. There was a certain aura around "The Department," or "External," as it was known until 1993 when its name was changed to Department of Foreign Affairs and International Trade. (I will refer to it as "Foreign Affairs" in this book.) It had been regarded as one of the senior, most prestigious ministries of government for much of Canada's history after Confederation; the prime minister himself had once held the portfolio. The cream of Canada's public servants of the preceding thirty years had either secured their start there or were still serving in its ranks. It was the department of Lester Pearson, winner of the Nobel Peace Prize; of Jules Léger, Canada's twenty-first governor general; of Norman Robertson, Hume Wrong, Escott Reid, Arthur Menzies, and Charles Ritchie – legendary figures of the glory years of Foreign Affairs and of Ottawa's mandarin class, who affirmed Canada's national sovereignty and place in the post-war world.

Entering the service was not easy. More than five thousand university graduates wrote qualifying examinations each fall: the top six hundred were interviewed over the winter months and usually no more than fifteen winners were offered jobs in the spring and started work the same summer. Prospects thus were not promising. However, I already had a job as a high-school teacher and was assured of fallback employment should my attempt to join fail. Hence I was in a relaxed mood on the November evening in 1965 when I entered the large examination room filled with some four hundred candidates at University College at the University of Western Ontario in London. I was the first to finish – always worrying – but scored high enough to be invited back for an interview.

In February 1966, after battling my way through a snowstorm from my distant place of work, I arrived thirty minutes late to meet an impatient interview board in London, its members anxious to wrap up its day's work and adjourn to a nearby hotel for a drink and a meal. I stumbled into the room, overcoat and hat covered with a thick layer of snow – an abominable snowman descending from the Himalayas – to present my reasons for being late, somehow spilling snow over the unsmiling chairperson. He stepped back in distaste as I nervously stammered out excuses and assured him that I was fine, thank you, rather than saying hello or asking how he was. Worse, I soon found myself embroiled in an argument with a board member who gave the impression that he was mortally offended at my opposition to the growing involvement of the United States in the Vietnam War. My chances of being accepted were ruined, I thought, not realizing that he was testing me to see how well I could defend my position. Then to the surprise of the examiners, I chose to discuss Native rights in Canada – of which they knew nothing and I only marginally more – rather than Quebec separatism when asked to reflect on the most important national issue facing Canada.

I received a job offer in April 1966. After comparing the advantages of being a high-school teacher in a remote part of Ontario for the rest of my life to those of joining the foreign service and seeing the world, I departed for Ottawa at the close of the school year in June to begin my diplomatic career.

Foreign Affairs in 1966

Despite my expectations, I found that the glory days of Foreign Affairs, now celebrated by nostalgic editorial writers and academics, were over by the time I reported for work. Certainly I detected no superhuman individuals wandering the halls of the East Block, the Langevin Block, or the five or six other buildings in downtown Ottawa that housed Canada's foreign-service elite until Foreign Affairs moved into its new home, the Pearson Building, in 1973. The three officers most cited for putting Canada on the post-war map, Hume Wrong, Lester Pearson, and Norman Robertson, were gone. Wrong had been dead for more than a decade. Lester Pearson was still around: he was our prime minister, but seemed to be more respected abroad than in Canada, where his foreign-policy triumphs were a decade old. Norman Robertson was still alive but deathly ill; I would occasionally see him in the Centre Block of Parliament as he carried out special advisory duties for his good friend and erstwhile rival, the prime minister.

Paul Martin, Sr., was foreign minister. Like all foreign ministers who followed Lester Pearson, he would labour in the shadow of Canada's only Nobel Peace Prize winner, whose accomplishments took on a mythic character with the passage of time. Marcel Cadieux was undersecretary, one of the best, despite spending most of his career in Ottawa, out of touch with the world outside of Washington, London, and Paris. The senior ranks were likewise a talented lot. They received the new recruits in their cluttered offices, desks overflowing with neglected papers marked with tags appealing for urgent attention, security cabinets bulging with files, and every available space adorned with enough kitsch from faraway places to do any garage sale proud. They would hitch up their suspenders, and take one last puff on the pipe every self-respecting officer seemed to possess in those days.

To us they would, of course, provide their views on Canadian foreign policy. Each in his own way would describe his specific duties and Canada's place in the world as seen from the perspective of his division or bureau. The sum of these parts did not, however, a whole make. Nobody, not even the undersecretary, was able to say if Canada had an overriding goal or goals in its foreign policy. I had the impression that no one worried too much about the matter, since the unspoken assumption was that the United States would do the worrying for us. Washington would defend us to protect itself and would ensure our economic well-being by providing a huge and stable market for our exports. And in the beneficent American shadow, Canada would have the luxury of choosing niche areas for foreign-policy attention, promoting good causes such as peacekeeping and environmental protection. Not much would change in the years to come.

With little prompting, the elders would tell stories of first postings, of eccentric ambassadors, of exotic capitals in areas off the beaten path, of fascinating people, of official visits gone wrong, of executive assistants acting as tyrants on borrowed power, of past triumphs, of occasional failures, of how their families coped, and of dangerous or funny events – just as I, in turn, am doing in this book. Consciously or not, they were describing their transitions from junior officers in small posts having the time of their lives to senior diplomats in major missions putting into practice decades of apprenticeship. For in those days, that is how officers learned their trade. Formal training did not exist as it does today; new officers were expected to pick up the art of diplomacy largely through a process of osmosis. And these sessions with experienced colleagues constituted the best training anyone could have for the profession of foreign-service officer – and perhaps for life in general.

The class of 1966 was larger than those of the past, which probably allowed me to make the cut. It was also different. For the first time, a large contingent of Quebecers and a high proportion of women had been hired. From the 1920s to the mid-1950s, recruits were generalist graduates in the humanities, often educated overseas, many of them "sons of the manse" if anglophone, or "sons of the notarial office" if francophone. The wave of outstanding Second World War veterans who had dominated the recruitment in the immediate post-war period and who were in control of Foreign Affairs in 1966 was largely drawn from this world and was similarly educated. In the class of 1966, there was a sprinkling of Oxford and Harvard graduates, but the majority were Canadian-educated lawyers, economists, and historians. Only a handful came from Canada's establishment. Most of us came from farming and middle-class families, and from working-class families such as mine.

There were also, I suspect, more entrants than before who were able to speak both French and English, to do business in difficult foreign languages such as Russian and Chinese, and to conduct negotiations in specialized subjects of growing importance to Canada such as trade and developmental policy. The class proved to be an exceptional one, with many moving to the highest ranks of the public service during their careers. Raymond Chrétien (ambassador to Washington and Paris), Gordon Smith (ambassador to NATO and to the European Union and undersecretary of state), Margaret Catley (president of the Canadian International Development Agency [CIDA]) and John Weeks (ambassador to the General Conference of the General Agreement on Tariffs and Trade [GATT] and later to the World Trade Organization [WTO]) were four among many stars. Margaret Catley would prove to be a trailblazer, defying the old guard to fire her when she married as custom demanded; they backed down and she was allowed to keep her job, setting a precedent for other women officers.

For all of us, it was a time of optimism. The pay was poor but we were young and the prospects for adventure and promotion more promising than they had been for years – and better than they would be for the next generation of foreign-service officers. The government was just beginning its rapid expansion at home and abroad and new embassies were being opened every year. Foreign Affairs was still one of the two or three most influential departments in town, together with Finance and the Privy Council Office, the department of the prime minister. Star performers from Foreign Affairs were still being recruited to staff deputy-minister positions elsewhere in the bureaucracy. Canada's place in the world, while starting its downward slide, was still high in this era when Canada had a decent-sized military, when the Europeans were building their new institutional structures, when colonies in the Third World were in the process of achieving their independence, and when newly industrializing countries such as South Korea, Malaysia, Singapore, Mexico, and Brazil had not started their economic takeoff.

Of course, in Foreign Affairs everything was not rosy, neither in its days of glory, nor when I joined. There were a few in our ranks, as there were buried here and there among the old-timers, who drew the wrong lessons from gaining entry, and considered themselves to be innately superior to other members of the human race, especially to colleagues from other departments. In an opinion shared only by themselves, they intimated to other lesser beings that foreign-service officers were the brightest, the best, and Canada's natural leaders at home and abroad. Many of these officers, after reaching the rank of ambassador, would be the ones who would forget their origins and exploit the personnel provided by the Canadian taxpayers to staff their official residences. People treated in this way do not forget. The cooks and maids, often recruited from Third World countries, would usually be too frightened for their jobs ever to complain. The officials they snubbed in Ottawa, however, would exact their revenge on everyone for the supercilious behaviour of a few when Foreign Affairs fell on hard times in the coming decades and needed the help of other government departments.

There were other problems. Few of the older officers were bilingual. Previous administrations had not thought it essential to provide the necessary training. Some of the most talented officers from their generation (Herbert Norman, John Holmes, and John Watkins), had been hounded to death or out the door after allegations of "character weakness" or treason by the RCMP Security Service (the precursor of the Canadian Security Intelligence Service [CSIS]) or by witch-hunting American congressmen. There were few women among the old-timers; many of the handful who had joined over the years had been forced to resign when they married. A similar fate awaited the gifted women officers who joined with me; most would leave. Homosexuals knew that they had to keep their sexual orientation secret lest they be hunted down. Many would be outed, told their security clearances would be revoked, and urged to resign by senior management. This was euphemistically called "counselling out." Fortunately for me, no one knew that my father, while never a communist, in a fit of rebellious Depression-era romantic enthusiasm had named me James Karl after Karl Marx. There were no African or Asian Canadians in the officer ranks. And, as far as I could see, I was the only aboriginal Canadian.

In 1966, all unilingual recruits were automatically sent on training to learn the other official language. All except me, that is. Reporting for work in early July, I expected to go for four or five months of intensive training with the other unilingual anglophones. A personnel officer told me, however, that my records indicated I was bilingual: there would be no language training for me. I could not speak French, but neither, it transpired, could the board members who interviewed me in February. Someone had asked me a question in halting French and no one had understood my muttered response, which they must have assumed was in the other official language. They marked me down as French-speaking.

I was told to report to the Langevin Block as desk officer for Belgium, the Netherlands, Luxembourg, and Switzerland, to start work as the replacement for an officer who had just departed on posting. Disappointment at not being sent to study French was more than offset by the prospect of being thrust into a weighty job involving the management of relations with no fewer than four major countries! Unfortunately, the countries in question were not quite as important as I originally believed, and their ties with Canada, while excellent, were so devoid of official content that I was not called upon to do anything, not even answer a letter from the public, in my time in the division. I traded stories with two other junior officers, John Paynter and Bob Blackburn, with whom I shared one small office and who would become firm friends. John, who was among the most talented members of the class of 1966, died at a tragically young age when serving as ambassador to China in the 1990s, and Bob eventually left the foreign service for a senior position in the private sector.

The rest of my time was spent reading files, doing research on issues that might arise, and listening to the stories of the officers of the division doing their part to help induct neophytes into Holy Orders, as it was so regarded. The senior officers were an all-star cast. James George, later high commissioner to India and ambassador to Iran, and replaced over the summer by John Halstead, a future ambassador to Germany and to NATO, directed the work of the division from behind a green velvet-covered door with a polished brass plaque proclaiming that the occupant was postmaster general. There had, it seemed, been no changes to the Langevin Block since Foreign Affairs eased out post-office management decades earlier. Blair Seaborn, later a senior deputy minister in Ottawa for many years, was deputy director for the East European section. Blair had previously been head of Canada's mission to the International Commission for Supervision and Control in Vietnam, where he played a major role acting as an intermediary for the United States government with the North Vietnamese government in trying to dissuade Hanoi from pursuing their full-scale offensives against South Vietnam. Full details of his role would come out later, but as a conscientious diplomat he breathed not a word of his role, at least not to his curious and garrulous junior colleagues.

Pierre Dumas was the deputy director for Western Europe. He was a close friend of Pierre Trudeau, which did not hurt his prospects in future years when he successfully put his name forward to be ambassador to Czechoslovakia and the Vatican. He was replaced by Claude Roquet, who later left Foreign Affairs to join the Quebec public service, eventually becoming Quebec's agent general in Paris. Claude was my supervisor, and hence responsible for writing my first rating report. In those days, managers did not have to show these reports to their juniors. Instead, they would call us into their offices, smile enigmatically, and read selectively from their evaluations. He told me only good things about my performance, of course. I shook his hand gratefully and left for my next assignment when the time came. Imagine my distress, therefore, when my personnel officer called me in to tell me in a tone of great disapproval that Claude Roquet had actually written that I was guilty of an "excess of enthusiasm and initiative" in the performance of my duties. This would not do, he warned me. I had traditions to uphold. I left his office chastised, determined to pay no attention to such ridiculous injunctions, but puzzled as to how it had been possible for me to display such qualities when I had done nothing of consequence throughout my assignment.

The United Nations
In the fall of 1966, a personnel officer handed me a red diplomatic passport and posted me on temporary duty to the Canadian permanent mission to the United Nations in New York as an advisor to the Canadian delegation of the General Assembly. At last I would have something important to do. Alas, the function of advisor, I discovered, had nothing to do with providing advice. My role was limited to trailing along behind a more experienced officer as a type of assistant, attending countless committee meetings as a note-taker, and drafting reports for headquarters that would be torn apart and redrafted by a succession of more senior officers. Each, it seemed, took malicious pleasure in searching out elusive split infinitives, run-on sentences, and dreaded Americanisms in spellings of words for which good British versions existed. The officer to whom I was assigned was important enough to have two advisors. Another junior officer and I accompanied our senior colleague to meetings of the fourth committee on decolonization and scribbled

furiously, taking down inane as well as pertinent points from long-winded speeches, the passion of all delegates to the United Nations. We did not dare stop writing: our chain-smoking superior would detect any let-up and hiss at us to keep scrawling.

The New York posting did, however, give me the chance to watch the Canadian decision-making process in action. Every morning, the permanent representative, George Ignatieff, one of the most senior and respected officers in Foreign Affairs, held a staff meeting. There, members of the permanent mission, delegates named by the government for the session, visiting members of Parliament, and lowly misnamed advisors would assemble to plan the work of the day. Decolonization issues, such as coping with the unilateral declaration of independence by Ian Smith in Rhodesia and the struggle for independence of the people of Southwest Africa (the future Namibia), were high on the agenda. Beijing's demand that it, rather than Taipei, should represent China at the U.N. was, however, the most contentious subject around the conference table.

Pierre Trudeau, then parliamentary secretary to Prime Minister Lester Pearson and a delegate to the annual General Assembly session, argued strongly for moving Canada's position from a vote "against" to an "abstention," which would represent a major foreign-policy change for Canada in those Cold War days. Foreign Affairs Minister Paul Martin disagreed, concerned at the reaction of Washington. I watched Trudeau lobby the Liberal members of Parliament on the delegation one by one. He then contacted Prime Minister Pearson, and instructions came from Ottawa for Canada to change its position.

As note-taker, I was assigned a seat at the Canadian table on the floor of the General Assembly, together with the permanent representative and deputy permanent representative. At the time of the vote, I prepared to push the button for "abstention" when the deputy permanent representative, who had not kept up with the latest developments, brushed my hand aside and pushed the "no" button. Trudeau's grim smile betrayed his fury but he said nothing. Fortunately, the vote had to be taken again for technical reasons. We then registered our abstention, a major milestone in Canada's move to support Beijing's membership in the U.N. and to recognize mainland China rather than Taiwan as the legitimate representative of the Chinese people internationally.

As it happened, Trudeau's room was next to mine at the Barclay Hotel and we often walked together to the offices of the Canadian mission. He was fascinated by foreign travel, told me some of his adventures as a backpacker, and was interested in my experiences in Europe a year earlier. We once shared a taxi to a diplomatic reception hosted by a Canadian diplomat. On arrival at seven in the evening, we were greeted by a remarkable scene of revelry and debauch. The host and several of the guests were so inebriated that they were on their hands and knees on the floor, laughing hysterically for no particular reason.

"We always have the best parties here," gushed one of the first people we met. Trudeau, for whom self-discipline was one of the highest virtues, was distinctly uncomfortable and left after a few minutes. I, naturally, remained to continue my wide-eyed education on how to be a diplomat. The behaviour of the host, I would later discover, was not typical of diplomats as a class. Never again, in more than thirty-five years in Canada's foreign service, would I attend a diplomatic function with such an atmosphere. Most were staid, even boring affairs designed to promote a specific national interest – trade, culture, or politics – and the consumption of alcoholic beverages was modest. This one drunken party in the fall of 1967 was to be historically significant, and damaging. I believe that his experience that evening in New York was one of the reasons Pierre Trudeau was so dismissive of Canada's foreign service after he became prime minister.

I was to run into Trudeau from time to time in my foreign-service career. The first several times, when he was minister of justice, he would stop to chat or cross the street to catch up on the latest news. I once even had the privilege of intervening with House of Commons security guards who were seeking to eject him from the building, not recognizing Canada's newly appointed justice minister, clad in shorts and sandals, trying to reach his office on a Saturday morning. After he became prime minister, the famous Trudeau forgetfulness for names and faces took over, and he would look at me blankly whenever we were introduced – obviously I had not made much of an impression. The last time I saw him was at a lunch hosted by Prime Minister Chrétien at 24 Sussex Drive in June 1994 for the visiting president of the European Commission, Jacques Delors. He was enjoying a green old age, as full of intellectual curiosity about the world as ever and destined to live another six years before, shattered by the death of his youngest son, depression and death overtook him.

Most advisors, myself included, had never been to New York, and we took full advantage of the free tickets available from the U.N. hospitality section. In the evenings, if there was time after committee meetings, we would hurry to take in Broadway shows or the opera. Whenever we could, we gathered to trade accounts of our daily adventures in a hospitality room set up for the use of our delegation in the hotel. There, friendships were forged that would last a lifetime. Often accompanied by members of Parliament, we would visit Greenwich Village for late-night meals. It was also the pre-Christmas rush in New York and there was excitement in the air. And not just excitement. The Barclay Hotel was located opposite a large department store which played the same side of a record of Christmas music over and over again for an entire month, driving me to distraction. I visited the store and asked them to change it; the management obliged, playing the other side non-stop for the next month.

Sundays I spent exploring the city, fascinated by the huge disparities in living standards of New Yorkers – wealth in Manhattan and urban decay in large swathes of Harlem. I had known poverty as a child, growing up on the wrong side of the tracks in rural Ontario. But what I saw in New York was of a different order: an urban squalor of uncollected garbage, old mattresses and sofas thrown negligently into backyards, and streets filled with the loitering and unemployed. President Johnson had launched his project for the "Great Society" to bring hope to this underclass. But the war in Vietnam was consuming the wealth of the country, and neglected American cities were rotting from the inside.

On April 4, 1968, less than fourteen months later, the Reverend Martin Luther King, Jr., was assassinated. He was one of the heroes of my generation. In December 1964, as a young backpacker in England, I had slipped into St. Paul's Cathedral seeking the tranquillity only to be found in churches in great cities. Dr. King, on his way to receive the Nobel Peace Prize in Oslo, entered and repeated his "I have a dream" sermon to the handful of people scattered here and there in the place of worship. It was a magical moment in my life. The area I had walked through, and similar ghettos right across the United States, would be consumed in riots during which desperate people trashed their own neighbourhoods. It would take sixty-five thousand troops to restore order; the cycle of black urban poverty would persist and worsen into the next century.

Canada's Centennial Year

Returning to Ottawa at the end of the General Assembly, I was assigned to work in the United Nations Division, staffed by a highly talented group of officers, including Geoffrey Pearson, the son of the prime minister, who told me in later years that he could not recall my ever having worked for him. The background papers I prepared for him on issues relating to Canada's role in

U.N. peacekeeping were likewise forgettable. I was then reassigned to the Office of State Visits, into a higher-profile job. It was 1967, Canada's centennial year, and the world had been invited to call. Elaborate machinery had been set up to welcome an average of three heads of state each week over a five-month period. A senior foreign-service officer was attached to the Visits Office; I was to be his assistant, and my principal responsibility was the organization of meetings between Prime Minister Pearson and the visiting leaders.

I established good relations with the security, protocol, and hospitality staff at Parliament, cultivated a network of links with local embassies, and developed ties with desk officers in Foreign Affairs who supplied material to prepare briefing notes for the prime minister. The drill for an official visit was supposed to be simple. I would meet the eminent visitor at the bottom of the steps to the Centre Block of Parliament and conduct him or her to an office close to the entrance to meet the prime minister. At the end of the meeting, I would bring in the press for photographs and then escort the visitor back to the entrance.

For the most part, the operation proceeded smoothly. Occasionally, I ignored the advice of the local ambassador on protocol matters. I was, for example, supposed to prostrate myself on the ground and crawl forward, face downwards, when meeting the King of Thailand. Afraid of ruining my one good suit, I simply bowed my head slightly and shook his hand. Another time, a visiting dignitary thought that the soldiers and band performing the ceremonial trooping of the colours for the benefit of tourists on Parliament Hill were there for him. He stood at attention as the troops marched by, oblivious to his presence; I solemnly stood by his side, playing my part in the charade. He left Ottawa happy that so many soldiers had been mobilized to do him honour.

Then there was the time it slipped my mind that President Nikolai Podgorny of the Soviet Union was scheduled to meet

Prime Minister Pearson. Sitting in my office on Sparks Street a couple of blocks away, I heard the sirens of the security vehicles. My blood froze. The president of one of the world's two superpowers was on his way and I would not be there to guide him in. I rushed out the door, sprinted through the honking traffic on Wellington Street, took a shortcut over the parliamentary lawn, jumped over the police barricade, and ran to the front door of the Centre Block, unaware that I was now being pursued by large, athletic, and armed RCMP officers who thought I was a terrorist intent on attacking the visiting head of state. The sergeant in charge recognized me at the last minute and called off his men. Chest heaving, I then calmly received the president and conducted him in to meet the prime minister. Pressing my luck, I manoeuvred my smiling face between those of the prime minister and the Soviet dignitary when the members of the press took their photos. I thought that the folks back home in Muskoka would be ever so proud to see that one of their own was associating with the great leaders of the world. The picture appeared in all the national papers the next day, but touch-up artists had brushed me out of it.

The visitor I really wanted to greet and escort into Parliament was President Charles de Gaulle, whom I had admired for years. France, however, was interested in promoting Quebec separatism and relations were difficult. Even greeting de Gaulle had proved to be difficult. A Canadian destroyer was scheduled to meet the French aircraft carrier transporting the president to Canada and to provide a ceremonial cannonade as it entered Canadian waters. Unfortunately, as possessors of St. Pierre and Miquelon, France disagreed on the location of Canada's territorial water boundary. Foreign Affairs, National Defence, and other government departments argued among themselves on the issue interminably. Finally, the commander of the Canadian ship, acting while others dithered, solved the matter by simply giving the ceremonial salute at the place he judged appropriate, forcing his French counterpart to respond in kind and thereby acknowledge Canada's claim to its territorial sea.

The next day I stood with a sinking heart before the television monitors in our operations centre watching the president make a triumphant tour along the north shore of the St. Lawrence River from Quebec to Montreal. My hero had feet of clay. De Gaulle, an official guest of our country, was seeking to divide Canada, and my respect for him vanished. As I watched him shout "Vive le Québec libre" from the Montreal City Hall balcony, I knew that the visit to Ottawa would not happen. Cabinet debated the issue for several hours before releasing a statement indicating that de Gaulle was no longer welcome in Canada. He left.

The summer of 1967 was a glorious one and, like most Canadians, the members of the foreign-service class of 1966 were determined not to let de Gaulle spoil Canada's birthday party. As the summer wore on some of us began to receive posting notices and depart for exciting destinations. For those who remained, there were barbecues at cottages in the Gatineau Hills and frequent trips to Montreal to attend Expo '67. A group of us rented a cottage at Lake Kingsmere, which became an informal gathering place. The last members then started receiving their posting notices and I began to feel forgotten. The call finally came in the late fall. A personnel officer called me in and offered me Bogotá, with departure from Ottawa set for February 1968. Would I accept? I did not let on that I wasn't sure where Bogotá was and said yes, Bogotá would suit me very well. I knew that it was in Latin America somewhere and hurried to an atlas to locate my future home. It was the capital of Colombia; at least there would be no shortage of good coffee.

2

Adventure in Colombia

After a night in a fleabag hotel, we boarded an old DC-3 aircraft filled with peasants, chickens, and pigs and flew northwest to Cravo Norte . . . landing in a tropical rainstorm and skidding down the tarmac out of control before coming to a safe halt.

My arrival in Bogotá on February 4, 1968, started a lifelong love affair with Latin America. The embassy was a small one, consisting of an unhappy ambassador, two trade officers, an administrative officer, two secretary-typists, and a third secretary – me. The embassy, not being important enough to merit a communicator, maintained links with Ottawa via commercial telex for routine unclassified traffic on trade, administrative, consular, and immigration matters. Every two weeks a diplomatic courier would visit the post to pick up confidential political and economic reports. In emergencies, we were authorized to resort to book cipher to send classified messages, but the process was cumbersome and rarely used. International telephone calls in those pre-satellite days were virtually impossible to place – as I discovered to my sorrow when my grandfather Bartleman passed away and I could not place a call to my grandmother.

Canada's Forgotten Diplomatic Outposts
In those days in Foreign Affairs, there was little interest in Colombia, or for that matter in Latin America. Having spent several days in the Latin American division at headquarters as part

of my pre-posting training, I was aware that most reports from Canadian missions in the region were sent to file after being read only by the junior officer responsible for the management of relations with individual countries and perhaps by his or her director. Little effort was made to comment on views from the field – unsurprising, perhaps, since the only countries that really mattered to the Foreign Affairs establishment in those days were Britain, the United States, France, and, of course, the U.S.S.R. as the common Cold War enemy. Latin America had not figured politically since the Second World War, when Canada had engaged in a flurry of post openings to bolster the Allied cause and help counter Nazi propaganda efforts in the region. Likewise, NATO, the U.N., and the Commonwealth were the only multilateral organizations that counted – certainly not the Organization of American States, regarded at that time as a tame creature of the American State Department. While it was recognized that Canadian missionaries had been active in Latin America since before the turn of the century, they were from Quebec and hence far from the heart of anglophone foreign-policy power and influence in the world of 1968.

Latin America was, however, important to Canadian business and thus to the Department of Industry, Trade, and Commerce. In 1983, the Trade Commissioner Service was absorbed into Foreign Affairs in an overdue recognition of the need for Canada to upgrade trade and investment as foreign-policy goals. Until that time, however, there was a strong rivalry between officers of the two departments at headquarters and abroad. Ambassadors with Foreign Affairs backgrounds tended to look on trade promotion as an activity unbefitting true diplomats, the roots of whose profession, they claimed, resided in the Middle Ages when true gentlemen abhorred anything akin to usury. They also sniffed that the entire business culture in Latin America was corrupt. Foreign businessmen often had to pay bribes to government officials and politicians via local "commercial agents" to win

contracts. Some of the mud, they claimed, was inevitably splat-
tered on Canada's trade commissioners, no matter how blameless
they may have been. The disdain was mutual. Ambassadors with
trade backgrounds were inclined to think officers from Foreign
Affairs were second-rate – poor managers often unable to speak
Spanish or Portuguese despite years in Latin America. They
claimed, correctly, that Foreign Affairs and the political world of
Ottawa did not accord sufficient attention to trade and investment
in Latin America. In their view, successive Canadian governments
would "discover" Latin America every decade or so, sending
high-profile missions, only to lose interest in the region and not
follow up opportunities.

My Responsibilities
I had no Spanish language training, but discovered that seven
years of Latin at high school and university made it easy to
acquire a proficiency in short order. My formal responsibilities
involved managing the consular section, issuing visas and passports, preparing economic and political reports, providing
hospitality to my Colombian contacts, and running the information program. My real job, however, was to listen to the stories
of ambassador Harrison Cleveland on his postings in Finland and
Nigeria and his assignment as director of the United States division. He had once had a distinguished career but was now bitter,
believing, probably correctly, that his talents were unappreciated
at headquarters. His situation, I would later discover, was not
unique. Many of our small and remote posts were headed by
older officers sent abroad to get them out of the way. The junior
officers sent to work for them paid the price.

Cleveland would enter my office early in the morning,
clutching a newspaper with an offending article, or a communication from headquarters that had upset him. As a respectful
junior officer, I would rise to my feet. Two or three hours of
heated grumbling later, he would glance at his watch and head

out the door for lunch at his residence. Exhausted from standing and feigning interest for such prolonged periods, I would then gratefully sit down and race to complete whatever work was on my desk, as he would be back early in the afternoon to repeat the morning routine.

There was rarely much to do. In theory, assistance to Canadians in distress was a major part of my work. But our approach to consular matters lessened my burden. In those days, heads of post were given much greater latitude in determining consular policy. My ambassador's orders, which of course I followed religiously in this first posting as I had not learned that my seniors were not infallible, were that under no circumstance was help to be given to any Canadian who was not morally above reproach. If someone was in trouble with the law, for example, it followed that he or she was obviously guilty of something. If guilty of something, then the person in question did not merit assistance. Fortunately, few Canadians visited Colombia in those days. And the one Canadian languishing without consular aid in the local jail managed to escape.

My visa responsibilities were likewise not onerous. In those days potential immigrants could apply for permanent-resident status at any immigration office in Canada if they could make it into the country. Colombians and other Latin Americans, not needing visas for temporary visits, simply pretended to go to Canada as tourists and applied for their visas, almost invariably granted, on the spot. Non–Latin Americans in Colombia requiring visas for tourism had to deal with me. I did my best, but in most cases I simply guessed whether the earnest individual sitting opposite me seeking a tourist visa was genuine or not. The person who came with a fried chicken and french fries, offering them with a wink on condition that I affix a visa to his passport, I turned down. Then there was the lucky person who received a visa only to return in tears to my office several days later. Hostile Canadian immigration officers in Montreal had subjected him to detention, a strip search, and expulsion from the country. I had inadvertently inserted his visa upside down in his passport; the officers in Montreal thought that I was sending them a secret message to scrutinize this person with greater than usual care.

The Fine Art of Diplomatic Hospitality

In this, my first posting, I was not expected to do much entertaining of Colombian contacts. The lion's share of the funding provided by headquarters for hospitality purposes was allocated to the ambassador. I was expected to invite my contacts to his receptions. In return, I was required to assist him in making guests feel welcome. This suited me well, since I needed pointers on how to be a successful host.

My initial start was good. I would arrive ten minutes before events at the ambassador's residence for instructions on who was who, then introduce guests to each other and make small talk when required. Seeing how eager I was, the ambassador decided to pay particular attention to this aspect of my diplomatic education. Complaining that his Colombian staff were doing a poor job in preparing for luncheons, dinners, and receptions, he invited me – as part of my training, of course – to join him before major events to help out. I would thus arrive dressed in my old clothes and struggle in the rarefied air of the high Andes to help him set up tables, erect marquees, and haul cases of soft drinks, beer, and wine from his locked storeroom. The household staff would watch quietly, hiding their amusement, as the ambassador and I sweated and strained doing their work. I would then rush home, change, and return in time to help greet the guests. The ambassador and his wife, products of the age when Canadian heads of post considered that their junior officers constituted a pool of cheap labour, were happy, and I knew no better.

The ambassador then accepted a speaking engagement in a remote part of the country, setting off a series of events that shattered this bliss. By coincidence, the more senior officers at the mission, who would normally have replaced the ambassador, were out of town. I would be in charge for the two days he would be absent. I was thrilled. What an honour! Here I was, a country boy from the hills of Muskoka, responsible for the management of a Canadian embassy!

I quickly rushed through the preparations for the ambassador's foray into Colombia's wilds. I first crafted what I considered to be an excellent speech: "The English Language as Spoken and Written in Canada and the United States: Some Nuances." The ambassador had given me no direction on what type of speech he wanted and I simply pulled the topic out of thin air, thinking any Colombian audience would be impressed by the erudition of the ambassador's speech writer. I likewise did not seek the preferences of the ambassador when I made his hotel reservations. This was a mere administrative detail that I delegated to a recently hired employee, who assured me that she had booked the best room in the town's best hotel. She neglected to tell me the hotel was the best because it was the only one in town. And how was she to know that it was also the town's bordello?

On the fateful day, I handed the ambassador his itinerary and speech and he departed. I could not have been happier. At last I was in charge of the mission! If I was lucky, the telephone would ring and the foreign minister of Colombia would be on the line seeking my advice on some important point of Canadian-Colombian relations. My answer would, I imagined, be so brilliant that the ambassador, on his return, would recommend me to headquarters for immediate promotion.

The telephone rang. It was the ambassador's wife, and it was not a call of encouragement. Instead, she demanded an account of everything that had gone on at the mission since her husband's departure. She, like many spouses of heads of post in that period, assumed it was her duty to keep an eye on junior officers left in charge of her husband's diplomatic mission. She obviously did not share my high opinion of my ability to manage the post.

Respectfully I told her that it was a normal day at the Canadian embassy: nothing had happened. One hour later, the telephone rang again. It was the ambassador's conscientious wife asking what I had been doing since she last called. "Nothing," I said, allowing just a whisper of irritation to appear in my voice. Every hour on the hour, for the rest of the day, she called.

A slow burn started from my chest and spread to my head, clouding all rational thought. What right, I asked myself, had this woman to interfere in the operations of the embassy? She was just a busybody. I, on the other hand, was an elite foreign-service officer, selected after a gruelling examination process, and able to manage any crisis that might arise in Colombia without her help!

Suddenly, something snapped. Rushing out of the office, I jumped into my car and sped off to the residence of my tormentor. Storming into the living room, I told her that since she thought she could do a better job in managing the mission, she should go to the office and take over officially. "Otherwise, leave me alone! And never ever call me again!"

I then returned to my office with a great feeling of satisfaction, leaving a stunned lady in my wake. I did not care about repercussions. I had done what I had to do.

The next day there were no telephone calls from the ambassador's wife. There were, however, no calls from anyone else. As the day progressed and my chance to prove myself faded, I started to think about what I had said in the ambassador's living room the previous afternoon. Like a repentant drunk the day after, I was now deeply sorry for my actions – and worried. There would be no letter to headquarters commending my management of the post. More likely the ambassador would request my removal for *lèse-majesté*.

The following morning a thoroughly unhappy ambassador appeared at the entrance to my office, but this time not to share with me his stories about the villainous nature of headquarters management.

"Mr. Bartleman, whatever led you to prepare a speech for me on an issue in which no one in this country could take the slightest interest? And the hotel with its wild women and their customers! And the room where I had to sit on the toilet to take a shower! And the cockroaches as big as lizards!"

And on and on. But no mention of my altercation with his wife or of revenge, for he needed my help: a load of fine French wines ordered from a Danish diplomatic supplier was being delivered to his residence that very morning. He wanted me to unload his treasures and transport them to the residence storeroom.

Of course I would help. Perhaps, I thought, he would let bygones be bygones. I returned home, changed into my work clothes, and reported to the residence. The wife greeted me frostily but the ambassador was all smiles, happy with the prospect of free third-secretarial labour. Then it happened. Carrying too many boxes of wine on a wheelbarrow, I hit a bump. A case flew off and landed on the concrete walkway in a crash of broken glass. The ambassador's face was ashen as he contemplated the fine French wine oozing out of the elegant wooden box stamped with the name of a famous French château. Insulting his wife and making him sit on a toilet to take a shower in a house of ill repute were nothing compared to this.

"Leave the premises," he said.

Never again would I be asked to provide free manual labour at his residence. I was henceforth to restrict my role at his hospitality events to that of a guest rather than a member of his household staff.

Embracing the Third World

I learned little about how to be a diplomat in this posting, but I did discover a lot about life. On weekends, accompanied by a Colombian friend, I would drive out of Bogotá on the highway leading to the Venezuelan border. Turning off onto side roads, we would stop at any of the small *campesino* or peasant households to hire a couple of the small wiry horses used by the people for transportation. Then we would be off, riding across the fields of the high altiplano at full gallop. Wearing a Colombian *ruana* – a type of poncho – with my then dark hair, black eyes, high cheek-bones, and a street Spanish learned from Hortensia, my live-in household employee, the locals took me for a Colombian peasant whenever we stopped for meals of rice and beans, the local fare.

Other times, I hung out with Canadian University Service Overseas (CUSO), Peace Corps, and Swedish Overseas volunteers, all of whom were closer to my age than my diplomatic colleagues and a lot more fun. Many of the young Americans had joined the Peace Corps to avoid being drafted to serve in Vietnam. As their assignments came to an end, however, they faced the bitter dilemma of either returning to their country to be called up to fight in a war they detested or of forsaking their country to take refuge in Canada or Sweden. Through the son of the owner of my apartment, a final-year student of law, I gained access to the Colombian university crowd. Although the offspring of the privileged Colombian middle class, they were as idealistic as students anywhere else, participating in street demonstrations calling for more democracy and being brutally beaten back by the police for their pains.

Colombia gave me my first exposure to a country of the Third World and I was fascinated and appalled by the enormous gap between rich and poor. Abandoned street children, some as young as three or four, wore cut-off adult clothes and slept under newspapers on the embassy steps in the cold of the High Andes, trying to survive by begging, theft, and prostitution. Almost every day on the sixth floor of our downtown office building, I would hear the roar of the crowd as people chased young pickpockets, administering vigilante justice on catching them by beating them senseless.

The rich (and the diplomats) lived in well-guarded homes and apartments in the north of the city fearful of the poor and criminals. Foreign Affairs, on the recommendation of the ambassador, decided to move the embassy offices to a safer area about halfway between the residential neighbourhoods of the north and the tough downtown. Our new location was certainly safer; it was also in the heart of Bogotá's red-light district, a detail that escaped the attention of the team of property experts who selected the site. While it was difficult for the staff to have lunch in one of the local restaurants (which doubled as brothels) without being offered dishes not on most menus, our special location had its advantages. The embassy enjoyed a popularity never before experienced as Colombians went out of their way to find some business to transact at Canada's prestigious new address.

A climate of violence was as pervasive then in Colombia as it is today. Over the previous twenty years, hundreds of thousands of peasants in rural areas had been killed in the *violencia*, a conflict marked by terrible cruelty of victors over vanquished. At its outset, the *violencia* was a non-ideological feud between the dominant traditional political parties. A massive influx of people, displaced in the fighting and accustomed to using force and torture to settle disputes, flooded into the cities in the 1950s. When I arrived in Bogotá, the flow of internally displaced political refugees was being swollen by large numbers of economic migrants seeking a better life in shantytowns, called *barrios*, around the cities. The drug cartels did not yet exist, but crime syndicates specializing in bank robbery, car theft, and kidnapping for ransom were prevalent.

No one was immune. One evening, walking briskly in the neighbourhood close to my apartment, I was stopped by a security guard who held a pistol to my head. Clearly, he thought I was a bad guy. I held my hands in the air and explained that I was an innocent Canadian diplomat out for my evening constitutional walk. He said nothing, probably not understanding my Spanish. We stood there for some time until I signalled to him that I was going to depart. I then backed slowly away, my hands still in the air as he continued to point his gun at me until I was far enough away to start running.

Another time, I returned home from a Saturday in the countryside to find my housekeeper, Hortensia, flustered and worried. Earlier in the day, she had seen someone running down the street. She shouted a general warning from our fourth-floor balcony that a thief was on the loose. A neighbour emerged from his garden, machete in hand, to pursue the individual until he caught him; he then brought his weapon down, cutting off fingers as the thief raised his arm to protect himself. The thief, however, turned out to be an innocent person running to catch a bus. He threatened to return to exact revenge, but nothing came of it.

With the insouciance of youth, I never worried about my personal safety, although I should have. Not until I was attacked during a posting to South Africa many years later did I really take my security seriously. Today, Foreign Affairs wisely does not permit its staff abroad to carry personal firearms for their protection, afraid they might accidentally shoot someone. In the Colombia of 1968, however, I possessed a .38-calibre pistol, bequeathed to me by my predecessor at the post, which had been handed down from one third secretary to another over the years. The theory was that on going to bed at night I was supposed to lock my bedroom door and shoot anyone trying to enter in the night.

I did have an encounter with Colombian crime on one occasion when I stopped my Ford Mustang, the first new car I had ever owned, to ask directions on a busy street. As I stood beside the car, someone jumped into it and drove off. I raced to the only store open in the neighbourhood to ask for help; everyone ran out, including the owner, who locked the door behind him after motioning me to leave the premises. They did not want to get involved. I stopped a taxi. The driver sped away when I told him what had happened. Finally, I waved down a passing police patrol, which took me to police headquarters. In those days, people implicated in vehicle accidents, injured or not, were taken to police stations for questioning before being allowed to seek medical care at hospitals. Thus, it was in the damp gloom of a Kafkaesque holding room among a collection of accident victims, some with broken bones lying on the floor moaning, that I was made to wait before being allowed to see someone in authority. The duty sergeant had little time to waste on my case. He told me to contact the thieves, providing precise instructions on how to ransom my car. I suggested that we work together to trap the gang. He thought I was naive, and obviously I was. The police were either too busy to look for car thieves or in cahoots with them. My car was never recovered.

Violence was not confined to the cities. In the mid-1960s, guerrilla groups inspired by the Soviet and Cuban revolutions took advantage of the injustices of rural Colombian life and the prevailing turmoil to establish themselves in force across broad areas of the countryside, areas that they control even today, in an unholy alliance with drug cartels. This became evident when I accepted what looked like an innocent invitation from a Canadian non-governmental organization to open a feeding station, a place providing food rations for poor malnourished children, in a remote area. I was puzzled when the invitation specified that I should go to a military airfield about fifty kilometres from Bogotá. A helicopter, complete with heavily armed military bodyguards, awaited me. Once aboard, I was flown to a distant area in the mountains, a soldier with his feet dangling from the open door scanning the terrain below, a machine gun cradled Rambo-style in his arms. The helicopter put down on a flat spot close to the facility, which was itself surrounded by heavily armed troops. I delivered my speech, ate a piece of fly-covered pork, and was marched back to the helicopter, which eventually delivered me to my car. The feeding station, I discovered, was located in the heart of guerrilla-controlled territory.

The challenges of living in Colombia included learning to live with earthquakes. When I first arrived, my new Canadian colleagues described in dismissive terms how their Colombian co-workers would run panic-stricken from the embassy and fall to their knees to pray in the street every time a tremor shook the building. Being "brave Canadians," they remained behind, continuing their work as if nothing had happened. I was certain that I would prove to be as cool and "Canadian" when the moment of truth arrived for me.

One night I was sleeping peacefully, my German shepherd watchdog on duty in the kitchen, the door to my bedroom locked as always, and my loaded .38-calibre pistol at the ready in my bedside commode to deal with human threats. I started to dream that the devil himself had come calling. I broke into a cold sweat as the evil one seized the bedposts with giant arms and shook it with such fury that I woke up. I found that a mighty earthquake was in progress, tossing my bed from side to side and up and down. The crystal chandeliers – I lived in an elegant apartment – were swinging crazily and tinkling madly. I leaped out of bed, forgetting that I was supposed to be a phlegmatic, brave Canadian, and dashed in my bare feet and pyjamas for refuge in the room Hortensia shared with her baby daughter behind the kitchen, yelling her name at the top of my voice. Pushing open the kitchen door, I stepped into something warm and gooey – the dog had relieved himself on the floor from fright – and I slipped across the room still calling her name. Hortensia emerged, turning on the light to reveal a room covered in small black cockroaches scurrying for cover, her brave employer with a compromised foot and a thoroughly frightened guard dog trembling in front of her. She never let me forget that evening, and I no longer felt so superior when confronting future earthquakes.

Native Peoples

As an aboriginal Canadian, I had often wondered what life was like in the Americas before the arrival of the Europeans. I was thus both captivated and repulsed by what Bernard Arcand, a young Quebecer who was doing field work with Indians for his degree at Cambridge, had to tell me. My new friend, who would later become one of Canada's most renowned anthropologists and brother of Denys Arcand, the famous film director, was living with native people in the hot interior region on one of the tributaries of the Casanare River, which flowed into the great Orinoco.

His hosts, members of the small Cuiva tribe, lived in family groups of ten to forty people in the forest fringe along the immense savannah that spread out across Colombia and Venezuela. Having largely avoided contact with white people, they retained the same language, culture, belief systems, and food-gathering methods as before the arrival of the Spanish in the New World. However, settlers, ranchers, and oil-exploration workers, seeking new land for exploitation, were moving into their territories, destroying their way of life, and even hunting them for sport on the weekends under the tolerant eyes of the Colombian authorities. Arcand was living with a group of about twenty who had been reduced to the condition of refugees, living on the land of a European expatriate who was running a ranching and smuggling operation in the interior. Despite his dubious activities, the European had a soft spot in his heart for the Cuiva and was protecting them.

Brian Moser, a producer for Granada Television, dropped into my office one day seeking leads on possible stories relating to Indians. I seized the opportunity to publicize the plight of this tribe and to visit them myself. Moser, an award-winning journalist featured in *Life* magazine, had made several documentaries and had recently been among the first to photograph the body of Che Guevara after his execution by Bolivian troops in the Andes.

We left Bogotá early one July morning in 1969, taking a public taxi from the cool altiplano 2,600 metres high to Villavicencio, some twelve hours away by road, at sea level in the hot Colombian rain forest. We brought hammocks for sleeping, since beds in the hotels were dirty, as well as all the supplies needed for an expedition in the Colombian wilds. After a night in a fleabag hotel, we boarded an old DC-3 aircraft filled with peasants, chickens, and pigs and flew northeast to Cravo Norte at the junction of the Casanare and Cravo Norte rivers, landing in a tropical rainstorm and skidding down the tarmac out of control before coming to a safe halt.

Cravo Norte was like a Wild West town in a Hollywood movie. There was no electricity and the one road was unpaved. Horses were tethered to hitching posts before the numerous *cantinas*, or bars, from which drifted raucous Colombian cowboy music. Not anxious to spend the night in one of the cutthroat hotels, Brian and I called on two missionaries, who agreed to provide accommodation for a small fee and to rent us their motorized canoe for the final leg of our journey.

Venturing out in the evening for some local colour and to escape the kind-hearted but boring missionaries, we strolled into what seemed to be the most respectable *cantina*, where we struck up a conversation with several of the locals. The patrons, however, were heavily armed and suspicious, not welcoming. Two tough characters identified themselves as members of the Colombian secret police and demanded to know what we were doing in Cravo Norte. They thought we might be Cuban agents sent by Havana to foment insurrection. Producing my diplomatic passport, I declared in a self-important way that I was third secretary of the Canadian embassy in Bogotá on an official mission. The secret police were unimpressed, perhaps wondering what official business I was trying to conduct in the *cantina*. The meaner-looking of the two, unshaven and with a scar running diagonally across his face, told me that anyone could falsify a passport. He was, he said, the law in Cravo Norte and did not take orders from anyone in Bogotá. We beat an undignified retreat back to the home of the missionaries.

The next day, we travelled fifty kilometres up the river until we came to the collection of thatched-roofed huts occupied by the Cuiva Indians. Unloading our possessions from the canoe, we spread them out and told the Indians to take what they wanted. We knew that they were hospitable, and so generous that they shared their possessions as well as the products of hunting or fishing with each other and expected visitors to do the same with them. I had brought a supply of steel hooks, with which they were unfamiliar, as well as rice and salt. After helping themselves, they shared their food with us for the period we were their guests.

I learned that social intercourse was marked by diplomatic courtesy and long-established custom. Anyone could walk unannounced into any hut, but each visitor was expected to shake hands and exchange formal greetings with the occupants on arrival and departure. For hunting birds and animals and spearing fish they used bows and a variety of specialized arrows. There were no fixed hours for meals. People ate when game was available, consuming virtually every part of the fish or animal. We shared meals of fish, birds, and, as a special treat, caiman, a member of the crocodile family. My salt was a big hit. I even contributed to the common pot by catching piranha from the immense schools infesting the river, fishing from a narrow dugout canoe using my steel hooks and trying not to think of how long I would survive if the boat tipped and I fell into the water.

The Antiques Roadshow

I then made a road trip to Peru which almost proved to be my last. The cultural attaché from the German embassy invited me to accompany him in his Volkswagen Beetle to Lima. His goal was to acquire as many antiques as possible; mine was simply to see more of Latin America. We departed Bogotá in high spirits, descending through the clouds from the high plateau where the Colombian capital sits to enter the so-called hot country close to sea level near Cali, later to become infamous as a centre of international drug trafficking. From Cali we headed south via the beautiful colonial city of Popayan, where an earthquake struck several years later, burying worshippers in the ruins of the cathedral just minutes after Canada's ambassador and wife of the time had walked out the door. We then moved on to Pasto, the isolated capital of the Department of Narino, where my colleague took me with him as he paid consular visits to members of the German community. He was welcomed enthusiastically but I was treated with wariness. The German colonists, my colleague told me, had left Germany in a hurry at the end of the war and did not want the outside world to know where they were. For my part, uncertain whether they had been Nazis or victims of Hitler, I was relieved when he finished his business and we were able to continue on our way.

The route from Pasto to Quito, Ecuador's capital, was terrible, often one lane only. Numerous markers indicated the spots where speeding cars, trucks, and buses had plunged over the edge into deep mountain valleys, killing the passengers. In Quito, colleagues at the tiny Canadian embassy took us in hand to show us the sights and extend hospitality, overjoyed to have visitors at their remote outpost. We then pressed on to Guayaquil, the hot, insalubrious port city of Ecuador where the road ended. Undeterred, we took the ferry to the southern bank of the Guayas River and followed back roads and trails to the border of Peru, where we met up with the paved coastal highway running through the Atacama desert. Two days later we were in Lima, capital of Peru, which still retained its charm as a small colonial city; in the coming decade the massive movement of the rural poor seeking a better life was to change its personality forever.

So far, so good. My German colleague had found antiques, in particular wooden carvings of saints that apparently were worth a fortune in Europe, and was satisfied with himself and with the trip. We were getting along well and looking forward to relaxing after our long drive in the quiet charm of Lima. The next morning, however, he burst into my room shouting that a *coup d'état* led by the military was in progress. We had to leave before roadblocks were set up around the city or we could find ourselves in the Peruvian capital indefinitely. As we scrambled to grab all of our belongings and get them to the car, he pulled out a revolver and said that it was to be used for our protection. The rules of engagement, as he described them, were simple: whoever was not driving (we were taking turns at the wheel) would ride shotgun and kill anyone who tried to rob us.

We set off at what I thought was a panic-stricken pace for the Ecuadorean border, the precious antiques under a blanket in the back and the revolver in the glove compartment with our passports. He did not appreciate my skeptical attitude. His mood worsened when I took the wheel and forgot that sand drifts on the highway along Peru's coastal desert were not as easy to plough through as snow drifts in Canada. I hit one at a hundred kilometres an hour; his car bounced high in the air and nearly overturned. He became downright nasty, however, when, after we crossed the border back into Ecuador, I almost drove his Beetle off a railway bridge into a deep gorge. About two hundred metres in length, the bridge was for trains, although limited road traffic was allowed over two narrow planks precariously laid along the tracks. Distracted by my excitable companion's back-seat driving, I allowed the front wheels to leave the planks. The front end of the car plunged downwards but was caught by a railway tie. He became almost apoplectic. To make matters worse, a train was coming. Several *campesinos* were watching all this with interest. As the sound of the approaching train grew louder, they came onto the bridge and lifted the car back onto the planks, allowing us to escape just in time.

Our next adventure was several kilometres down the road. We were travelling on a dirt track almost blinded by dust and burning refuse from banana plantations. My colleague had taken the wheel and was no longer talking to me. Suddenly, out of the smoky haze, a band of about fifteen men confronted us. They looked like actors from an old Pancho Villa movie, armed with shotguns, pistols, machetes, and bandoliers full of ammunition wrapped around their shoulders. My companion had no choice but to stop the car. I was riding shotgun and knew that my duty was to shoot our way free. But I simply reached into the glove compartment and pulled out our diplomatic passports. I did not know where the safety catch was on his damned pistol. Even with my trusty .38, I would not have engaged more than a dozen wild-eyed Ecuadoreans in a gunfight.

I think my companion was relieved that I had not taken literally his injunction to use firepower to blast our way out. But our trouble worsened. The gang could not have cared less for the diplomatic passports and told us to get out of the car with our hands up. My colleague was torn between saving our lives and saving his antiques. The antiques won. He put the car into gear and drove straight through the crowd, pushing the gunner aside with the bumper. We left behind a gang of outlaws so surprised that they did not open fire, although I was glad when we rounded the first corner. When we reported this encounter to the Ecuadorean authorities, they told us that the area was frequented by notorious criminal bands. We were lucky not to have been killed.

We returned to Bogotá in silence and did not make further trips together.

I would not see South America again for eleven years after the end of my posting to Colombia. When I returned, respectably married with two children, my days of wild adventure over, it was to be *chargé d'affaires*, or acting ambassador, at the Canadian embassy in Lima; my mission would be to oversee the provision of proper consular services to look after Canadian prisoners in Peruvian jails. The first event that my wife and I would attend would be the swearing in at the National Assembly of Peru's first democratically elected president in years. The new head of state would be none other than Fernando Belaúnde Terry, the same leader who had been overthrown during the *coup d'état* that precipitated my flight from Lima with my German colleague in 1969.

3

Ottawa

What I saw . . . was not pretty.

On my return to Ottawa in February 1970, I was assigned to the Security and Intelligence Liaison Division as an analyst. I looked forward to being admitted to the hidden world of spies and counterspies. Sadly, the Canadian intelligence establishment turned out to be modest in size and ambition with a variety of departments and agencies assigned specific roles for the collection, production, and consumption of foreign intelligence. Foreign Affairs was responsible for economic and political intelligence; National Defence for military intelligence; the RCMP Security Service for national-security information; and the Communication Branch of the National Research Council for the collection of signals intelligence from its network of listening posts, mainly on Soviet military matters. The Joint Intelligence Committee met each week, with a senior officer from Foreign Affairs in the chair, to coordinate the interdepartmental effort.

Unfortunately, it was rarely possible to persuade anyone in any position of authority in the government, including the prime minister, to read the reports we produced. They obtained their news from the *Globe and Mail* and *Time*, which was written in a far racier style than was allowed in the intelligence world. Moreover, liaison contacts with our more glamorous cousins in the Central Intelligence Agency and the British Secret Intelligence Service were the exception rather than the rule. But

I was not disappointed when it became clear I would not be a James Bond. Ted Rettie, the director, and Peter Johnson, the deputy director, were outstanding as officers and as individuals, and they provided me with my first solid professional guidance since joining Foreign Affairs.

There were three of us in the analysis section, which was located behind locked doors on the floor above the post office on Sparks Street, and we were responsible for producing written intelligence reports for Foreign Affairs and for senior members of the government on key issues affecting Canada's interests around the world. Since there was no possibility that the three of us could fulfill such an ambitious worldwide mandate, we worked in close collaboration with the political divisions responsible for managing Canada's relations with the various geographic areas of the world, persuading or browbeating regional experts into helping us. I was responsible for covering Latin America and the Middle East. When one of us was away, the others covered.

The World in 1970

Although I had been away from Ottawa for only two years, it could have been a generation. When one is young, time goes by slowly. As one grows older, it speeds up – days, weeks, months, and then years flash by with accelerating velocity – like a train picking up speed leaving a station. There had been great changes in the world outside Colombia of which I was aware from reading month-old newspapers, but I had not fully grasped them in that era before the Internet. The first man had stepped on the moon. The Soviets had crushed the Prague Spring. The Americans were deeply mired in Vietnam. The Reverend Martin Luther King, Jr., and Robert Kennedy had been assassinated. Pierre Trudeau was prime minister. The public was caught up in "Trudeaumania" – a bout of untypically Canadian mass hysteria and matched in its passion only by the fervour about Princess Diana thirty years later.

A new wave of foreign-service officers, predominantly male with long hair, sideburns, and beards, was now swamping Foreign Affairs. Taken on in their hundreds to staff the growing number of new embassies and high commissions, they had come of age with the youth rebellion in France, Germany, and the United States, and its fainter echo on Canadian university campuses. They helped sweep away the cobwebs of a foreign service overly reliant on rules from another era, questioning the edict that female officers must resign if they marry and rebelling against the practice whereby spouses served as unpaid labour for heads of mission, and even for their wives. Their defiant spirits sometimes spilled into excess. One group of recruits drank its way across Canada on a familiarization tour. The low point occurred when a junior officer descended from a charter flight at Fort McMurray, Alberta, in a drunken stupor to urinate against the tire of the air-craft. He then turned and waved a welcome of sorts at the party of local notables waiting on the tarmac to welcome Canada's new generation of diplomats to the oil-sand capital of the country. They were not impressed.

In time, even these most irreverent of recruits would fall into line, conform to the institutional culture, and be productive members of the foreign service. Nevertheless, it boggles the imag-ination to think of a Lester Pearson, Hume Wrong, or Norman Robertson ever behaving in such a way. Likewise, such conduct by the highly educated, superbly motivated, and computer-literate classes of the 1980s and 1990s, who now soberly run Foreign Affairs, would have been inconceivable.

Too often a Foreign Affairs officer returning from a posting abroad finds life in Ottawa dull. For me this period was one of the most fulfilling of my life. Purchasing a small rudimentary cottage on the Gatineau River opposite Wakefield, Quebec, I converted it into a winterized home and a place of refuge. Mesmerized by the sound of rapids just metres from my bedroom window, I would rise in the night to test myself, battling the current in the dark until I could go upstream no farther, my canoe crashing against logs being borne downstream to the mills on the Ottawa River. Lifting my paddle, I would allow myself to be swept back downstream through the heavy mist, where cold air met warm water, in company with groaning tangles of wood pungent with the smell of wet bark – cedar, hemlock, and spruce.

My new neighbours, scattered in a mix of hippie and conventional houses along the river and on the heavily wooded hills behind, were an assortment of locals, professors from Carleton and Ottawa universities, federal public servants commuting to their jobs in Ottawa, and long-haired American draft dodgers and their spouses. The latter, remnants of the counterculture that had passed me by, were ardently committed to the social and political issues of the day and to the "Gatineau Gold" marijuana they quietly grew in small plots hidden deep in the bush. This was the period of the Kent State University killings in Ohio, and they were passionate participants in anti–Vietnam War demonstrations. I shared their convictions on Vietnam but not their fondness for marijuana.

The October Crisis

I thought it ridiculous that I had managed to learn Spanish but still could speak only one of Canada's official languages, and was determined to become bilingual and to learn something about Quebec society and culture. The only francophones I knew personally were strong federalists; I wanted to know the other side of the story. Foreign Affairs authorized two three-week intensive French-immersion courses in Quebec City at a five-star hotel. I thought I had died and gone to heaven. Every minute of the day was devoted to learning French. Charming francophone counsellors accompanied the students at every meal and coffee break, ensuring that French was spoken outside as well as within the classroom settings. Political, cultural, and academic speakers came to address us on Quebec's place in Canada and in the world. I made friends with students from the Laval School of Music who had been providing entertainment to the patrons in the dining room; they in turn introduced me to a cross-section of university students, public servants, and young professionals. All were democratic nationalists committed to the independence of Quebec, but neither they nor I permitted our differences over the future of Canada to affect our relations.

Then in October 1970, James Cross, the British trade commissioner in Montreal, was kidnapped by the Front de Libération du Québec (FLQ); Pierre Laporte, the justice minister of Quebec, was later seized and murdered. Prime Minister Trudeau, in the interim responding to appeals for help from jittery leaders in Quebec, invoked the War Measures Act. Hundreds of suspected FLQ sympathizers were rounded up and thrown into prison. Many were treated badly by their guards and none was charged with any crime. Thousands of soldiers occupied Ottawa and the major cities of Quebec to head off an "apprehended insurrection." Quebec, the government said, was about to be engulfed in a wave of uncontrollable violence. I did not share these worries, aware from reading so-called secret reports (containing information available to the general reader in *Time*) that the organization did not enjoy the support of the Quebec population and in no way threatened the viability of the institutions of Quebec and Canada. A quick-tempered prime minister, unrestrained by a charter of rights that would have proscribed such behaviour, abused his power for short-term political purposes. And the Canadian public, despite its deep respect for human rights, allowed itself to be stampeded.

My friends in Quebec City were in a state of shock. Many people they knew had been arrested and beaten in nighttime police raids. They could not understand, and nor could I, how such a thing could happen in our democratic country. With a sense of shame, I read that a refugee from Algeria, a close friend of the late Nobel Prize–winning author Albert Camus, had been caught in the net, thrown into jail, and pulled from his cell and beaten by prison guards when the news of the murder of Pierre Laporte broke. I would trudge to work in an Ottawa under siege followed by the watchful eyes of nervous nineteen-year-old soldiers standing in doorways holding their automatic weapons at the ready. Returning home in the evening, I would look up to see military helicopters ominously silhouetted against the purple-grey sky, their clattering rotor blades drowning out the cries of the Canada geese heading south.

The silence of the public was deafening. It was a scene more appropriate to Colombia than to Canada. In later years, I would think of October 1970 when I saw the movies of Costa-Gravas describing the slide to military rule in Greece and Chile. From that period came my deep-seated conviction that democracy and respect for human rights is a fragile thing and needs constant nourishing even in my beloved country.

Despite my doubts, which I dared not air for fear of ending up in prison myself, I was caught up in the management of the crisis, assigned as a duty officer to the special task force that had been set up in the operations centre of the East Block of the Parliament buildings under the authority of Foreign Affairs. Prime Minister Trudeau maintained a close watch over developments and periodically visited the centre for briefings. One question he asked, and to which he could not obtain an answer, was whether the FLQ had links with other guerrilla groups elsewhere in the world. Were the FLQ actions part of a broader international conspiracy?

The intelligence community was asked to provide the answers and a senior officer was assigned to prepare an assessment. He had little background on the issue and could not deliver. The director then appeared in my doorway on a Friday afternoon with a worried look. He had noticed that I had drafted several reports in recent months on Latin American guerrilla movements. Could

I help? The prime minister was pressing. With my Latin American background and knowledge of Spanish, which allowed access to documents in the original language, I was prepared to try. I combed the files of the division, paying particular attention to reports received from other intelligence services, and reviewed my own books and papers throughout the Saturday. Then, fortified with cups of strong black coffee and an ample supply of chocolate bars, I wrote non-stop from early Sunday until six o'clock Monday morning. At eight in the morning, I was back at my office, where an anxious director, uncertain whether I would be able to deliver the goods, awaited me. My report demonstrating that there was no international conspiracy, and describing the key revolutionary movements in the Americas as well as the better-known ones in Europe and the Middle East and Africa, was what was needed.

Counterterrorism

I thus became the government's "expert" on the subject of international terrorism. What I learned, drawing on sources of information available only to those in the intelligence world, was not pretty. I saw young followers of Carlos Marighella, the Brazilian guru of the Latin American revolutionary left, try to deal with Latin America's endemic problems of social, political, and economic injustice by waging urban warfare in the megacities of the continent. The kidnapping of ambassadors in exchange for cash and the freeing of political prisoners was a favoured tactic. The first two or three times ambassadors were kidnapped, the guerrillas got their way; political prisoners were released and flown to Algeria.

Then there was a change in tactics. The security forces decided to deal with the problem once and for all by murdering all remaining political prisoners in their jail cells after torturing them to obtain information; they then routinely killed all suspected guerrillas captured in raids on safe houses. The revolutionary movement was wiped out in Brazil, Uruguay, and Argentina for the time being. When it resumed some years later in these countries, the security forces applied the same scorched-earth tactics they had learned earlier, but this time their victims numbered in the tens of thousands, routinely abused and in many cases tossed from aircraft into the sea.

Other members of Foreign Affairs and some colleagues at posts abroad had little confidence in the capacity of our small unit to find out what was happening in this highly secretive world. I recall sending a flash message (one that takes precedence over all others in the system) to a senior ambassador in a Latin American post, telling him to cancel all social engagements immediately and not to leave his residence unless accompanied by carloads of heavily armed bodyguards. Given the sensitivity of the source, I could not tell him why he was being subjected to such drastic measures. The ambassador sent me messages of ridicule, telling me that he knew local conditions better than I did and that my instructions were ruining his professional and social life. What I could not tell him was that his name was on a list with two other ambassadors as terrorist targets. The other two were duly kidnapped while Canada's ever-complaining head of mission remained at liberty.

Another time, I learned that an uprising was about to occur in an Asian country and much bloodshed was expected. I sent a flash message to the post, giving instructions for the mission to close and for the staff to seek safety. I received two messages in short order. The first was to advise me that the officers at the post were aware of local conditions and that I was being alarmist and unprofessional. The second reported that heavy firing was taking place in the vicinity of the high commission, that local radio was reporting that hundreds of bodies were floating down a river, and that the mission was being closed indefinitely.

Abroad Again

When the time drew near for my second tour abroad in the spring of 1972, I was more wary than I had been in 1967 when approached for my first foreign assignment. I did not want to repeat the experience of working for an ambassador who was bitter about Foreign Affairs. In fact, I did not want to work for any ambassador at all, if I could help it. In March, the first call came. I was to be sent to Cuba as deputy to the ambassador. Afraid that we would not be compatible, I advised my posting officer – speaking only from a security perspective, of course – that a bachelor should not be sent to Cuba. I told him that I would succumb to the charms of the first beautiful spy Castro sent my way, spilling all of Canada's deepest secrets.

He bought my story and returned in April with a new offer: head of chancery (responsible for the overall management of a diplomatic mission under the ambassador) at the Canadian embassy in Addis Ababa. I would have loved living in Ethiopia but was again worried that I would not get along with the ambassador. I was also concerned by reports that an inordinate amount of time would be spent at empty formal state functions at the court of Emperor Haile Selassie. I told my posting officer that I had suffered from altitude sickness throughout my posting to Bogotá at 2,600 metres above sea level – a true, if self-serving, statement. Addis Ababa was 2,750 metres above sea level. I began to detect a certain impatience and skepticism. My posting officer returned one week later with a tailor-made offer: to open Canada's first high commission in Dhaka, Bangladesh. The country was only three feet above sea level and there were no communist spies. I could not say no.

I was delighted. My supervisor in this posting would reside 3,200 kilometres away in Bangkok and visit only infrequently, if at all. I would have the task of establishing a diplomatic mission from the ground up, renting an office and quarters for staff, establishing

links with the new government, and assisting in the reconstruc-
tion of a country. Lest I gain a swelled head from being given such
authority so early in my career, my posting officer told me, only
half in jest, that it had been decided to offer me the assignment
since Foreign Affairs did not want to risk sending a valuable officer
to a country in turmoil, where he or she could be injured or killed.

The director of the South Asia division then summoned me
to his office to give me my marching orders. A former colonel in
the Canadian army who had seen active service in the Second
World War, he could scarcely conceal his unhappiness at the personnel division for daring to send such a junior officer to head
up a mission in his territory, but did his best to prepare me.
Accompanied by his deputy, who puffed malevolently on a foul-
smelling pipe and indicated with body language that he shared
the doubts of his boss on my unsuitability for the assignment, the
director sat me down in front of a map and proceeded to brief me
on the history, culture, and demography of Bangladesh and the
challenges facing it as if his audience were composed of a roomful
of military officers about to prepare their troops for the Normandy
landings. If I occasionally looked bewildered as he recited facts and
figures, he would poke at the map with a pointer to bring me
to attention.

The director told me that there already were two CIDA officers,
Terry Glavin and Emile Baron, who were among the finest I
would know, working out of a temporary office in Dhaka. I was
to proceed to Bangkok, where I would be accredited to the Thai
government as a first secretary at the Canadian embassy, my base
from which to open the office in Bangladesh. He expected me to
spend two weeks of every month in Bangladesh, where I would
be acting high commissioner; the other two weeks I was to spend
in Bangkok, but he was rather vague as to what I was supposed to
do there before returning to the horrors of Dhaka. Foreign Affairs
had assigned me a senior clerk and secretary who were supposed
to accompany me in my travels to and from Dhaka every two

weeks. I would be authorized to hire as many local Bangladeshi staff as I judged necessary for the efficient operation of a medium-sized Canadian diplomatic mission. Given the high profile Bangladesh's suffering had assumed in the Canadian media, the CIDA section would be authorized to exceed the fifty-million-dollar annual budget allocated to the program.

I supplemented the briefings from the South Asia division with extensive research of my own on Bangladesh, drawing heavily on British, American, and Australian intelligence sources. I tried to become as familiar as possible with the relevant facts: its origins as the East Pakistan homeland for Muslims fleeing the violence that had accompanied Britain's granting of independence to India and Pakistan in 1947; its history of cataclysmic natural disasters; its troubled unequal partnership with West Pakistan over the preceding twenty-five years that had provoked bloody civil war; and finally, the intervention of the Indian army and air force, which had defeated Pakistan's armed forces and cleared the way for the emergence of the newly independent country of Bangladesh in December 1971.

After a farewell party at my Gatineau River home, I departed for Asia not knowing that it would be 1977 before I returned to live in Canada. A powerful sense of liberation from the personal and professional entanglements built up over the previous two years swept over me as I boarded the Air Canada flight. I looked forward to new adventures, new friends, new challenges, and the exoticism of life in a part of the world I had heard so much about. There were similarities, I thought, between the foreign service and the French foreign legion. Those joining (if they remained single) were assured of being able to make fresh starts in their lives at periodic intervals and of being paid for the privilege.

Hong Kong, my first stop, did not disappoint. I felt like the hero in Joseph Conrad's *Youth*, who, after an arduous and lengthy sea voyage from grey England at the turn of the century, awakens one morning in an Asian port in a magical world. I disembarked from an aircraft after a fourteen-hour flight almost a century later, but the impact was the same. A chauffeur in a white uniform, wearing white gloves and flashing white teeth, held up a white sign with my name on it before seizing my suitcase to take me to a white Mercedes and conduct me to a white five-star hotel with white marble floors. The clerk in the Foreign Affairs travel section who had made the reservations for this two-day "rest break" had pulled out all the stops. Luxury and personal attention such as this I had not experienced in Latin America.

The Hong Kong of 1972 was the Hong Kong of five excellent made-to-measure suits or two dozen fitted dress shirts for one hundred dollars, delivered, of course, to the white hotel within twenty-four hours; of open-air restaurants selling fresh dog and snake meat; of monkey brains served on a lacquered spoon; of prostitutes calling from red-light bars to passing sailors and diplomats; of tenements crammed with refugees from mainland China, with shirtless men leaning out of the windows smoking, spitting, and gossiping; and of overcrowded sampans housing tens of thousands of people on the water, as in an old Pearl Buck novel.

Then it was on to Bangkok, my destination, flying over a Vietnam whose villages were giving their names to battles in the headlines around the world. Then we flew over Cambodia and through tropical thunderstorms to rendezvous with the Foreign Affairs team assembling to open the Dhaka mission. No uniformed driver met me at the airport, but I did not care. The price of the fare, like everything else in Thailand, had to be negotiated. I forced the driver to cut his opening offer in half, but his broad smile as I climbed in indicated that he had won the negotiation. The traffic was heavy, the air charged with heat, humidity, exhaust fumes, and the smell of garbage and open sewers. There was then another five-star hotel; an overwhelming fragrance of jasmine; open-air markets selling stolen American war supplies and pirate tapes of Joan Baez and Leonard Cohen protesting the Vietnam war; air-conditioned shopping malls where a Coca-Cola cost more than the day's labour of a woman mixing cement at a construction site; and the welcoming staff at Canada's embassy to the Kingdom of Thailand where I, in principle only, was a first secretary in the political section.

Headquarters' edict that I divide my time between Bangkok and Dhaka made no sense, and I decided to move the operation to Bangladesh permanently. When I left for Dhaka my baggage contained two unusual ingredients: the twelve-hundred-pound safe the security division, in its wisdom, insisted I bring along to store any classified reports that I might generate; and, as a fan of Second World War American war movies in which enterprising G.I.s always obtain what they want from populations in war-ravaged areas with cigarettes and nylon stockings, I also brought a generous supply of Lucky Strike cigarettes for barter in case the Bangladeshis would not accept dollars. Nylon stockings I dispensed with, afraid of offending the local mores.

4

Canada's First Mission in Bangladesh

*Despairing women and children congregated daily at the entrance
to my house, their hands thrust through the gates, mutely appealing
for something to eat.*

Bangladesh would be one of the shortest yet most intense of
all my foreign-service assignments. More than three decades
later, images reappear: smallpox victims; street children; fleets of
magnificent square-rigged sailing boats; a blind beggar and his
guide waiting patiently for me to relent and give them a handout;
a grizzled patriarch's giggling teenage wives, who cast furtive
glances my way; a fierce tongue-lashing from a senior official from
headquarters for lack of deference; a KGB spy; André Malraux;
water buffalos, wooden ploughs and the calm of village life; a rat
scuttling across the floor; men and boys, their hands bound
behind their backs, squatting on a lurching flatbed truck; rifle fire
shattering the midnight silence outside my bedroom window;
shouting, people running, and evasive answers from the authorities the next day; and people, people, and more people.

Apocalypse Now
The goals of the small team of one brand-new acting high
commissioner, two CIDA officers, one clerk, one secretary, and
eventually one communicator, were to deliver a massive aid
program, consolidate diplomatic relations with the new government, launch a program of political and economic reporting, and

set up a functioning high commission from scratch. In principle, the CIDA officers ran the aid program and I was responsible for everything else. In fact, we worked closely together. Although the CIDA officers did not have to involve me, they often did. Although I did not need to consult them, I would not have dreamed of acting without their advice.

Bangladesh was in terrible shape in 1972. It would be years before the infusion of aid and the energy of its people would start to lift it from its status as the world's worst basket case. With seventy-five million people in an area the size of New Brunswick, it was heavily overcrowded and desperately poor. The effects of war were visible everywhere: bridges destroyed, power lines down, the railway not functioning, and famine in the north and hunger everywhere. Huge refugee camps, administered by the International Committee of the Red Cross, housed millions of people driven from their homes and jobs for siding with Pakistan in the civil war.

As one of the leading aid donors, Canada participated in a special U.N.-led effort to coordinate the relief effort for the country. We sent experts to Singapore to buy small cargo vessels able to get up the rivers to deliver wheat to the starving. Transport aircraft and crews, flown in from Canada, delivered food to the most-affected areas. Canadian engineers arrived to help re-establish the power grid; others worked to rehabilitate locomotives sabotaged in the fighting. We brought in equipment for thousands of tube wells to provide fresh water. I signed an agreement allowing work on a ground satellite station, planned before the civil war, to resume, providing the country with reliable international telephone communications for the first time.

I pitched in to help my CIDA colleagues, acting as an observer for aircraft crews as they loaded wheat and flour in Chittagong and delivered it to famine-affected villages, inspecting the progress being made in boring wells, and accompanying non-governmental aid workers in their trips to refugee camps. The purpose of the high commission in Dhaka, we all understood, was to deliver aid. There were no other reasons for Canada to set up a diplomatic mission there. In those days, few Canadians owed their ethnic origin to this part of the world. Trade prospects with such an impoverished nation were nil. And in strategic-security terms, Bangladesh did not count. Thirty years and several billion dollars in aid later, there is a large and thriving Bangladeshi community in Canada, but the other aspects of the relationship remain unchanged.

The Father of the Nation
Where I was really useful to the CIDA officers, however, was in cultivating good relations with heads of diplomatic missions, with Bangladeshi ministers, and with the prime minister to smooth the way for my CIDA colleagues to do their jobs. One of my early priorities was to establish links with Prime Minister Sheikh Mujibur Rahman, who had been released from a political prison in West Pakistan and flown to Dhaka some months before I arrived.

Sheikh Mujib, as he was affectionately known, was fifty-three when I met him. The son of a middle-class rural landowner, he had been educated in Calcutta and Dhaka before throwing himself into the struggle for Bangladeshi independence. In 1949, he was a founder of the Awami League political party, was repeatedly elected to both the regional and national legislative assemblies, and was frequently imprisoned. Like Nelson Mandela, whom I was to meet many years later when I was high commissioner in South Africa, he did not become embittered by the long years in prison. Unlike Mandela, Sheikh Mujib had no sense of what to do with power once he achieved it, and had only a hazy notion of the world beyond his own corner of it. Coming back from the Commonwealth summit in Ottawa in 1973, he told me in wonder that the streets were deserted when he looked out his window at night. Were there no people in Canada's capital?

The culture shock he experienced in his encounter with Canada was just as great as mine in meeting Bangladesh.

Bangladesh's prime minister radiated charisma, as the leader who had led his people to independence. Sheikh Mujib was another Fidel Castro as an orator, able to hold millions of people in the palm of his hand when he gave speeches lasting for hours at giant outdoor rallies. He cultivated his links with the people, making himself available to all Bangladeshis in daily audiences, during which he provided advice and promised help in the manner of a village headman. Personally, he was unfailingly cour-teous, even kind, taking me for walks in his garden and showing me his favourite pets in a small private zoo. He was always pre-pared to meet the occasional Canadian visitor, such as Ivan Head, who once came with a message from Prime Minister Trudeau.

The same masses who loved their prime minister in 1972 would turn against him in 1975, and the armed forces would kill him. His military bodyguards saluted as an assassination squad of soldiers rolled onto the grounds of his residence one evening in June of that year. They shot him, his wife, those family members unlucky enough to be at home, servants, guests, and even the small animals in his private zoo. The army chief of staff then seized power, inaugurating years of political instability.

Hunger and Disease

The highlight of my thirty-five years in Canada's foreign service was being associated with the World Health Organization cam-paign that eradicated smallpox in Bangladesh. When I arrived in Dhaka, a major epidemic was raging, which had been touched off by an outbreak in refugee camps established in West Bengal during the civil war and carried back by the ten million exiles who had streamed home in January and February of 1972. People died in the tens of thousands. The virus, we all knew, was highly infec-tious and spread by direct contact from one person to another or by exposure to bodily fluids or contaminated clothing or bedding.

Several times after I had attended a dinner at a private home, the worried host would telephone me to say that a member of their household staff had come down with the disease. Was my vaccination up to date? Embarrassed silence would greet my question on the fate of the unfortunate cook, waiter, or watchman. Bicycle-rickshaw drivers were paid handsome fees to haul away the condemned who were left to die at the entrances to Dhaka's few overburdened and underequipped hospitals.

I was thus sympathetic when the head of the World Health Organization approached me to ask if Canada could provide ten million dollars to fund the supply of sufficient vaccine to stem the outbreak. My CIDA colleagues in Dhaka were in agreement and CIDA headquarters provided authority for us to spend the money in record time. I was summoned by the senior Bangladeshi official responsible for managing aid flows and was royally chewed out. I had not followed channels, he said; there were committees that should have been consulted. Despite his unhappiness, the World Health Organization soon had the vaccine to begin a massive smallpox-eradication effort. Teams fanned out over the country, literally chasing people over rooftops when necessary to ensure that everyone was vaccinated. By the time I left Bangladesh at the end of 1973, the world's last smallpox epidemic was being brought under control.

A Planeload of Babies

I was less successful in dealing with a demand from headquarters that I round up several hundred babies to be sent to Canada for adoption. Tens of thousands of women had been raped as part of the Pakistani policy of intimidation, foreshadowing the approach taken by the Bosnian Serb army three decades later, and many became pregnant. In conservative Bangladeshi society, it was unheard-of for families to tolerate the presence of such offspring within their family circles. Scandinavian doctors established a clinic and worked overtime throughout the spring of 1972 performing abortions on young women. The Sisters of Charity religious order, under the direction of Mother Teresa in nearby Calcutta, set up shop and saved as many of the babies as possible.

The Bangladeshi Ministry of Information, in a propaganda effort to encourage the flow of more aid money to Bangladesh, claimed that more than two hundred thousand women were pregnant as a result of rapes. Enormous publicity was given to this allegation in the international press, prompting a huge demand from people in Europe and in Canada to adopt these babies. Without seeking confirmation that the scale of the problem was as great as depicted in the media, the Canadian Cabinet authorized the dispatch of a special flight of a Canadian Forces 707 to Dhaka to pick up a planeload of infants for adoption in Canada. Foreign Affairs sent instructions telling me to select at least three hundred of these infants supposedly awaiting placement. Once I had gathered them together, a team of Canadian nurses, pediatricians, and social workers would arrive on the special flight to pick them up.

I visited the nursery where Mother Teresa's Sisters of Charity had set up a temporary home for the babies. There I learned that the Bangladeshi government had greatly exaggerated the number of babies being born as a result of rapes, and Scandinavian families had adopted all available infants. There were none left. This was wonderful news, of course, but not for me. I frantically visited orphanages throughout the country and consulted international agencies active in helping children, to find that there were older children but only a few babies available – certainly not enough to fill a 707. Foreign Affairs was furious. Obviously I had not looked hard enough. How could they explain this to the prime minister, to the Cabinet, to the non-governmental organizations, and to the Canadian public? The director of the South Asia division sent a nasty message telling me that I was not doing my job.

The team of Canadian pediatricians, nurses, social workers, and even a lawyer arrived unannounced at my office to press me to do as I had been told. I took the team to the nursery and arranged for them to visit orphanages to see for themselves. The disgruntled Canadian team soon gave up on me and decided to take direct action, barging into the residence of the prime minister and staging a sit-in. Not wishing to offend one of his country's largest donors, Sheikh Mujib went out the back door, turned off the air conditioning and lights, and let his uninvited guests stay until they grew hot and tired and left the premises. He then summoned me to his office the next day to berate me for their behaviour.

"What would your prime minister have done if a group of Bangladeshis had invaded his residence in Ottawa? He would have had them arrested. Some Canadians believe that they can act here with impunity because Bangladesh is a Third World country and you give us a lot of money."

I stammered out some lame excuses, but he was right.

With my help, the Canadian team eventually found fifteen babies and children, including abandoned street waifs, and departed with them on a regular Air-India flight for Canada via Calcutta. At the time, I was glad to see the last of them. But I was humbled when I met one of the children twenty years later and realized what a difference the intervention of these private Canadian citizens had made in his life.

Canada's Diplomatic Presence

Six months after my arrival, the Canadian staff had increased to seven and the locally engaged contingent to fifty. We moved from a small house originally rented by the CIDA officers to more spacious quarters and installed an emergency generator. No longer would we have to work with towels around our shoulders to soak up the heavy flow of perspiration that poured onto our papers when the overhead fans failed. Just as important, we established excellent links with a diplomatic free shop in Bangkok that kept us supplied with beer, otherwise unavailable in a Muslim country.

Now we were left with two main problems: obtaining decent accommodation and remaining healthy.

Since Canada was one of the first to establish a diplomatic mission in Bangladesh, we had first pick of available houses and quickly rented seven for the Canadian staff. Unfortunately, we had no furniture. Headquarters tried to be helpful by sending the very best furniture Ottawa stores had to offer, by air at enormous expense. Nothing was too good, they said, for Canada's brave employees in Dhaka. The thought was commendable, the initiative excellent, but the execution faulty. Apparently the only people in Canada unaware that East Pakistan was by then Bangladesh were the Foreign Affairs shipping experts who dispatched our precious cargo to the Pakistani capital of Islamabad, for onward transit. Pakistan and Bangladesh were still in a formal state of war, and links between the two, other than via the Red Cross, were non-existent. We never saw our furniture.

By this time, we were thoroughly fed up with the artificial existence of hotel life and longed for homes of our own. Every night we faced the same menu in the dining room. Every night the same group of expatriates sat down to eat. Every night the same band of octogenarian musicians, outfitted in the same frayed tuxedos, played the same renditions of what was truly the world's most awful Dixieland music. As I look back, I see myself as the anti-hero Phil Connors in the cult movie *Groundhog Day*, condemned to relive the same day, day after day, as punishment for some mortal sin. Then one night, several hip young Bangladeshis came to listen to the strange music. A young Newfoundland member of the air crew flying grain then violated local custom and asked one of the Bangladeshi girls to dance. She said no but he insisted. Her brother escorted her out the door.

I thought that was the end of the matter and went to bed. An hour later, the senior high-commission clerk, Denis Ryan, who had become a close friend and constant companion, and with whom I had just had dinner, pounded on my door. There had been mayhem in the hotel, he said. The young Bangladeshi had returned with a gang of his friends. He was, it turned out, a member of the ruling party, a war hero, and someone with sufficient clout to order all the Bangladeshi hotel staff to clear out and let him exact revenge for an insult to his family's honour. Seizing the Newfoundlander, who was sitting quietly in the dining room with Denis, they started to beat him, but he broke free and fled howling like a pig being slaughtered, first to the reception area and then to the kitchen. Denis did not intervene, aware of the diplomatic code of conduct that discouraged employees from engaging in brawls; and besides, there were too many of them. With no one coming to his rescue, our hero seized a rake left by a gardener at the kitchen door and used it to beat off his attackers before racing through the back rooms of the hotel and losing his pursuers on the stairs. I made arrangements for him to leave the country on the first flight out the next day.

The hotel, it was evident, was either too boring or too exciting. Making an executive decision, I bought furniture at the local market to furnish our empty houses. If Bangladeshis could sleep on mattresses stuffed with the shells of betel nuts, sit on chairs and sofas as hard as boards, and forgo curtains and other effete luxuries of the developed world, then so could the Canadians. My doubtful team agreed, moved to their newly furnished homes, but were not happy. They apparently did not appreciate the scorpions, spiders, and cockroaches that occasionally crawled out of the stuffing to visit. I came up with another solution.

Aware that the high commission in New Delhi was about to move into an up-to-date office and residential complex, complete with new furniture, I received permission from headquarters to take my pick of the castoffs. It would be up to me to find a way to move my hoard to Dhaka, 3,200 kilometres away over the Indian and Bangladeshi road network, the latter still devastated by the war. Our colleagues at the high commission would not help

– the Dhaka mission was too puny to merit attention. Denis and I travelled to New Delhi, to Calcutta, and to the border crossing between India and Bangladesh, to make the arrangements ourselves. The Indian authorities, infamous for their red tape, initially refused to authorize the export of used furniture. We sat in the Foreign Ministry office in Calcutta pestering the local officials until they finally gave in just to get rid of us. They stamped our documents and approved the dispatch of two separate convoys of fifteen trucks each. Fortunately, by this time it was winter, the dry season; the drivers were able to cross the parched beds of the smaller rivers whose bridges had been destroyed and to use ferries to cross the giant Bangladeshi Meghna River.

I had achieved great savings for the Canadian taxpayer and my Canadian colleagues in Dhaka were delighted. There was one drawback. The furniture, pockmarked by cigarette burns and stained by coffee and wine spills, was Scandinavian modern and virtually indestructible; it was not replaced by Ottawa for a decade. The staff who succeeded my team and had to live with New Delhi's leavings was not as enthusiastic as we had been at our coup.

Health was the other main concern, particularly for staff who had children. Aside from smallpox, cholera and tuberculosis were the big killers. The first was spread through contaminated water, dehydrating victims so rapidly through diarrhea and vomiting that death followed quickly if treatment was not provided. All visitors entering the country and all passengers departing the airport had to show proof of an inoculation no more than three months old. My World Health Organization friend advised me, however, never to submit to the painful and unhygienic procedure at the Dhaka airport.

It was timely advice. I once arrived at the airport to discover that it had been four months since my last shot. The needles produced to inoculate me reposed in a dirty basin filled with blood and water. I refused to accept the risk of contracting hepatitis A,

B, and C, and who knows what else. Putting ten dollars in my immunization booklet, I handed it to the doctor, who returned it to me stamped up-to-date with the money gone. Then I went to a clinic in Thailand and received a sanitary inoculation.

Tuberculosis was even more widespread and insidious, since it led to a lingering death during which the sufferer continued to infect those around him or her. The situation was all the more tragic since the illness was treatable, but neither the international community nor the country itself could even begin to make available the resources required. It was with a sense of helplessness that I was obliged to dismiss a number of our first local Bangladeshi staff who had been hired on the understanding that they pass a medical examination. Their reports came back showing severe tuberculosis infection and we could neither keep them nor provide medical assistance.

In those days, the Canadian Department of Health and Welfare would send their doctor from Kuala Lumpur to Dhaka to ensure that we received proper medical care. We dreaded his visits. Not, as you may think, for what he did to us. The first time he came, I invited him to lunch at my home. Talking garrulously, he swallowed a piece of chicken without chewing. I rushed him to a local doctor who received him in his bare feet in his combination bedroom-office. He then probed and poked in his throat with a metal instrument to no avail before saying it was not long enough. Perhaps, he said, he should cut open our doctor's throat and extract the offending bone *manu militari*. First, however, he would need an X-ray. My National Health and Welfare colleague agreed, at least initially.

The sole X-ray machine at the local hospital was a foot-operated contraption that looked somewhat like my grandmother's old sewing machine. The Canadian doctor did as he was told, entering a small room and sitting still. The technician started working the treadle as a small crowd of the curious gathered to watch a foreign doctor be treated Bangladeshi style. When he had reached maximum velocity, the technician pushed a button. There was a mighty flash in the next room where the X-ray machine was located to capture an image of the throat of its victim. The X-ray plate was so dirty, however, that no one among the gathering of onlookers who rushed to provide their opinion could distinguish between dirt and bone.

My colleague, who now had his doubts about the wisdom of an operation in Dhaka, left the premises in a hurry. His throat raw from the ministrations of his Bangladeshi counterpart and pierced by bone, he suffered for thirty-six hours until he could leave the country. On his second visit, he contracted pneumonia. The third time, he caught an illness that left him confused and that no one in Dhaka could diagnose. We put him on a flight to Bangkok and thankfully never saw him again.

I found that I could remain healthy as long as I avoided meals where everyone ate with their hands from a common bowl. This was not always possible, since few Bangladeshis used cutlery in their homes. Everyone digs in to scoop rice and curry out of common dishes on the table with their right hand, the left being reserved for use in the toilet. The illness that I did contract regularly was a bloody diarrhea accompanied by a high fever, an illness familiar to all those who have served in South Asia. I would visit the one expatriate doctor in the city, submit to a test or two, and be prescribed medication from the stock that we kept on hand at the high commission (there were few reliable drugs on the local market). My other illness, which was more of a nuisance, was a tropical scalp infection. Since no medicine in our high-commission pharmacy could ease my discomfort, the doctor doused my scalp with gentian violet, a mainstay remedy used by First World War doctors treating trench foot and other unmentionable soldierly diseases. Gentian violet is indelible, and my hair and neck remained purple throughout the posting.

The one serious illness I contracted was avoidable. With an Australian colleague I had been invited to an event hosted by the Dhaka Ladies' Business Club. The dessert was a cold, milk-based delicacy, something I normally avoided eating at open-air public events because of the risk of contamination from flies. I looked at my Australian colleague, we both shrugged, and I swallowed the goody. The Australian did the same. I got typhoid fever; he contracted hepatitis. I left on emergency medical evacuation to a clinic in Thailand for a difficult two weeks, returning to Dhaka weak but eager to resume my duties. My colleague departed for Australia, never to return.

Other staff members remained healthy, although a spouse became seriously ill after leaving Dhaka at the end of her husband's assignment. She began to suffer excruciating pain throughout her body and was consumed with relentless itching that no amount of scratching could relieve. She thought she was dying from a rare and undetectable form of cancer because her disbelieving doctors could neither diagnose her ailment nor ease her distress. Was it all in her head? Then, to her relief mingled with horror and disgust, she discovered worms burrowing out of her skin. Walking barefoot in her home in Dhaka, she had picked up a South Asian parasite which had incubated in and fed off her innards for months. All too often, our diplomatic families bring more than memories home with them.

The Face of Evil

The Bangladeshi people had suffered greatly through natural disaster and war and during my time in the country were still enduring great hardship despite the aid flowing in from abroad. Most were charming, gregarious, and fond of telling and listening to amusing stories. Some were outstanding in their dignity, piety, and compassion. I was often invited into private homes for tea and meals and was made welcome whenever I visited mosques. However, as always when countries and societies suffer turmoil following civil unrest and warfare, the worst as well as the best in human nature is exposed.

At the national-day reception of his country, a celebrated Bangladeshi war hero, decked out in ceremonial finery and covered in medals, helped entertain the guests. He had recently been promoted to the position of military aide-de-camp to the president and was proud to be associating with diplomats. As his contribution to the small talk, he explained how he had managed to escape house arrest in West Pakistan during the war and make his way to Bangladesh to join the freedom struggle of his people. He had, he said, hired a guide to take him over the border through the dangerous mountains separating Pakistan and Afghanistan. He had then killed his guide.

"You understand why I did it, of course," said the ever-so-charming young man. "I needed to save money for my onward journey to Dhaka. And now you must try our chapatis. Our kitchen is the best in the city."

On a visit to a remote city in the north, a stern Bangladeshi security official visited me at the guest house where my companions and I were lodged. I had, he said, no right travelling in this area without official approval, and he warned me specifically not to visit the local refugee camp. My curiosity piqued, I saw a camp where dirty secrets were kept hidden. All the men and older boys had been removed to be shot or imprisoned; the camp was filled with starving children whose abused mothers implored me to publicize their plight.

Likewise, no mercy was shown to the vanquished in Dhaka. Young members of the governing party would cordon off sections of camps housing hundreds of thousands of people who had supported Pakistan in the civil war and who had been driven from their homes by the winners. They would rape the young women and steal the miserable possessions of the occupants. Canadian volunteers working in the camps told me the police and the army simply looked on. And injustice to them came not only from their Bangladeshi conquerors. I once accompanied the Swiss delegate of the International Committee of the Red Cross on a tour of one of the giant camps. Scabies-infected people, formerly middle-class members of society, waited with quiet despair for word that they would be accepted as refugees in Pakistan, their former protector. A tall distinguished-looking refugee approached to ask my companion a simple question, only to be coldly rebuffed. I thought that it was sometimes easier to love humanity as a concept without caring for people as individuals.

Similarly, corrupt Bangladeshi officials in Chittagong collaborated with Indian officials in Calcutta to siphon off wheat provided by donor countries and sell it on the black market in India. It was often only possible to buy fuel for my car by paying exorbitant prices to gas-station owners who hoarded available stocks. I had to pay bribes for the smallest service and was once even on the receiving end. Representatives of a wealthy minority handed me a sack of black pearls, not for any special favour rendered but to keep me in a sympathetic frame of mind if their community was forced to emigrate to Canada in a hurry, in which case they would need visas. They were incredulous when I handed it back.

La Condition Humaine

The posting was, in its own way, as full of adventure and colour as Colombia had been two years previously. Five times a day, the air was filled with the cries of the mullah calling the faithful to prayer. During the monsoon, rain pounded down with a ferocity unknown in Canada, transforming dust, feces, and garbage into mud, and bringing fresh outbreaks of cholera, worsening the already miserable condition of the people. Despairing women and children congregated daily at the gate to my house, their hands thrust through the entrance gates mutely appealing for something to eat. I averted my eyes, aware that if I gave food to even one person, a mob of thousands would materialize and a riot would ensue. Desperate to find some way to help other than through the mission's aid program, I took to driving through the worst slums and rapidly handing used clothing or a gift of food to some desperate-looking person and then fleeing back to my car before a mob could form. To obtain a sense of the life of an ordinary Bangladeshi, I once hired a bicycle-rickshaw operator, and asked the surprised driver to trade places with me and be the passenger while I did the pedalling. Although in good shape physically in those years, I nearly collapsed from exhaustion after pedalling through ten kilometres of traffic. The life of a Bangladeshi, I realized, was as nasty, brutish, and short as the life of any medieval European serf, and probably worse.

Every day brought new encounters with unique personalities, each with a story to tell. There were Irish and Indian nurses seeking to alleviate the suffering of the flesh; priests and nuns anxious to minister to the spirit; the occasional CIA or KGB spy trying to recruit people of influence; CUSO volunteers; oilmen with American accents claiming to be Canadians, attempting to talk the new government into granting them concessions to drill for gas offshore; and Soviet helicopter pilots counting the days until their assignments were over.

I met André Malraux, one of the great French intellectual figures of the twentieth century and author of *The Human Condition*, who spoke in aphorisms when I met him briefly at the Alliance Française. A long-standing supporter of independence for the Muslim people of East Bengal, Malraux had come to see the new state and despite his ill health was exploited mercilessly by the propaganda arm of Bangladeshi government, who kept him busy and on the move. He died shortly thereafter. I accompanied Lotta Hitschmanova, the legendary founder of the Unitarian Service Committee, on some of her rounds by rowboat to isolated villages; although constantly surrounded by an ensemble of saffron-robed Buddhist acolytes, she interacted with the poorest of the poor in a way that maintained the dignity of donor and recipient.

I shook the hand of Kurt Waldheim, the United Nations secretary-general, whose black wartime record was then unknown; seeing my smiling non–Bangladeshi face in a receiving line, he could not resist whispering some condescending remark on the backwardness of his hosts. Then there was Geoffrey Rippon, British minister of trade, who was in town to inform the Bangladesh government of Britain's "irrevocable decision" to join the European Common Market, as it was known at that time. Listening to his debriefing over lunch at the residence of the British high commissioner, I did not then appreciate that he was really saying that Britain was turning a page; the economic ties linking the Commonwealth would soon be a thing of the past.

Once my initial culture shock was forgotten, I had a wonderful time. The Marine Club bar was my hangout on Friday nights – the beer was cheap, the music and laughter loud, and the company good. It was a place to unwind and forget the troubles of the week, to meet new arrivals, and to plan expeditions to tea plantations in the Sylhet Hills, to refugee camps in the interior, and to major cities along the coast. There, too, we planned trips to Calcutta – surreal, polluted, ugly, overpopulated, and throbbing with life – for we all wanted to escape every so often to the world outside Bangladesh, a place in some respects where time had stood still. In Chittagong, my Canadian hosts, members of a Catholic religious order implanted in the region for the past hundred years, kept referring to the "recent" visit of Pierre Trudeau as a backpacker. He had, it transpired, been their guest a quarter of a century earlier.

The posting coincided with the dying years of the Vietnam War. In my liaison trips to Bangkok, the bars were filled with thousands of American servicemen on leave from the action. The mood was one of *fin de régime*. They were losing the war and no one supported them, not even their own people. Then came the American bombing campaigns of North Vietnam of December 1972 – the infamous Linebacker II Christmas bombings that killed thousands of civilians in Hanoi, which constituted the last gasp of American involvement in the war. The bombings inflamed a Bangladeshi population already hostile to the United States for siding with their former oppressor, Pakistan, against India in the war leading to the independence of their country a year earlier. Mobs roamed the streets carrying iron bars ready to do in any American they found. No one was ever caught. Our American friends simply placed Canadian flags on their cars and pretended to be Canadian.

Last Days in Bangladesh

However emotionally satisfying, Dhaka was difficult and I spent an enormous amount of time bolstering the morale of the other members of the staff. I often invited them to my place for informal dinners and film evenings. We sat outside on lawn chairs in the evening, drinking imported Thai beer and watching ancient National Film Board of Canada classics such as *Life in the Marsh* or *Paddle to the Sea* as our battered old sixteen-millimetre projector hissed and sputtered its reedy soundtrack into the humid night air. I introduced flexible office hours to allow staff who so wished to start at seven in the morning and leave at three in the afternoon, giving them time before darkness fell to play a round at Dhaka's one golf course. Constructed years before by occupying Pakistani troops for the amusement of their officers, the course had its own special "hazards," which I, fortunately, never encountered: cobras and the occasional anti-personnel land mine left over from the war.

To my staff, I repeated the mantra that Dhaka, while not without its problems, was a wonderful place and we were all making a contribution to relieving human misery. This was true and my staff were a happy lot, bonding together in a way I would see nowhere else in my foreign-service career. The highlight of the posting for my original team was Denis's marriage to Jean Androchow, a secretary who joined our staff in the late fall of

1972. I was proud to be Denis's best man when they tied the knot in Dhaka's modest Roman Catholic church. I was, however, ready to move on, and was happy when told in late 1973 that, as a reward for my services in Dhaka, I would be given a choice assignment in Belgium at the Canadian delegation to NATO. The personnel at the high commission then decided to play a joke on me. One week before my departure date in November 1973, the communicator entered my office looking very serious and handed me a message from headquarters: "Posting to NATO cancelled for operational reasons. Another offer will be made in six months."

I lost control of myself, crying to the ceiling: "How can they do this to me? I want out of this hole now! Who in their right mind would stay here any longer than they absolutely had to?"

I added a few choice phrases and looked around to see the Canadian staff and their spouses staring at me with stunned expressions. The communicator had written the message himself and had assembled everyone to witness good old Jim rejoice at his good luck in being granted more time in Dhaka. Smiling thinly and crumpling the message, I said that of course I knew it was fake. No one believed me, but I was forgiven. I think.

5

NATO During the Cold War

Edward Teller, the fanatically anti-communist father of the hydrogen bomb, who could have been a character from Stanley Kubrick's Dr. Strangelove, *came once and scared me with his assumption that there could be a winner in a nuclear war.*

The culture shock of arriving in Brussels in 1973 was almost as great as it had been when I first saw Dhaka. Dhaka had been poor, hot, and dirty, but teeming with people and full of the vitality of their struggle for survival. Brussels was the rich capital of Europe, cloaked that dark November in thick fog and undergoing the heaviest snowfall and coldest weather in decades. The discomfort of the populace, huddled indoors, was made worse by a shortage of fuel resulting from the oil embargo imposed by Middle Eastern countries in the wake of the just-ended October Israeli-Arab war.

In Dhaka, I had been entrusted with broad responsibilities even many ambassadors did not have in terms of budgets, personnel, and post programs. In Brussels, I was just one of five or six first secretaries, each with specialist responsibilities but buried well down in a pecking order in which various colonels, counsellors, and a deputy permanent representative ranked higher on a list that culminated in the exalted position of the permanent representative. In Dhaka I had a house with servants – albeit barefoot – as well as a car and driver. In Brussels, I was assigned a poorly maintained apartment with paper-thin walls two hours by car from the office.

The Madness of Man

I accepted this fall in status without too much difficulty, but it was a shock to be exposed in short order to two different faces of the madness of man: the consequences of brutal ethnic conflict in Bangladesh, and the preparations for a war that could end civilization as we knew it in Europe. In Dhaka I had worked as part of an international effort that included close collaboration with the Soviets, Hungarians, and East Germans together with the Americans, British, and Dutch towards a common humanitarian goal. In Brussels, twenty-four years of Cold War had hardened attitudes. Warsaw Pact countries were the enemy. A million and a half men faced each other, fully mobilized, ready to fight the greatest tank battle in history across the central European plain. And thousands of battlefield nuclear weapons on both sides were kept in a high state of readiness.

First Impressions

Arriving in Brussels on a direct flight from Montreal late on a Saturday morning, I took a taxi the short distance to NATO headquarters in the suburb of Evere. I expected the staff to be on duty even though it was a Saturday, and they were. Jacques Roy, later to be Canadian ambassador to France and a good friend, welcomed me. He introduced me to the deputy permanent representative and then to the permanent representative himself, Arthur Menzies. Arthur had joined Foreign Affairs in 1940 and belonged to the generation of officers who had put Canada on the map in the post-war period. He and his wife, Sheila, took me in hand and provided the guidance about diplomatic life abroad that would stand me in good stead for the rest of my career. Arthur was replaced several years later by another outstanding senior officer, Gerry Hardy.

A huge cold edifice, the headquarters was originally constructed as a hospital but was turned over to NATO when de Gaulle ordered the alliance out of France in 1966. It housed the civilian and military delegations of NATO's fifteen member states as well as facilities for the international civil and military staff. Delegations occupied offices along separate corridors, and when you walked along them you got the impression of a cloister with industrious monks quietly carrying out their devotions. Their leaders were the permanent representatives, drawn from the highest ranks of their diplomatic services. They formed the North Atlantic Council, the most senior body in NATO; along with the members of the Military Committee (the military body representing the chiefs of staff and subordinate to the council) they behaved as if they were princes of the Church. Their work was vital to the security of their countries and was treated with the utmost seriousness, and they expected the same treatment. They knew each other intimately and considered NATO to be an exclusive club of the initiated. All had come of age during the Second World War. Many were veterans, and all of them had been marked profoundly by the consequences of conflict. The German ambassador, who had lost an arm in submarine warfare, and a fellow countryman, the chairman of the Military Committee, badly burned in a tank battle, were visible reminders of the cost Germans had borne for the folly of their leaders.

A number of the Europeans were drawn from the nobility, and were addressed in meetings as "Baron," "Count," or even "Prince" in a style dating from another era. I found this pretentious in the extreme, particularly since I had no title. Several of them frequently sprinkled their speeches with Greek and Latin allusions, showing off their classical education to the rest of us peasants. As a note-taker sitting behind the Canadian permanent representative in the council chamber, an important part of my job seemed to be to laugh at the jokes of the Belgian permanent representative, funny or not, and to express existential sadness when the Danish permanent representative, wearing a perpetual scowl and imagining himself a fitting inheritor of Kierkegaardian angst, described the fate awaiting humanity were NATO to fail.

As had been the case for a generation – and as would be the case seventeen years later when I took my turn as Canada's ambassador at the same table – the permanent representatives of the United States and France, each vying for the security leadership of Europe, could be counted on to clash on all issues, big and small, whatever their merits. Their combat in my initial years at NATO was worthy of the two great nations. Donald Rumsfeld, scion of a wealthy Chicago family, Princeton University graduate, and captain of the wrestling team, an American filter-tip cigarette always in hand, faced off against the Compte de Rose, haughty, brilliant, and Cartesian, and never without a potent Gauloise in his ivory cigarette holder. We all enjoyed the princely combat and felt cheated when Rumsfeld departed to become chief of staff to President Gerald Ford (and was later secretary of defence for the Ford and George W. Bush administrations, and a prominent player during the 2003 war with Iraq). His replacement was the legendary David Bruce, a cultured, wealthy Southerner, who had been European head of the Second World War Office of Strategic Services (precursor to the CIA) but was now a septuagenarian past his prime. The Compte de Rose was victorious in every dispute with Bruce, who had to rely on cue cards in the cut and thrust of council debate.

The weekly meetings of council, in conference room number one, were the heart of NATO activity. With so much testosterone in the air, the power and energy of a primeval beast radiated from the room. With only a limited number of seats available for each delegation, note-takers ranging in rank from third secretaries to counsellors waited expectantly outside the council room. They would then file in discreetly when it came their turn to sit behind the great ones. Summits and ministerial meetings with presidents, prime ministers, foreign ministers, defence ministers, generals, admirals, air marshals, and political directors – all impeccably dressed in the most expensive and conservatively tailored suits and with shoes so highly polished they positively glowed – were periods of amplified drama. Their body language conveyed the message that NATO – not the United Nations – was the real centre of world power and that it was the arbiter of the destiny of the West. After all, as Stalin is said to have asked about the Pope in the Second World War, how many divisions did the Vatican have?

A flashing green light would call the mighty to take their seats. The session would be called to order by Secretary-General Baron Joseph Luns, a former Dutch foreign minister, who would try to cut through the pomposity with earthy humour – inevitably upsetting the Netherlands delegation, which would have preferred him to display a more sophisticated face of their country to the world. Clerks would then scurry from delegation to delegation, handing out copies of speeches and draft language for the communiqué to be issued at the end of meeting. Silence would descend as the representative of the United States, always the first to take the floor, spoke. The hum of a dozen languages would issue from the earphones of delegates, transmitted from interpreter booths around the room. The representatives of Germany, France, or the United Kingdom would then take the floor. Canada or Italy would follow, and the others, in no particular order, would come after. Attention would flag after the first few speakers. The great had pronounced and the views of the others were not of great interest, although attention to their views would be feigned – the appearance that all were equal, even if some members were more equal than others, had to be maintained.

The review of defence plans and the examination of budgets were standard items on the agenda. More interesting were consultations on specific political issues, such as the situation in the Soviet Union and in regional hot spots. Almost every week senior personalities came to provide briefings. Edward Teller, the fanatically anti-communist father of the hydrogen bomb, who could have been a character in Stanley Kubrick's *Dr. Strangelove*, came once and scared me with his assumption that there could be a winner in a nuclear exchange. An occasional visitor, always providing a much-needed balanced perspective on East-West relations, was Canada's veteran ambassador in Moscow, Robert Ford, a Kremlinologist and man of letters.

At the military level, priority was given to keeping up-to-date the long-standing plans to repel a possible invasion by Warsaw Pact troops across the north German plain and through the mountain passes of Austria. Since the Warsaw Pact forces outnumbered those of NATO in personnel and equipment, they had the capability to strike deep into Germany with less than two days' warning. NATO's flexible-response strategy sought to hold back the onslaught by conventional, or non-nuclear, forces in the first instance and by battlefield nuclear weapons in the second. If the battlefield nuclear weapons did not work, nuclear weapons would be fired from the continental United States and from American and British submarines at targets in the Soviet Union.

Every year, NATO held paper exercises (a type of war game without the actual involvement of military forces) to test how it would handle a real crisis with the Warsaw Pact. Given that any conflict was likely to start in Europe, European cabinet ministers dropped other duties to participate. In Canada and the United States, where the threat was more distant, public servants usually assumed the roles of their ministers. I was involved each time during my years in NATO as a senior exercise officer for Canada during these two-week-long deadly serious games. In the preplanned scenarios, we would have to cope with a simulated buildup in tension with the countries of the Warsaw Pact leading to war. It was always assumed that NATO would be unable to hold back the massive tank armies of the Warsaw Pact, which would rapidly punch their way through allied defences in Central Europe and roll westward.

Then the exercises became really interesting. Following the script, we would draw selectively on NATO's stock of battlefield nuclear weapons to simulate explosions on land and on sea to save

Western Europe from the Red Army and its Central European colleagues. At this point, the war game or exercise simulation would end. No one wanted to deal with the reality that our use of nuclear weapons in this way (called "first use" by the initiates in strategic-military jargon) would probably lead to a general nuclear exchange between the superpowers that would destroy the world. The choice facing NATO should war begin was a defeat at the hands of the conventional forces of the Soviet Union and its allies, or nuclear war in which no one would win.

Trying to Change the Doomsday Scenario

To deal with this doomsday scenario, a twofold approach was followed to control the use of nuclear weapons and to rectify the imbalance in conventional forces. For the first problem, the Americans launched direct negotiations with the Soviets to reduce the size of their strategic nuclear arsenals. The first phase had concluded successfully the year before I arrived in Brussels, when the Strategic Arms Limitation Talks (SALT) agreement of 1972 limited intercontinental and sea-launched ballistic missiles. On the second problem, NATO had been pushing the Soviet Union for years to deal with the imbalance in military personnel in Central Europe. The Soviets, however, were not interested. They had no desire to give up their military advantage. Then in the early 1970s, NATO found something to trade. The Soviets wanted recognition for the border changes they had imposed on Central Europe after the Second World War and called for the convening of an international conference for that purpose. The countries of NATO eventually agreed, confident that they could safeguard their interests. The two processes were then launched: the Mutual and Balanced Force Reductions talks and the Conference of Security Cooperation in Europe.

In 1975, both NATO and the Warsaw Pact gave up trying to reach a deal on Mutual and Balanced Force Reductions. By that time, the countries involved in the Conference of Security

Cooperation in Europe negotiations had signed the "Final Act," which spelled out agreement by the parties on a complex package of economic, military, and human-rights issues. The Soviets thought they had achieved their goal of obtaining recognition for their border changes and were in no hurry to make military concessions on non-nuclear forces where they held the advantage. The United States, for its part, seems to have recognized that these talks were going nowhere and thereafter gave little priority to them. Neither side was prepared, however, to take responsibility for ending the negotiations; they were to drag on for years.

Learning on the Job

Unfortunately, my main job was as a staff officer representing the Canadian delegation on these ill-fated talks. It was an exercise in frustration. Those of us in Brussels and Vienna, labouring away on the issue of non-nuclear forces in Europe, were largely forgotten by our headquarters and by the other members of our delegations. Making matters even more difficult for me, I had only a rough familiarity with arms-control negotiations and even less with the arcane field of technical military tactics and strategy. Nevertheless, I found myself on a technical working group, along with a group of colonels from the other delegations, preparing background studies on issues relevant to the negotiations. These papers – on standardized definitions of troop categories, permissible sizes of military manoeuvres, notification of troop movements, and examination of different verification regimes – were sent on for consideration by the political committee of senior diplomats hammering out common NATO positions for the ambassadors negotiating with their Warsaw Pact opposite numbers in Vienna. Good-natured military officers did their best to provide me with advice and keep me out of trouble.

Luckily, the depth of my ineptitude was suspected by none of my superiors. The subject matter was so detailed and technical they did not try to understand the issues, and never sought to find out what I did with my days. It did not hurt that I was also Canada's representative on the political committee, most of whose members had even less of a grasp of the issues than I did, since I at least had the benefit of being exposed to the subject matter at the technical level.

Fortunately, I had other, more rewarding work, serving as a general dogsbody and backup officer to the ambassador on the crises of the day, as the NATO council met continuously to monitor the effect on the alliance of the overthrow of the military dictatorships in Greece and Portugal. Despite the brave words to the contrary in its 1949 treaty, NATO tolerated among its members a number of countries which were not democracies and had poor human-rights records. As has always been the case when the vital security interests of states were at stake, *realpolitik* trumped shared values. Churchill, speaking of the West's partnership with communist Moscow during the Second World War, said that he would ally Britain with the devil himself to defeat Nazi Germany. In addition to Greece under the colonels and Portugal under Salazar, Turkey was a member in good standing despite being consistently condemned by the Council of Europe for its treatment of prisoners and minorities. During the Cold War, NATO even maintained a close but quiet relationship with apartheid South Africa, anxious to use its ports in case of hostilities with the Warsaw Pact.

Since usually I was not fully occupied, I took the initiative to start sending to Ottawa assessments of major developments on NATO and East-West relations. Ambassador Hardy, under whose signature the reports were sent, and who received the credit from headquarters, was happy. Ottawa called for more and I produced appraisals on a wide variety of issues, such as NATO's evolving relationship with the European Community, the rise of Euro-communism, and the ongoing United States–France rivalry for security leadership in Europe.

A new supervisor, through whom I had to submit my texts, was opposed to my continuing to send them, for reasons he never explained. At first he urged me to desist, but I persisted. He then complained loudly and criticized my work severely each time I submitted a draft paper. Ignoring him, I spent most of the remaining two years of the posting on these activities, consulting with colleagues on other delegations, reading learned journals, and attending colloquia – in short, obtaining familiarity with strategic issues that would stand me in good stead later in my career. At the same time, I took advantage of my low-level position as a note-taker at council meetings to watch the giant personalities of the 1970s formulate and implement East-West policy.

The United States in Temporary Decline

In this period, the ability of the United States to provide leadership to the West was undermined by developments at home and abroad. The Watergate affair left the country unable to exploit the genius of President Richard Nixon and Secretary of State Henry Kissinger, two of the most talented foreign-policy leaders it ever produced. The two American leaders had acted boldly at the beginning of the decade to exploit the growing tensions and fear of war that had developed between China and the U.S.S.R. By cultivating China, or "playing the China card," the United States had forced the U.S.S.R. into a policy of practical peaceful co-existence with the capitalist world. Nixon's resignation in August 1974 would badly damage the prestige of the United States, weakening its credibility within NATO and with the U.S.S.R.

I was present when Nixon visited NATO headquarters in June 1974, just two months before he was driven from office. Little deference was shown to him by the European permanent representatives, who muttered privately that their time was being wasted. The president, they said, was using his Brussels stop as a photo opportunity to show the American people that their leader, under siege at home, was still a respected statesman. They did not want to be props for an American domestic public-relations exercise. We all stood when the president, accompanied by Ambassador Rumsfeld, entered the council chamber to be greeted with curiosity rather than respect. He was smaller than I had imagined. In what was almost a caricature of the images I had seen of him on television, his smile was fixed on a doll-like face heavily covered with make-up for the television cameras. His analysis of East-West relations was cogent, but he exuded no special magnetism. Years later, when I saw the mummified corpses of Lenin in Moscow and Ho Chi Minh in Hanoi, I thought of him.

Henry Kissinger, who survived the Nixon presidency to serve as secretary of state under President Ford, had an altogether different impact. An intellectual heavyweight who sounded like a European with his measured, grating, and accented English, he was the dominant Western statesman of the 1970s. Born in Germany in 1923, he emigrated to the United States to escape Hitler in 1938, served in the United States army, and was educated at City College in New York and Harvard. While he was still at Harvard, his books on strategy were so influential that they shaped the American and NATO approach to fighting war in Europe. He was the architect of NATO's interpretation of *détente* – a dynamic process in which the West's policy of containment of the U.S.S.R., adopted in the late 1940s, was to be converted to one of co-operation. Linkage was an integral part of this approach: if the Soviets conducted policies inimical to those of the United States and its allies, they should be made to pay the price; if they co-operated, they should be rewarded.

When I first saw Kissinger in action in the fall of 1973, he was at the height of his international renown. He and the North Vietnamese negotiator, Le Duc Tho, had just won the Nobel Peace Prize for the agreement that allowed the United States to pull its troops from South Vietnam. Throughout the fall of 1973 and winter of 1974, he was heavily engaged in high-profile shuttle diplomacy to separate Israeli and Arab forces following the Yom

Kippur War. He must have thought this record of success would allow him to succeed with his 1974 "Year of Europe" initiative.

The secretary of state was of the view that the alliance would be stronger if a declaration were issued reaffirming the strong links between NATO's North American and European members. France strongly objected. It pointed out that such a declaration would run at cross purposes to the movement in Europe for greater European unity. The Economic Community of six nations (France, Germany, Italy, Belgium, Netherlands, and Luxembourg) had just expanded in 1973 to nine members with the addition of the United Kingdom, Ireland, and Denmark. France, which wanted to be the dominant voice in the new Europe, suspected that the United States was seeking to suborn the new institutions. I watched Kissinger and the French foreign minister, Michel Jobert, engage in a brutal, highly theatrical verbal duel in the council chamber on the issue. NATO Secretary-General Joseph Luns cut off the discussion by calling a coffee break. When the session resumed, no further mention was made of the issue. In due course, a watered-down text papering over differences and extolling allied unity was issued.

As time went on, the lustre of Kissinger's accomplishments started to fade. The North Vietnamese tore up the agreement he had signed with Le Duc Tho, invaded South Vietnam, and chased the remnants of American diplomatic and military power from the country. He was then reduced to being an impotent witness as the American Congress, in the beginning of what was to be termed the "Vietnam syndrome," began to prevent the administration from responding to communist-supported insurgencies around the world. From my seat in the back row of the Canadian delegation in 1976, I listened to a bitter Kissinger tell the council that the United States was being forced to abandon Angola to the U.S.S.R. since funding for a CIA operation had been vetoed by Congress. He also complained that Senator Henry Jackson's amendments, seeking to force the U.S.S.R. to permit the large-scale emigration of Soviet Jews as a condition to being accorded most-favoured-nation trade status, were killing *détente*.

The secretary of state was also a bully. I once watched him physically brush aside Canada's foreign affairs minister, Don Jamieson, when he tried to discuss an East Coast fishing dispute with him outside the NATO council chamber. "I have no time for your eternal fish concerns," he snarled at the red-faced Jamieson, humiliating him in front of several European ministers.

Another time, during the 1974 NATO foreign-ministers' meeting in Ottawa, I was taking a shortcut through the narrow tunnel between the convention centre in the old railway station and the Château Laurier. There, in the middle of the tunnel, stood Kissinger, loudly chewing out one of his aides for providing him with a text that did not meet his standards. I tried to return to the convention centre, but an unsmiling Secret Service agent refused to let me pass, even though I was a representative of the host government. I squeezed by the hectoring Kissinger only to be blocked on the other side by another American agent.

"I could have prepared a better text with one arm tied behind my back! You call yourself a professional!"

The victim and I stood quietly waiting for the verbal storm to end. I don't know who was the more embarrassed – the errant American foreign-service officer or the Canadian witness to his humiliation. I would meet my American colleague, who would rise to the top ranks of the State Department, often in the years to come. We never mentioned the incident.

Alexander Haig, a White House colleague of Kissinger's under Nixon, was the third larger-than-life figure to appear on my NATO horizon. Named Supreme Allied Commander Europe, or SACEUR, by President Ford in December 1974, he at first was looked upon by the NATO permanent representatives as an unsophisticated general who had been given the most senior

European command to get him out of Washington. Haig did not improve matters at the outset by becoming involved in minor scandals involving the use of his official car to chauffeur his dogs, being caught with bottles of alcohol in his official shipments, and issuing orders for the permanent redeployment of NATO forces without seeking political agreement. Yet Haig was no fool. He saw that the U.S.S.R. was taking advantage of the weakness of post-Vietnam America and the desire of many NATO countries to persevere with *détente* even in the face of unfriendly Soviet actions. He began a crusade to pass the message that the Soviet Union was building up an immense arsenal of nuclear and conventional weapons, and argued that *détente* carried dangers, that the warning time for a Warsaw Pact attack in Central Europe was now dangerously short. NATO simply did not have the means to halt a massive tank attack.

Haig drummed this message into the political leadership of NATO Europe and propagated it in widespread media interviews. Attitudes changed. Dressed in a tailored combat uniform, he became the darling of the press and captivated many of NATO's permanent representatives. From my back-row seat in the Canadian delegation, I would watch as he strode with a determined air into the council chamber, accompanied by gold-braided aides bearing his charts and his pointer to deliver another dramatic warning about the threat from the East. He gave the impression somehow that he expected the permanent representatives to rise and salute him, but they remained glued to their seats, aware that they represented the civil or political authority of the alliance, which always took precedence over the military.

Nevertheless, Haig got his way. NATO countries agreed to raise their defence budgets by 3 per cent. Defence tactics were changed. Large numbers of anti-tank weapons were added to the arsenals of NATO countries, as well as one hundred tank-busting fighter aircraft to back them up. President Jimmy Carter reappointed Haig to his SACEUR position after the elections of

November 1976; he then departed in January 1978, eventually becoming President Ronald Reagan's secretary of state.

Canada Loses Ground

And what was Canada's role throughout this period? Our military contribution, and hence our influence, was in decline. In the late 1940s and early 1950s, European countries were weak economically and militarily while Canada had a strong economy and the capacity to have a credible presence, providing ground forces integrated into the British army on the Rhine and a major air component based in eastern France. At that time Canada, together with the United States, agreed to help European countries build a military infrastructure of pipelines, airports, submarine pens, and so on, without insisting that they receive any economic benefit in return. As the years went by, the Europeans developed a greater capacity to provide for their own defence, leading to a relative decline in Canada's importance. The inept handling of defence policy in the 1960s under the Diefenbaker government further weakened Canada's voice. In 1969, the Canadian government, believing that *détente* was irreversible, cut its land and air forces stationed in Europe by 50 per cent and slashed defence spending.

The impact was dramatic. Canada was never to be taken seriously again as a major player in NATO, although we continue to make a disproportionate contribution to the consultative process through the quality of our military and civilian representatives. Even here, our views were sometimes greeted with condescension. The British permanent representative, who should have known better, given Canada's role as a close, early ally in two world wars, once questioned our right to take a strong position on some issue relating to NATO strategy, saying that Canada's small military presence in Europe and low defence spending meant we should be silent on major issues of alliance concern. No one spoke up for Canada, leaving our ambassador to twist slowly in the wind, our legitimacy as a full member of NATO challenged.

At the next council meeting, however, the Dutch ambassador asked for the floor under "any other business" to read a statement supplied by his foreign ministry. The Netherlands, he read out to an indifferent audience, would never forget the sacrifices of Canadian troops in his country during the Second World War, and objected to those who would deny our right to participate in NATO as a full member. The lesson I took from the incident, and what I would often think about when I returned as Canada's ambassador, was that good ideas could take you only so far in the often rough-and-tumble debates in NATO. Real influence depended on the credibility derived from making a real military contribution as well as producing good ideas.

In the four years I was at NATO, a succession of Canadian leaders and foreign and defence ministers came to participate in the high-stakes sessions: Pierre Trudeau, Mitchell Sharp, Allan MacEachen, Don Jamieson, Barney Danson, and James Richardson. Prime Minister Trudeau, perhaps uncomfortable following his decision to slash our contribution to NATO some years earlier, came only once. He spoke eloquently on East-West relations to a special council meeting of permanent representatives who pretended interest in his views. Then, one after another, in an obviously planned, concerted effort, they cynically lavished praise on Canada's contribution to Western security before moving in for the kill: appealing to Trudeau to upgrade the ancient Centurion tanks used by Canada's military contingent in Germany. German chancellor Helmut Schmidt applied similar pressure during a separate Trudeau visit to Bonn. Then, word came that Canada would replace the Centurions with German-made Leopard tanks. Regardless of the merits of the decision, it was galling to see Canada's prime minister make it as a result of outside pressure.

Mitchell Sharp and Allan MacEachen stood head and shoulders above their Canadian peers. I will always remember a briefing session for Sharp organized by Ambassador Menzies at the Hotel Amigo in central Brussels on a Sunday afternoon in late November 1973. The streets were deserted. All traffic, other than emergency vehicles and cars with diplomatic licence plates, had been banned to conserve oil in that period of Middle East oil embargo. It could have been a scene from Nevil Shute's *On the Beach* in the aftermath of a nuclear attack. Inside the hotel, John Halstead, whom I had not seen in action since I had worked for him in the summer of 1966 and who had emerged as one the greatest foreign-service officers of his generation, put the minister in the picture with a model briefing. I watched carefully, storing up lessons I would put to good use more than two decades later when I would be called upon to brief the prime minister regularly.

Allan MacEachen, for his part, was a man of strong moral convictions, a guardian of the public purse who insisted on travelling economy class on transatlantic flights no matter how uncomfortable they were, and the archetypical moody Cape Breton Islander who could have fitted easily into Alistair MacLeod's *No Great Mischief*. I felt the lash of his tongue once when I woke him up to hand him an urgent message. He was one of the finest foreign ministers for whom I would ever work.

A Personal Alliance

During a flight to Vienna in 1974 on arms-control business, I met my future wife, Marie-Jeanne Rosillon. She was a Belgian born in the former Belgian Congo, where her father had been a doctor, medical director of the province of Kasai, and a member of the Allied military expedition during the Second World War that trekked into Ethiopia from the south to free it from Italian rule. Marie-Jeanne returned with her family to Belgium before the chaos that shook the Congo following its independence. She was only twelve when her parents passed away. Odette de Wynter, Belgium's first female notary, then took a close interest in Marie-Jeanne and became, in effect, her adoptive mother.

We set the wedding date for September 12, 1975. Three months before that date, Marie-Jeanne, driving her small sports car, was hit by a Belgian military ambulance running a red light, causing a hairline fracture to her skull. Her recovery went well until one week before the wedding day, when she sustained another head injury. Marie-Jeanne and I were afraid that if we did not get married at that time we never would, so we went ahead with the wedding. I assisted her up the stairs of the city hall of Waterloo, just outside of Brussels, for the ceremony, and then back home. The reception, with the wedding party replete with top hats and morning coats and including Ambassador and Mrs. Menzies, and my mother, sister, and brother-in-law from Canada, was held with the bride upstairs in bed.

Odette welcomed me warmly into the family and her circle of Belgian friends, dramatically improving the quality of my life. Her home, with notarial offices on the ground floor, was an inviting house with large lawns and flower gardens. Like many members of the Belgian bourgeoisie, Odette was well served by a devoted household staff, had a well-stocked wine cellar, and was a superb cook. Her house became our home away from home in Europe, a haven of smells, light, sounds, and tastes: the musty odour of notarial files, the fragrance of masses of freshly cut flowers, the bouquet of old burgundy wine, the rich smell of strong coffee, the scent of apple blossoms, the golden light flooding in through the huge windows overlooking her garden, the distinctive cooing of doves that nested under the eaves, the savour of the French-Flemish dishes that emerged twice a day from her kitchen, and the creamy succulence of Belgian chocolate to celebrate every family gathering.

In November 1976, our first child, Anne-Pascale, was born at the Saint Pierre hospital in Brussels after a wild ride to reach it in time, the car radio blaring out the American presidential-election results that would bring Jimmy Carter to the White House. Laurent would follow eleven months later at the same hospital.

And after a long wait of twelve years, Alain was born in an ambulance on the Ottawa Queensway, unwilling to hold off his arrival until we could reach the hospital. All three grew up making frequent visits to their Belgian grandmother, who provided stability for them in a life of constant travel around the globe until Odette's death in 1998.

6

Turmoil in the Caribbean Basin

There was evidence of civil war everywhere; disabled cars and trucks, pockmarked by bullet holes, littered the sides of the roads, and windows in shops and homes were shattered.

I returned to a sombre Ottawa in July 1977, with everyone still in shock over the victory of the separatist Parti Québécois in Quebec the previous fall. It had been five years since I had last lived in Canada, and the changes in my personal circumstances were profound. Gone was my carefree bachelor life. I was now thoroughly domesticated with a wife, eight-month-old Anne-Pascale, Laurent expected in October (when Marie-Jeanne would return to Brussels to be with her family for the birth), and a dog and cat. The cottage I had constructed on the Gatineau River at Wakefield in 1970 was no longer mine. I had been forced to sell it after it nearly floated off in a flood when I was away in Bangladesh. We moved into a house in the woods near Chelsea, Quebec, from where I commuted daily to my new job in Foreign Affairs.

Foreign Affairs in 1977

Foreign Affairs had also undergone profound changes since I last worked at headquarters. It was now an unhappy place – or at least many of its employees professed to be discontented while cheerfully carrying on with duties they loved. Many complained about being gathered together in the newly opened layer-cake-style Pearson Building on Sussex Drive, far from the amenities of central Ottawa and the heart of power. They complained about poor pay, the arbitrary nature of the promotion system, the general chaos of a unique personnel system developed to deal with government employees who were expected to live most of their working careers abroad, and the hostility of other government departments.

There were also deep concerns about the gradual erosion of the Foreign Affairs mandate. Every government department in town with interests abroad now seemed to be sending direct instructions to Canada's heads of post for action. Even worse, they were posting their own officers to work at embassies and high commissions but leaving it to Foreign Affairs to foot the bill for accommodation, office space, and office support. Canadian society was changing and Foreign Affairs was running to keep up. Families were now dependent on two incomes and yet spouses in the foreign service (of officers and non-officers alike) usually had to quit their jobs to follow their husbands or wives abroad. Support staff (secretaries, clerks, security guards, and communicators) complained about their dead-end jobs and started speaking out against diplomatic practice, sanctioned in nineteenth-century international law, that saw only officers receive tax-free benefits, red diplomatic passports, and immunity from local laws when abroad.

I was thrown into this bubbling cauldron of grievances in my new job as head of the officer-assignment section. I did not want it, much preferring the NATO desk. With a family to support, I gritted my teeth and reported to work on September 1 to meet my new colleagues, whose paths would often cross with mine in the coming years. We had almost total control over postings abroad and assignments at headquarters for all foreign-service officers, staffed the promotion boards, prepared draft lists for ambassadorial nominations, and, in our spare time, wrote policy papers on how to reform the system. Suddenly, everyone was my friend. Jim Bartleman, who by nature was not an extrovert, was the most popular officer in the cafeteria. There was keen interest in my just-completed postings. And was I free for lunch? Why not bring Marie-Jeanne and come home for a meal with the family? By the way, could you post me to Washington, London, Paris, or Rome? No one, I discovered, asked for Third World postings. I sent one friend to Bangladesh (he went reluctantly, but came to enjoy Dhaka) and the importuning diminished.

The talented amateurs, who included such outstanding officers on my team as Michael Kergin, future ambassador to Washington, and Jim Judd, later to be deputy minister of defence, made some inroads on the policy side, putting in place procedures to give everyone a chance to be considered for the posting or assignment of his or her choice, establishing career streaming, lessening the attrition of women, and formulating the first plan to recruit Native staff. I did not, however, enjoy personnel work; I was equally fed up with abuse from every employee who had a grievance and with the orders passed down from individuals high up in the system to post their favourites to choice locations, despite our new guidelines to bring fairness to the system. We nevertheless had our small triumphs, winning battles with senior officers who "instructed" us to fire officers abroad who had incurred their wrath for offenses such as not being deferential enough to their wives or not providing sufficiently elaborate hospitality to them when they travelled. Our memoranda to senior management declining to take action would be sent back with nasty comments and marked with ink blots indicating, we hoped, that expensive fountain pens had been destroyed in the venting of rage.

I was looking forward to leaving as soon as my two-year assignment was over. My heart sank when John Hadwen, the irrepressible director-general of personnel, told me that my next assignment would be as director of the seventy-person division itself, on the departure of the incumbent. I would, he said, be able to expand my focus from dealing with foreign-service officers only to trying to solve the problems of everyone – a task I likened to attempting to clean the Augean stables. Fortunately, in a perverse twist of justice, Marie-Andrée Beauchemin, who had specialist personnel skills and whom I had helped recruit from outside the foreign service, was thrust into the position ahead of me at the last minute. I was cut loose to find myself something else.

The Commonwealth Caribbean

It was by then early July 1979, and almost all of the directorships had been filled with people I had myself proposed. There was only one left, that of director of the tiny Commonwealth Caribbean division. The incumbent had a health problem and was being moved elsewhere on short notice. I was happy to take the job. The incoming director-general, Richard Gorham, who would be my immediate boss, was a no-nonsense officer who was not afraid to delegate work and to stand up to anyone, no matter how senior, in defence of his staff. Moreover, the region that I would be responsible for was undergoing rapid change and there was growing Canadian concern for its future. I was also fortunate in having as deputy director Robert Poetschke, a highly capable, long-suffering, and quiet-spoken officer who had been carrying the weight of the division's work on his shoulders essentially alone for the past year. The heads of post in the field were a gifted foursome: Terry Sheehan, on immigration in Jamaica, Allan Roger, on public relations in Barbados, John Graham, on public policy in Guyana, and Paul Laberge, on trade in Trinidad and Tobago.

Now that Joe Clark was prime minister and Flora MacDonald was foreign minister, the government had directed that a fundamental review of foreign policy be conducted. Great progress had been made towards its completion, but one area had not been touched, which worried Allan Gotlieb, the undersecretary. He was convinced that the Commonwealth Caribbean was the only part of the Third World that really mattered to Canada. In his view, declining living standards and high population-growth rates could cause social and political turmoil, leading to the people turning to communism on the Cuban model. The *coup d'état* of March 1979 in which Maurice Bishop, leader of the Marxist New Jewel Movement, threw out the corrupt premier of Grenada, would be a harbinger of the Caribbean's future if concerned outside countries did not act to deal with the roots of regional instability.

The undersecretary's wishes were passed down, in the time-honoured hierarchical fashion common to all foreign ministries, to the deputy undersecretary, to the assistant undersecretary, to the director-general and finally to me: the Commonwealth Caribbean division was to pull up its socks and ensure that Canada's interests in the region were safeguarded. I was to oversee the drafting of a memorandum to Cabinet and to find ways of strengthening Canada's collaboration with the United States and Britain, the two heavyweight "metropolitan" powers in the region. No new resources would be provided, but an oversight committee, chaired by the deputy undersecretary and including all members of the undersecretarial management team, was established to supervise the written product of the drafting team.

The drafting team was composed of one solitary officer – me. And I had never been to the Caribbean. I resolved to balance the dearth of staff in my minuscule division at headquarters by using the resources of the posts, and to profit from the unique talents of each of the high commissioners. I telephoned all four heads of post and departed on a two-week tour to the region. I left my number two in charge, reasoning that since he had already managed the division for a year, two additional weeks should not make a difference. The region, I discovered in my travels, was indeed low on everyone's priorities. Our high commissioner in Guyana, for example, told me that he had discovered that for six months the communicator at the post had been ill; he nevertheless came to the office each day. Rather than work, however, he spent his days sleeping behind the locked doors of his communications centre and routinely tossed out all the classified political and economic reports submitted to him for encryption and dispatch. Throughout the six months of silence, the high commissioner told me, no one in Ottawa had noticed.

The heads of post thus welcomed the undersecretary's intention to upgrade Canada's relations with their countries of accreditation. They were, however, doubtful that anything would happen. All experienced high commissioners, they could scarcely hide their amusement at my ambitions. They nevertheless patiently answered the hundreds of questions I put to them and agreed to produce a series of background papers on what they perceived to be Canada's current and future interests in the countries of their accreditation, and to provide feedback on my own drafting efforts. I also sought help from other government departments, in particular from CIDA, and the Departments of the Solicitor General, Transport, National Defence, Employment and Immigration, Finance, and Industry, Trade, and Commerce. A flood of reports washed onto my desk in short order.

I went home, drank gallons of black coffee, ate chocolate bars to satiety, and produced a succinct five-page assessment together with what I thought to be brilliant new policy directions. The oversight team did not share my high opinion of my effort. I was summoned to the large conference room located on the hallowed eighth floor of the Pearson Building, where the undersecretary and his most senior officers held court. On one side of the table was Jim Bartleman – the drafting team. On the other, the Foreign Affairs elders who smelled blood – my blood. Each one was a self-professed expert on the Commonwealth Caribbean. All had been to the region on holiday at one time or other in their lives. Several had even had postings there, even if twenty-five years previously. Everyone held strong opinions, however out of date, on the character of the people and the relationship Canada should have with their governments. No one came to my defence and my draft was savaged.

I bit my tongue and left the room, vowing to myself that no one would be able to criticize my next draft. I put aside my five-page synthesis and embarked on a project to produce a major background paper on the economic, social, cultural, security, and political changes that had occurred in the area over the preceding decade, together with a hard-headed look at Canada's interests. My colleagues at the director level from other government departments, in particular CIDA, went out of their way to be helpful. The Department of Finance, concerned that new spending might be required, sought to discourage me. I prepared laborious draft after laborious draft, but was in no rush to return to my eighth-floor Chamber of Inquisitors.

My understanding of the issues deepened as I participated as a member of the Canadian team in secret talks on the future of the Commonwealth Caribbean with counterparts from the United States and Britain. Philip Habib, later replaced by the haughty Thomas Enders (who refused to shake hands with or even speak to mere directors), was the assistant secretary of state for Latin America who headed the American team. Nicholas Ridley, open, frank, and friendly despite his aristocratic credentials, and minister of state for Foreign Affairs in Margaret Thatcher's Foreign Office, directed the British side. Jacques Gignac, assistant undersecretary for Latin America and the Caribbean in Foreign Affairs, with me as deputy, constituted the Canadian side. We met in Washington, New York, and London. Canada and the United States agreed that much more attention should be paid to the region, the decline in aid flows should be reversed, increased security should be provided, and access to our markets for trade products should be improved. Ridley did not disagree, but said the United Kingdom could not provide new resources to a region already receiving a disproportionate share of British overseas funding. He proposed instead that Canada take on responsibility for one or more British Crown territories, mentioning the Turks and Caicos Islands, but his proposal was ignored. The Caribbean Basin

Initiative, the most important American program ever launched to assist the Caribbean-rim countries, resulted from these talks. A series of recommendations for an enhanced Canadian engagement in the region contained in the memorandum to Cabinet which I was drafting would be Canada's response.

By the time I was ready to face the oversight committee again, Joe Clark's government was no more; Pierre Trudeau was prime minister once again and Mark MacGuigan was foreign minister. One of the first acts of the incoming government was to scrap the foreign-policy review, which had the misfortune of being tabled in the House of Commons just hours before the Clark government fell. The new government was unaware of the efforts conducted at my lowly level to produce a companion piece, and I did nothing to enlighten them. As a result, the new minister took ownership of my project. I then returned to the oversight committee, which this time pronounced itself satisfied. The undersecretary was happy and sent my report to MacGuigan. He read it, made a series of marginal comments, and directed that it go forward to Cabinet for approval.

The Department of Finance, having promised to support the text on condition that I make the recommendations as cost-free as possible, lived up to its reputation for perfidy by opposing the proposal in Cabinet. It nevertheless passed. Minister MacGuigan then organized a meeting of Caribbean foreign ministers in Kingston, Jamaica, to outline its main conclusions. In my inno-cence, I thought the Caribbean leaders would welcome a new policy which provided for the doubling of aid over a five-year period, not to mention the provision of police, military, and civil defence training and a package of related measures. I secretly hoped, after putting so much effort into the preparations, that they might even say good things about it.

They were, however, singularly unimpressed. The people of the Commonwealth Caribbean, they said, had been exploited by colonial masters for hundreds of years. Ignoring the fact that

Canada had never actually possessed any colonies, they said that we owed it to the people of the region to do even more. Why stop at doubling aid? We should have agreed to increase the levels threefold at the very least. And so on. Despite the complaints, the policy formed the basis for the Canadian government approach to the area for the coming decade.

Trouble in Central America

In the spring of 1980, the director-general asked me to take on responsibility for Central America, Cuba, and Haiti in addition to my existing duties for the Commonwealth Caribbean. Central America was the area of greatest concern. Vicious civil wars, marked by gross violations of human rights, were raging in El Salvador and Guatemala. The Sandinistas had just overthrown the regime of the Nicaraguan dictator Anastasio Somoza, and with Cuba's help were seeking to export their model of revolution elsewhere in the region. Panama was stable under a left-leaning military dictator, but Honduras, despite its history of maintaining domestic harmony in the face of an enormous gulf between rich and poor, was being sucked into the maelstrom of violence on its borders.

Mark MacGuigan found himself in the hot seat. At home he was strongly criticized, not for Canada's policy towards Central America, but because we were not sufficiently opposed to Washington's approach. A well-organized campaign led by church groups and non-governmental organizations lobbied members of Parliament. "Letters to the Editor" columns were flooded with condemnations of Canada's position. Hundreds of letters of complaint arrived on Mark MacGuigan's desk each day and the political opposition seized on the issue to belabour the government in Parliament. All sense of perspective was lost.

What was really happening, however, was a phenomenon peculiar to Canadians. Every so often, such as during the Vietnam War, we become confused about our foreign-policy identity.

Editorial writers, demonstrators, and opposition parliamentarians criticize American foreign policy as if they were American citizens, and attack the Canadian government as if it were responsible for American policy. A visitor from outer space would have had the impression that Canada was the source of all the suffering of the people of Central America.

Canada was actually strongly critical of the right-wing regimes and supported efforts in the United Nations and the Organization of American States to hold the repressive governments in the area to account. We lobbied the countries concerned to treat their people more humanely, but we were rebuffed. The president of Guatemala even told Canada's ambassador that he supported the death squads who were torturing and massacring peasants suspected of being leftist sympathizers. He was reported to have said, "If Canada does not like Guatemala's use of death squads, then Canada can go to hell."

We also encouraged the United States to pay greater attention to the social and economic roots of the conflict and not just focus on military solutions. The United States was really not the devil painted by its critics, but it had much to answer for because of its support for corrupt right-wing dictatorships sympathetic to American business interests over the previous hundred years. President Carter, who was in the White House at this time, had an impeccable human-rights policy and had withdrawn American support for Somoza at the critical moment, thereby facilitating the Sandinista victory.

To deal with the paperwork associated with the growing criticism and pressure, Foreign Affairs had only one overworked junior desk officer. We were not much better off in the field. Unlike the Commonwealth Caribbean, with its deep and long-standing ties to Canada, we had few interests in this part of Latin America. Canada's official presence was limited to two small embassies headed by trade officers: one in San José, Costa Rica, for Costa Rica, Panama, El Salvador, Honduras, and Nicaragua; and another under a chargé d'affaires in Guatemala. The Canadian government was basically operating in the dark. We had no feel for the history of the area, nor for underlying social and economic conditions. We were reliant on newspaper stories and a flow of information from the U.S. State Department, Pentagon, and the CIA designed for American rather than Canadian decision-makers. The time of my newly constituted division was spent on drafting replies to the mountain of mail to the minister from concerned Canadians rather than on devising policy.

Central America in 1979

I resolved to try to follow the approach I had used in dealing with the Commonwealth Caribbean in the preceding year: visit the area on a fact-finding mission and prepare an assessment of the situation with policy recommendations for the government. An early opportunity to visit the area came in the spring of 1980. A vice-president of CIDA was scheduled to visit Nicaragua to assess aid requirements. Minister MacGuigan asked me to go along to deliver a political message: Canada wanted to be generous in the provision of aid, but expected the new government to adhere to the publicly stated principles of its revolution, which included respect for democracy and for private property. Specifically, Canada would not deliver a promised shipload of wheat if this commitment was not given.

Douglas Sirrs, the Canadian ambassador resident in Costa Rica and accredited to Nicaragua, briefed our team at the Canadian embassy in San José, and we then departed for Managua. A Hieronymus Bosch landscape of the end of the world greeted us. Rubble from an earthquake years earlier still clogged the centre of the city, and beggars scrounged for food among the ruins of the cathedral – a visual confirmation that the massive aid sent by the international community to help the people in the aftermath of the tragedy had been funnelled into the bank accounts of the now-exiled former dictator. There was evidence of civil war everywhere: disabled cars and trucks, pock-marked with bullet holes, littered the sides of the roads, and windows in shops and homes were shattered. Young slogan-shouting fighters with red Sandinista scarves around their necks, looking like Garibaldi's nineteenth-century Italian revolutionar-ies, stopped us to check our identification every few kilometres at roadblocks adorned with banners and flags proclaiming the victory of the Sandinista revolution.

We called on the president, Arturo Cruz, a respected former senior official of the World Bank, who told us that we could assure the Canadian government that democracy and respect for private property would be fully guaranteed by the revolutionary government. The same message was given to us by a variety of young ministers, recent idealistic recruits from the expatriate Nicaraguan community attending Ivy League universities in the United States. (Most, disaffected with the new regime, would drift back to the United States in the coming years.) However, we had not yet met any of those who represented the real power in the country: the Sandinista commandants.

At my insistence, our hosts finally arranged a meeting with the minister of the interior, Tomás Borge. We were driven to a heavily fortified building, conducted though corridors lined with murals depicting short, dark-haired guerrillas slitting the throats of blond-haired oppressors, and into the office of the min-ister himself. All went well until I delicately delivered Minister MacGuigan's message.

Borge's reply was unambiguous. The Sandinistas were grateful for our sympathy. They needed our aid. There was a great short-age of food, and wheat was required. But if Canada insisted on linking aid to adherence to the stated principles of the revolution, he told me, his voice rising, we could keep our help. Sandinistas would never be dictated to by anyone! Aid had to be given without conditions! Moreover, Nicaragua would never accept our definition of democracy. Canada was being hypocritical. He

"knew" that the Canadian army was the servant of the ruling
Liberal Party and would come to its defence if it were threatened.
The army in Nicaragua, he said, would in the same way serve as
the army of the victorious party. He then dismissed us.

As I left his office, fuming, I dismissed him as a pompous ass.
Imagine, kicking a well-meaning Canadian envoy out of his
office when he came offering gifts, with just a little gratuitous
advice. I told myself that this man was merely an ignorant dandy.
Why else would he sport a silver-handled revolver and dress in a
khaki uniform that made him look like a miniature version of
Fidel Castro?

When I calmed down, I grudgingly realized that I had been
the author of my own misfortune. What would my reaction have
been had I been in his shoes? He was, after all, one of the original founders of the Sandinista movement and had been captured
and tortured repeatedly. Should I have expected someone who
had spent most of the past decade hooded and in solitary
confinement in a tiny cell to be sympathetic to the case I had tried
to make? Should he have understood what a Western liberal-
democratic government really was? He had never lived under one
as I had all my life. And as for myself, I had an intellectual but not
a visceral understanding of what he had endured in prison, and
of what Nicaraguans had suffered under half a century of
Somoza's dictatorship. Our dialogue had been one of the deaf –
of mutual incomprehension, and the fault was not all his.

From Nicaragua I flew to Guatemala to be briefed by the small
Canadian team at the embassy. On my arrival, a soldier met me
at the aircraft door, carrying an automatic rifle. He would be my
bodyguard until I was delivered back to the airport for my departure several days later. Apart from that, my first impressions were
positive. Guatemala City was stunningly beautiful, with lush veg-
etation covering its volcanic hillsides. The streets were filled with

Indians in their national dress, each tribe displaying distinctive clothing and headgear. In contrast to the desolation of Managua, the city centre was modern and there were chic upscale shops and restaurants in abundance.

There were also frequent patrols of sinister-looking security troops wearing what looked like surplus Second World War German army helmets. At the United States embassy, where I attended an outdoor evening reception, evil-looking security guards fingering their weapons were so omnipresent that they even sat up in the trees, looking like vampire bats awaiting the fall of night to begin their wicked work. In those days, the vicious civil war was at its height. The Canadian briefing team explained to me that endemic conflict between left-wing guerrillas and right-wing paramilitary forces supported by the military had ravaged the countryside since 1954 when the CIA masterminded a military coup to overthrow the legitimately elected government of President Arbenz; he had been considered by the banana companies and Washington to be too left-leaning for their taste. Hundreds of thousands of people, largely Indians, had been killed. Conflict had spread from its original base among the tiny minority of Guatemalans who were proud of their "pure" Spanish bloodlines and the larger group of Ladinos of mixed Spanish-Indian origin into the large Indian majority of Guatemalans who had maintained much of their culture since pre-Columbian times. All sides displayed savagery, particularly the right-wing death squads.

Respect for human dignity disappeared. An officer at the Canadian embassy told me of an incident he had seen just before my arrival. Coming to work in the morning rush-hour traffic, he saw the vehicles ahead of him on the highway hit a bump, one after the other. When he arrived at the spot, he discovered that there was a corpse on the road and no one was bothering to drive around it. The trade officer told me that another time, a Canadian businessman had just come in to say that he had advertised in the newspaper and hired a local security company to patrol the premises of his small business. He then noticed that certain employees, especially those associated with the labour union, were no longer coming to work. The security company had interpreted its mandate broadly, killing with impunity those workers it considered might cause problems for the management.

Our embassy staff was not immune. In the coming months, a first secretary had to depart in a hurry after he witnessed an assassination. Returning to work after lunch one day, he brought his car to a halt behind another one waiting at a red light. A man with a pistol got out of the car behind him and walked calmly past him to the car ahead and shot the driver twice in the head. The killer then strolled back to his car after taking a careful look at the Canadian diplomat and his licence-plate number. Later the same day, the Canadian received an orchid – the code indicating that he was next on the hit list. I ordered him to leave the post at once. We later repatriated another staff member who was chased home by an attacker who riddled his car with gunfire but did not hit him.

On the Defensive

I returned to Ottawa to advise Minister MacGuigan that the situation in Guatemala was hopeless, and it was unlikely Nicaragua would follow a liberal-democratic path. In my view, it would only be a matter of time before Nicaragua would seek to follow Cuba in establishing a form of communist dictatorship, perhaps with a more human face than those in Eastern Europe. Canada should, however, provide aid since the basic human needs of Nicaragua's populace after so many years of war were enormous. The pressures from the coalition of church and other non-governmental groups to support Nicaragua, right or wrong, were in the end decisive. Although he might have wanted to, the minister discovered that it was politically impossible to use aid as a lever to bring about democratic change. He accordingly authorized a large aid program, starting it off with the shipload of wheat that I had offered to Tomás Borge, but with no strings attached.

In the coming year, the conflict in Central America intensified, particularly in El Salvador, where outrages, including the murder of Archbishop Oscar Arnulfo Romero of San Salvador, became regular features on the Canadian national news. I produced my policy paper but the minister, while accepting its general directions, did not feel any need to take the matter to Cabinet. We increased aid flows to all the countries of Central America, adopted a vocal approach in international organizations condemning human-rights violations, reinforced ties with moderate Guatemalans, and, despite my abortive initial efforts, continued to seek a dialogue with the Sandinistas. We also established links with a diplomatic commission representing both Salvadoran and Nicaraguan revolutionaries working out of Mexico City, seeking to gain international support for their cause.

When two representatives came to Ottawa, Minister MacGuigan was reluctant to meet them in his office, afraid that their sponsors, a coalition of Canadian supporters, would turn the event into a media circus. So I invited them to my small office and persuaded the minister to speak privately to them. A young woman, not yet twenty, was their spokesperson. Her face was childlike, her demeanour calm, and her gaze direct. There was nothing in her behaviour to indicate that, prior to her assignment as spokesperson for her cause abroad, she had been imprisoned, tortured, and repeatedly gang-raped by soldiers of the right-wing junta in El Salvador before escaping to wreak her revenge in a rampage of killings in the hills.

The meeting with the minister was, I thought, like the encounter I had with Tomás Borge the previous year when I had played my bit part in trying to push the new Nicaraguan government to adopt a Western liberal form of government. The voice of the girl was soft as she stated her case. I knew that neither

MacGuigan nor I would ever be able to comprehend the suffering she had undergone – nor her awful retaliation. As the minister lectured her about the dangers of accepting Cuban aid, she nodded vigorously, her smile as angelic as ever. But she was just being polite, and there was no meeting of minds.

The government remained on the defensive before an aroused public opinion, despite vigorously defending its position in special House of Commons debates in March 1981. Minister MacGuigan could not answer for the United States, but the critics wanted Canada to force Washington to change its policy. As I drafted the speech he would use, he insisted against my advice on inserting an ambivalent message: "We are prepared to contest the U.S. policy of military aid, but not to protest it; we are prepared to pronounce on it but not to denounce it; we are prepared to criticize it but not to condemn it. . . ." The press roasted him mercilessly for being indecisive and ambiguous.

I left the division in June 1981, leaving the hot potato for my successor to manage. The pressure on the Canadian government would be unrelenting until the situation on the ground changed in the mid-1980s when President Reagan used the CIA to beat back the forces of revolutionary change. Canada would eventually provide peacekeepers to help try to introduce democracy in the region. With the end of the Cold War, however, the region would lose its strategic importance. In an era of globalization where making a profit replaced ideological and security competition as the goal of international behaviour, Central America would revert to its traditional role of Latin American backwater. The social and economic injustices that stirred revolt in the 1970s and 1980s would remain unaddressed. Minister MacGuigan died in 1998, and the disputes over the nuances of Canadian policy that seemed so important to so many for a few short years in the 1980s would be forgotten.

7

Crisis Management

I told them to block the runway with police cars and force the pilot to disembark the woman. I had no idea whether I had the authority to issue such an order, but it certainly felt good.

Although preoccupied with the Commonwealth Caribbean and Central America in 1980 and 1981, I did not neglect Cuba, the largest and most demanding of the countries in my area of responsibility. I became acquainted with the Cuban ambassador, a tough, uncompromising ideologue who saw the world through the prism of the class struggle. He was, however, very friendly to me and introduced me to the new leader of Grenada, Maurice Bishop, when he made a private visit to Ottawa, sponsored by the Cuban embassy, shortly after he seized power. He also arranged an official trip to Cuba for Gerald Regan, the minister of state for sports, in the spring of 1981. I attached myself to the official delegation in order to obtain a first-hand look at the regime. We were wined, dined, and cultivated by the Cubans, who received few visits at the political level from any Western country. The delegation essentially did nothing but holiday at Cuba's expense for ten days, play baseball with our Cuban liaison officers, party at hotels in Varadero, and listen to Fidel Castro for hours in his office.

The Cubans graciously provided an excellent protocol house, complete with microphones in the walls to record all conversations for the benefit of the Cuban Ministry of the Interior.

Whenever the Cuban ambassador to Canada, who accompanied the Canadian mission as a type of high-level liaison officer, wanted to speak discreetly to a Canadian, he would put two fingers to his lips and motion for his interlocutor to follow him into the garden. He would then seek to conduct a frank exchange of views supposedly out of reach of the technical devices of the sinister Cuban security agency. I suspected that there were microphones in the bushes but thought the whole thing hilarious. After all, what secrets could our band of happy-go-lucky visitors have that could conceivably interest the Cuban Ministry of the Interior? Microphones or not, everyone had a good time, especially the Canadian official who had too much to drink and fell off the stage at a nightclub, landing on a table among bottles of rum, buckets of ice, and stony-faced Soviet military officers and their spouses.

Incident at Gander

My relations with the Cuban embassy in Ottawa were sometimes abrasive. Late one afternoon, the director of the security division walked into my office to tell me that an East German Interflug aircraft flying from Berlin to Havana had landed on schedule for refuelling at Gander, Newfoundland. As the passengers were disembarking, two Cubans, a man and a woman, broke away from the others and ran towards the RCMP constable on duty to seek asylum. This was not unusual: two or three Cubans obtained refugee status in Canada each week from aircraft refuelling in Canada en route to Cuba from Eastern Europe. This time, however, the other passengers, all Cuban, took up the chase. The man escaped, but the woman was captured. About eighty passengers surrounded her in the transit lounge. Thirty RCMP special constables were brought in to maintain order.

What was the government to do? The airport authorities did not believe that Canadian law applied to transit-lounge passengers, and did not want a violent confrontation between the RCMP and the passengers of the Interflug flight. There were no rules to govern cases like this, and I was just a junior director. I quickly visited the office of Leonard Legault, Foreign Affairs legal advisor and one of Canada's leading experts on international law. Did Canadian law apply to aircraft from foreign countries landing at our airports and to foreign passengers in the transit zones of airports? The answer was an unequivocal *yes*.

I resolved to obtain the freedom of the woman. After checking with my director-general, who gave me carte blanche to manage the crisis, I tried to persuade the Cuban ambassador to tell the Cuban passengers that they had no right to hold anyone prisoner on Canadian soil. He did not want to help, pleading that he was too busy to become involved. At the same time, I maintained contact with the RCMP Security Service, which in turn kept in close contact with its officers at the airport in Gander. With the ambassador unwilling to co-operate, I sought to enlist the support of his deputy, but the embassy refused to give his unlisted home telephone number to me. This was no problem. The Security Service knew where he was and put me on the phone with him. Initially reluctant to become involved, he eventually agreed to speak by telephone to the senior Cuban among the passengers to ask them to co-operate with the authorities in Gander. I stayed on the line to see if the Cuban diplomat would indeed be helpful. Perhaps he thought that I could not understand Spanish, but he was mistaken. Far from making an effort to encourage the passengers to co-operate with the Canadian authorities in Gander, he acquiesced to their plans to coerce the refugee back on the aircraft. He then telephoned me to say — a blatant lie — that the woman, of her own free will, wanted to return to Cuba.

I then spoke to the airport manager, saying that he should interview the woman alone. If she said that she wanted to leave, then of course she could do so; otherwise, she should be allowed to remain. The manager eagerly agreed and I heard no more for over an hour. The Security Service then called me from Gander to say that the manager had done nothing. There had been no interview and the woman had been forced to return to the aircraft by the other passengers. The aircraft had taxied to the end of the runway and was awaiting clearance for takeoff. What should be done?

I told them to block the runway with police cars and force the pilot to disembark the woman. I had no idea whether I had authority to issue such an order, but it certainly felt good. The police obeyed with alacrity, sending two squad cars out with lights flashing to take up positions on the tarmac in front of the aircraft. The door opened, a truck with mobile stairs pulled up, and the woman emerged, to be interviewed alone.

Of course, she wanted political asylum in Canada. In the evening news coverage, it was reported that the Canadian government had acted with dispatch to help a woman seeking freedom in Canada. The minister and senior management said they were happy. I was well aware, however, that if matters had turned out differently, there would have been the devil to pay. Jim Bartleman the hero would have been Jim Bartleman the goat.

The Cuban ambassador called on me in my office to express his outrage. He said President Castro had recently allowed more than one hundred thousand disloyal Cubans to depart from the port of Mariel for Florida, overwhelming the capacity of the United States to deal with them. He was instructed to tell me that any repetition of the antics of the night before would lead Cuba to unleash thousands of boat people on Canada. I rather undiplomatically asked if he had looked at a map recently: Nova Scotia was somewhat farther from Cuba than Florida.

Saving Saint Lucia

My crisis-management skills were tested one last time with less than glorious results before my assignment ended in the summer of 1981. Working late one evening, I received a telephone call from the duty officer at the National Defence Operations Centre, who said that an urgent message had come in from the commander of a Canadian destroyer on a friendship visit to Castries, the capital of the small Caribbean island state of Saint Lucia. The Canadian high commissioner and the associate undersecretary together with the ship's commander were in the process of hosting a shipboard diplomatic reception.

The local prime minister had approached them at the party to say that he expected his political opponents to launch a coup attempt that night to seize power, in much the same way as Maurice Bishop had in neighbouring Grenada in 1979. His request, supported by the ship's commander and the two senior members of Canada's diplomatic service on the spot, was for the Canadian Forces personnel on the ship to intervene to prevent the coup. The commander recommended that heavily armed members of the ship's company as well as a Jeep with a mounted machine gun be deployed ashore to protect vital installations from a potentially hostile takeover. The message ended with a plea for urgent instructions.

I did not know what to do. My director-general and the legal advisor who had given advice and encouragement during the incident at Gander were unavailable. I knew the views of the associate undersecretary, the senior official to whom I would normally turn in a crisis situation of this severity – he was on the ship recommending that we intervene. I did not know any high-ranking uniformed members of National Defence and thus could not turn to the military chain of command for help. The deputy minister of defence was so senior that I was afraid to call him. I plucked up my courage and called the assistant deputy minister of defence responsible for policy, whom I had met during my days at NATO headquarters, and explained my problem.

His response startled me. He said that, of course, Canada should act. Democracy in a part of the world of key importance to Canada was being imperilled. He would call the "Chief" (as the chief of the defence staff was known to initiates) to seek authority. Five minutes later, the assistant deputy minister breathlessly called me back. The Chief was completely onside. I had authority to send instructions authorizing the ship's commander to deploy the ship's company as recommended. At this point I got cold feet. True, as I had so eloquently written in my memorandum to Cabinet on Canada's relations with the Commonwealth Caribbean, it was in our interest to foster stability in the region and thus, presumably, to ward off coups. I had a strong inkling, however, that the recommended course of action could go terribly wrong. It did not occur to me that I (and the Chief for that matter) needed political authority for the commitment of military force and for the establishment of rules of engagement. My gut instinct told me that the whole enterprise was bizarre. What if nervous, heavily armed Canadian sailors were to shoot innocent people by mistake as they drove around Castries in the dark? Worse, what if they were to shoot themselves?

I then did what any sane foreign-service officer would do in similar circumstances. I sent a message telling the commander to rid his ship of his guests, pull up the gangway, and not permit any member of his crew to leave the ship until further notice, no matter what transpired onshore. If he and his Foreign Affairs colleagues still wanted to intervene in the morning, we could think about it at that time. I then went home to bed. The next morning at seven I turned on the CBC news hoping that the first item would not be coverage of a bloody coup in a friendly island state of the Caribbean under the tolerant watch of the crew of a Canadian destroyer. Fortunately, all was calm. On arrival at my office I found a message from the high commissioner waiting for me on my desk: Perhaps he and the associate undersecretary had overreacted to the request from the prime minister. Please disregard the recommendation of the previous evening.

When I related my adventures to my director-general, he assembled dozens of earnest military officers, RCMP personnel, and representatives of the departments of the Solicitor-General, Justice, Foreign Affairs, the Office of Emergency Measures, and the Privy Council Office to try to figure out how situations such as I had encountered at Gander and Castries should really have been handled. Fortunately, I was sent on posting just as the interdepartmental committee started its work. I never did find out the conclusions.

My personnel officer told me that I was to be offered an ambassadorial posting that summer either to Cuba or to Peru. The choice was mine. My wife and I were delighted. I had just turned forty and had not expected to receive the call for some years yet. Peru and Cuba were both appealing, but we opted for Cuba because it appeared to provide me with greater opportunity to spend time with Anne-Pascale and Laurent, aged five and four. We hoped the Cubans would overlook the little incident at Gander and my subsequent contretemps with the ambassador. *Agrément*, or approval for my nomination as ambassador, was quickly received – but the Cubans had not forgotten.

Return to Peru
Before I reported for duty in Cuba, however, Foreign Affairs asked me to spend the summer in Lima on special duty as chargé d'affaires to try to sort out some difficulties that had arisen in recent months. We seized the chance. Marie-Jeanne would have the opportunity to learn Spanish and I would be able to brush up on a language that I not spoken since leaving Colombia eleven years earlier. I was also looking forward to showing Marie-Jeanne a city and country that I had visited in 1969 on my first posting. Despite the unfortunate timing of that visit with my difficult

German companion, the place had made a lasting impression on me with its old-world colonial charm reminiscent of Thorton Wilder's great novel, *The Bridge of San Luis Rey.*

I was also curious to see what was going on at the mission. A series of bizarre messages had been sent from the embassy in recent months. The most alarming of these solemnly reported that an astrologer had predicted that a giant earthquake, with its epicentre just a few kilometres off the Pacific coast, would occur in early July: half of Lima was supposed to fall into the sea and the other half would be destroyed in the resulting giant tidal wave. Many of the good citizens of Lima were fleeing the city, the local Peruvian staff at the embassy were agitated, and even the stalwart Canadian personnel were worried and seeking guidance and solace from distant Ottawa.

Headquarters was also concerned by some of the inventive suggestions advanced by the embassy for dealing with the threat of terrorist attack. It was true that guerrillas were active in the country and the mission was commended for taking the threat seriously. And yet . . . one proposal to protect the ambassador in case of an attack was ingenious but perplexing: a fireman's pole was to be installed in the ambassador's office to allow him to slide down three floors to ground level and run out the back door. The post had not explained how their plan would work in practice. Clearly, the Canadian ambassador would have to be in good physical shape to be able to carry out this operation. He would have to engage in regular exercise and train assiduously in sliding down the pole to be ready when the moment arrived. A system to reserve the pole for the use of the head of post would have to be worked out; it would not do to have less important staff members making use of the pole in times of crisis since otherwise there would be a risk of a pileup at the bottom. There was also the problem of what the ambassador was to do when he ran out the back door. Should the Canadian government pay to keep a driver and a fast getaway car available at all times? The post wanted these and other weighty matters investigated. Headquarters was starting to wonder if the team at the mission had drunk too many pisco sours, the potent local drink, and asked me to look into the situation over the summer.

What Foreign Affairs was really worried about, however, were reports in the Canadian press about the allegedly bad job the embassy was doing in providing consular services to more than a hundred Canadian citizens, men and women, who had thought that they could visit Peru and pay for their holiday by transporting cocaine back to Canada, but instead found themselves in overcrowded jails in Lima. To make matters worse, in the eyes of the critics, most of the Canadians had been arrested as a result of sting operations run by the RCMP liaison officer working out of the embassy in co-operation with the Peruvian police. The embassy was accused of being in conflict of interest: helping to arrest Canadians and then providing consular help to the same people after their imprisonment. Embassy personnel were apparently doing a better job of the former than the latter. Minister MacGuigan was being subjected to a barrage of questions in Parliament and so welcomed the proposal that I go to Peru to shake up the mission.

Marie-Jeanne, Anne-Pascale, Laurent, and I arrived in Lima early one morning in late June after an overnight flight from Toronto. The city we entered in 1981 was very different from the one I had visited with my German colleague in 1969. Gone was the small clean city with its colonial personality. In its place was a megacity overcrowded with rural migrants who had fled the countryside looking for a better life for their families. We drove in from the airport in a jam of trucks and buses belching black smoke, past burning garbage that littered both sides of the road, and the bloated bodies of dogs killed in the traffic. Unending miles of slums with their tangles of unpaved alleys and shacks with polyethylene plastic roofs stretched off into the distance. A grim black cloud, a combination of ocean fog and industrial soot, hung over the city, coating everything, including the leaves of the trees, with fine dirt. I wondered how people could tolerate such conditions without exploding into revolt.

The ambassador departed Lima for good on the day of our arrival, leaving a half-eaten plate of canapés at the official residence as a farewell gift for us. While too polite to say so, he indicated that if I thought I could do a better job than he had, then I was welcome to try. I did not have to do much. I found that the post already had an elaborate security system in place to protect the staff, and the hare-brained scheme to install a fireman's pole had been quietly dropped. The astrologer who had predicted the destruction of the city allowed that she may have been a little hasty in her conclusions; those staff members who had been worried about their fate calmed down. The consular officer responsible for assisting the incarcerated Canadians, who had been on medical leave for six weeks, returned to work and rapidly brought order to his files. The RCMP officer in charge of the anti-narcotics program went on leave, temporarily reducing the arrest rate in Peru of young middle-class Canadians out to make a fast dollar from the drug trade.

We thus were able to spend our time getting to know Peru, visiting the tropical rain forests to the east of the Andes where the rivers drained into the Amazon and calling on Canadian volunteers providing technical assistance to Indians. We went up into the high Andean Sierra to Cusco, the ancient seat of the Incan empire destroyed by Francisco Pizarro in 1531, where its strong local Quechua population still retained its Indian personality. Suffering from altitude sickness, I entered a church for a moment of rest and reflection. The church was dark and cool. Candles flickered, illuminating the Creole faces of Christian martyrs from another era in ancient portraits on the walls. There was only a handful of people in the pews. A group of young people were playing guitars and singing subdued Joan Baez–style hymns to peace and human rights. A young priest started to speak, and to my surprise I found that he was denouncing the power structure of Peru, calling for a revolution in thinking to bring social justice to Indians and other marginalized peoples. He was an Indian himself, with dark-brown skin, most likely chosen by the parish priest to be educated in a seminary, and the son of proud *campesinos* happy to see a member of their family move up a social class.

Both Joseph Stalin and Fidel Castro, I recalled, had been educated in seminaries before going on to embrace the secular faith of communism, which excused human-rights abuses of entire classes of people in the expectation of a better tomorrow that would never come. Would this young priest preaching liberation theology be able to resist excusing violence or turning to violence himself in the face of his country's crushing social, economic, and political injustices?

After the obligatory trip to Machu Picchu on a mountaintop some fifty kilometres by train from Cusco, we departed to see the Lines of Nazca and other vestiges of the rich cultural past of Peru. In Lima we attended the inauguration ceremony of Fernando Belaúnde Terry, the president driven from office when I was in the Peruvian capital on holiday twelve years previously. He had been replaced by a series of left-wing military dictatorships, all of which had tried but failed to solve Peru's endemic social and economic problems.

The ceremonial highlight of our stay was the national-day parade during which tens of thousands of troops marched past reviewing stands filled with the high officers of state and members of the diplomatic corps. A radical leftist revolutionary group, the Sendero Luminoso (Shining Path) – with more in common with Pol Pot's Khmer Rouge in Cambodia than with Castro's Twenty-Sixth of July Movement in Cuba – was already stirring revolt in the mountains. It would, I thought, have no chance against such firepower. I was wrong. It would not be long before appeals from priests such as the one I had heard at Cusco and from intellectuals inspired by the writings of Mao would set the Andes on fire. The insurrection would continue for decades, costing tens of thousands of lives.

I was to have no further connection with Peru until fifteen years later, when I would be engaged in an operation to free a Canadian ambassador captured by urban guerrillas who were ideological soulmates of the Shining Path. In late August, we left Lima for Havana on a Cubana airlines flight to learn about revolution from the godfather of the Latin American left himself, Fidel Castro.

PART TWO

THE AMBASSADOR

1981–2002

8

Cuba in Castro's Days of Glory

My message was blunt: "Call off your goons!"

The posting as ambassador to Castro's Cuba marked a transition in my career, although I did not know it at the time. I had spent fifteen years in the foreign service, never with a master plan. Trying to live life to the fullest, I had by good fortune bounced from one fascinating job to another. The same lack of design would prevail in the remaining years in my diplomatic career, which from that point on would be spent always as an ambassador or high commissioner when serving abroad. Focusing on family life and the job at hand, I would be constantly surprised with these postings, although in retrospect they formed a pattern, preparing me to become foreign-policy advisor to the prime minister in 1994.

Infatuation and Disillusion

My interest in Cuba went back a long way. In high school, I followed with admiration Fidel Castro's guerrilla war in the Sierra Maestra mountains in Oriente province and his eventual victory over dictator Fulgencio Batista. In those days, Castro was an international hero. The media, including American publications such as *Life*, *Time*, the *New York Times* and even *Reader's Digest* portrayed the Cuban revolutionary as a modern-day synthesis of Simón Bolívar, Abraham Lincoln, and the great nineteenth-century Cuban poet and activist, José Martí. No one could quarrel with Castro's goal of turning around more than three hundred years of oppressive Spanish colonial rule, followed by half a century of American military rule and indirect control through weak corrupt governments after the Spanish-American war of 1898. He was respected for tackling racial discrimination against blacks, gambling, prostitution, and gangsterism exported by the Mob from Miami, and the enormous inequality between a small upper class and the rest of the population.

By the early 1960s, when I was a university student, his halo had cracked. To be sure, Castro was still in the news. The social and economic revolution that he had launched, leading in short order to the eradication of illiteracy, the provision of universal medical care, and the end of discrimination against blacks and mixed-race Creoles, was widely admired. But the hundreds of executions following summary courts-martial after his seizure of power, his nationalizations of sugar mills, banks, utilities, and other private property belonging to Cubans and foreigners alike, combined with the flight of almost the entire Cuban middle class to seek refuge in the United States, disillusioned many of his erstwhile international supporters.

A realignment of Cuban foreign policy happened at lightning pace. In February 1960, Soviet vice-premier Anastas Mikoyan led a large delegation to Cuba and signed important trade contracts, whereby the U.S.S.R. agreed to supply technicians to replace those who had fled to the United States. An outraged President Eisenhower authorized the CIA to back Cuban émigrés to overthrow the Cuban revolutionary government. The failed Bay of Pigs invasion by fourteen hundred CIA-trained émigrés followed during the presidency of John F. Kennedy in 1961. Castro's declaration that he had been a Marxist-Leninist since his university days established him firmly in the communist camp at the height of the Cold War – a decade after the establishment of NATO, the communist revolution in China, and the Korean War – and turned the United States into an implacable enemy. The next year, Nikita Khrushchev sought to install medium-range missiles, bringing on the Cuban missile crisis – arguably the most dangerous showdown of the entire Cold War era. It was resolved only when the Americans blockaded Cuba and the Soviet leader agreed to withdraw his weapons on receiving a secret assurance from President Kennedy that the United States would not invade Cuba.

Castro's Views
In dozens of discussions with me (and with the visitors I brought to call on him in the 1980s and 1990s), Castro loved to reminisce about that period. He scoffed at suggestions that he had been converted to Marxist-Leninism only after the Americans turned against him. He had been, he repeated, a Marxist-Leninist from his early university days. It was thus natural that he would adopt communist economic and social policies and turn to the Soviet Union for financial and military help as relations with the United States deteriorated. He remained bitter, however, over the Soviet retreat in the face of American pressure during the missile crisis. Castro's eyes would flash when he recounted what had happened. His pride at crushing the invading force in 1961 was matched by his anger at the Soviet leadership, especially Khrushchev, whom he never forgave for not consulting him before cutting his deal with the Americans. If he had been consulted, Castro said, he would never have agreed to the withdrawal of the missiles. As it was, he once told me, he had not hesitated to push a button to launch a surface-to-air missile that brought down an American U-2 spy plane overflying Cuba in the midst of the crisis. The subtext, which I was always too discreet to mention, was that the Cuban leader, but not Khrushchev, was prepared to risk nuclear war to preserve his revolution.

Anger at the Soviets for their betrayal in 1962 would remain an open wound for decades, and Castro would have other

quarrels with the Soviets, over economic policy, ideological direction, and management of the war in Angola. These problems,
however, were quarrels within one ideological family – a point
driven home to us when Marie-Jeanne and I, invited in error,
attended a meeting of the faithful in Havana at a stadium filled
with Cuban communists. The guests of honour were the ambassadors from the local communist embassies, as well as delegations
from communist countries. It was like a giant revivalist Christian
meeting, but the gods worshipped were Marx and Lenin. The
"International" and other Marxist songs were the hymns, a
chanted pledge of adherence to Marxism-Leninism the Nicene
Creed. The martyrs were the comrades who had fallen in action
in the fight against "Yankee imperialism" in Africa and Central
America and whose names were roared into the night air by the
crowd in angry defiance of Washington.

As Castro never tired of repeating, the real enemy was the
United States. At least half of all discussions I had with the president were taken up by anti-American tirades. His hostility was
visceral, based on the real and imagined unjust treatment of
Cuba in the years leading up to his assumption of power. It was
also, however, tactical. He realized that fanning the embers of
incipient Cuban resentment of the United States, an essential
component of Cuban nationalism, guaranteed a certain level of
popular support for his regime. The United States played into his
hands by implementing a full trade embargo against Cuba in
1961 and by pressuring the OAS to have its members break diplomatic and economic ties with the Castro government. Only
Mexico refused to follow suit.

Canada and Cuba

Canada, not being a member of the OAS, took no part in the decisions to isolate Cuba, but was asked nonetheless by Washington
to cut off ties. We refused and benefited: trade that Cuba normally

would have conducted with the United States was diverted to Canada. Exporters of agricultural products such as seed potatoes, beans, corn, wheat, bagged flour, and a wide range of processed foods and industrial products gained an instant market. The Cubans and Soviets (who were underwriting their economy) paid cash. Castro accordingly never failed to mention Canada's defiance of the United States and the special place Canada held in Cuba's heart every time a Canadian visitor or group of visitors came calling. The Cuban leader, I believe, was sincere in his gratitude, but was under no illusion about Canada's basic position as a committed member of the Western alliance on the other side of the ideological divide throughout the Cold War.

In fact, political relations between Canada and Cuba were never particularly close, despite the myth to the contrary. From a distance, Cuba's revolutionary image, Castro's charisma, and Havana's defiance of the United States were attractive to Canadian governments, starting with that of John Diefenbaker, who was prime minister when Castro seized power in early January 1959. Diefenbaker supported Castro out of a desire to demonstrate to the United States that (in certain non-essential areas, to be sure) Canada would not allow itself to be dictated to by Washington. All subsequent Canadian prime ministers followed the same policy, with varying degrees of enthusiasm.

After Diefenbaker, Lester Pearson adopted a minimalist position, wishing to use his diplomatic credit with Washington to differ over something really important – the United States's involvement in Vietnam – rather than engaging in polemics over Cuba. From my position as a junior foreign-service officer arranging the programs of heads of state visiting Canada as official guests during our centennial year in 1967, I recall Prime Minister Pearson giving instructions that Castro not be invited to Canada. He allowed a Cuban minister to represent his leader but decreed that the welcoming ceremony be moved at short notice from the usual afternoon time slot to one early in the morning when there would be no crowd and few reporters. Relations were correct but cool.

Under Pierre Trudeau, relations improved markedly, the high point being the official visit of the prime minister and his wife to Cuba in 1976, during which Margaret sang to Castro and Pierre shouted "viva Castro" to the crowd. The two countries, however, remained so far apart on human rights, political freedoms, and foreign policy that the warmth of the relations between the leaders was never reflected at the official level. When Cuba dispatched troops to Angola, Canada phased out its aid program and downgraded relations. Castro never lost his high regard for Trudeau, however, whom he regarded as a fellow visionary.

My Views

Having seen the social and economic inequities of Colombian and Peruvian life, and since I was familiar with conditions in Central America, I had deep admiration for what Cuba had accomplished under Castro. Canada also owed a debt of gratitude to Cuba, I believed, for agreeing to accept the FLQ kidnappers of James Cross in exchange for his liberation during the October Crisis in 1970. Nevertheless, I was not blind to Cuba's dark side. The economic and social justice provided by the revolution had not been matched by political justice. The country had become a gulag with total press censorship, jails full of political prisoners, summary executions, and people encouraged to spy on each other. The most efficient institutions were the armed forces and the Ministry of the Interior. The spirit of private enterprise had been snuffed out and an atmosphere of suspicion prevailed among the general population.

Cuba had fallen slavishly into line on all the issues of vital importance to the U.S.S.R. Castro had even justified, in self-serving terms, the Warsaw Pact's crushing of the Prague Spring and the Soviet invasion of Afghanistan. He sought and obtained

The author (far right, first row), aged 7, at Port Carling Elementary School, Ontario, 1947.

James Bartleman, aged 12.

First foreign assignment to the U.N. in 1966; James Bartleman in Central Park, New York.

On a second continent. Acting high commissioner to Bangladesh, in his garden, Dhaka, 1972.

Children at work on the street, Dhaka, 1972.

Collecting alms to bury the displayed body of a loved one, Dhaka, 1972.

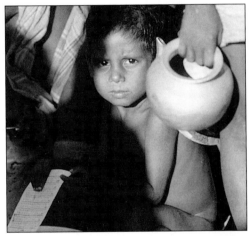

Losers in the civil war.
Hungry refugees in a camp
in Bangladesh, 1972.

High-level talks. Sheikh Mujibur Rahman, leader of Bangladesh, Ivan Head
(Prime Minister Trudeau's envoy), and James Bartleman.

Marriage, September 1975, in Brussels. Left to right: Pierre Pat Rosillon, Octave Rosillon, Marie-Jeanne Rosillon, James Bartleman, young bridesmaid, and Maureen Bartleman.

On holiday in Venice in 1977 with Marie-Jeanne and Zaka – who was later poisoned by the Cuban secret police.

Nicaragua 1980: car riddled with bullet holes in the aftermath of the
Civil War.

Two officials talk in front of the mural in the Nicaraguan Ministry of the
Interior. Note the peasants killing blond CIA or U.S. army agents.

1981. The new Canadian Ambassador to Cuba presents his letters and credentials to Fidel Castro, while Marie-Jeanne looks on.

1982. Fidel Castro drops in for dinner.

After dinner, Castro holds forth to an audience of visiting Canadian MPs. The photograph is signed: "Para Jim Bartleman, fraternalmente Fidel Castro."

leadership of the Non-Aligned Movement and shifted its orientation from one of equidistance between East and West to one aligned with the U.S.S.R. and its foreign policy. The Cubans provided the Soviets with airport and naval facilities to refuel long-range bombers and submarines carrying nuclear weapons, whose role was to patrol the coasts and skies off North America. He authorized the Soviets to station a combat brigade in Cuba to protect an extensive Soviet signals-collection spy complex targeted against defence installations in Florida and Panama.

Cuba, it was evident, had been well rewarded for these services. The Soviets provided massive economic assistance indirectly in the form of subsidies for sugar imports and directly in the provision of machinery, foodstuffs, and petroleum products. Cuba was, in effect, receiving far more for its loyalty to the U.S.S.R. than Batista ever obtained from the United States for his anti-communist stance in the 1940s and 1950s. In return, the Soviets turned a blind eye as Castro carved out a lead role in supporting revolution in Africa and Central America. As the direct inheritor of Lenin's mantle, the U.S.S.R., in theory, supported revolution in the Third World. But the flame had long since gone out. Moscow was more interested in mobilizing support for its Cold War confrontation with the United States than in fanning the flames in areas far from its borders where it had no chance of matching American military power should matters deteriorate. Cuba, however, was led by first-generation revolutionaries who still believed in radical change and had no such inhibitions. It dragged along an often cautious and always reluctant U.S.S.R.

The Good Years
The period of my posting was a good one for Castro internationally. Jimmy Carter was president of the United States. Castro saw him as weak and non-threatening. The Cuban armed forces, provided with the latest Soviet armaments, had never been as well equipped and were confident of their ability to defend Cuba

against anything but a massive American invasion. Cuba emerged as the major power-broker in Africa, with large concentrations of troops in Ethiopia and Angola and a presence propping up friendly leaders in a dozen other countries. It had fought the South Africans to a draw in Angola, and its greatest triumphs in that country were yet to come. It would not be until 1996, when I was on a special mission on behalf of the prime minister, that I would learn directly from Castro himself the details of Cuba's massive involvement.

Central America and the Caribbean were Cuba's greatest priority areas. Havana rejoiced in the overthrow of the Eric Gairy government by the leftist New Jewel Movement in Grenada and of Somoza by the Sandinistas in Nicaragua. These areas were also where the stakes were the highest. In contrast to Africa, the Caribbean region was in the backyard of the United States and its future was considered vital to Washington's interests. The Cubans applied the same logic, convinced that their revolution would never be secure until their neighbours embraced the same political ideals and the communist system. Castro barely concealed the support that Cuba provided to Central American guerrillas, and poured in more resources than Cuba could afford in order to support its champions. Cuba sent men, equipment, and materials to Grenada to construct a new airport and dispatched military advisors, military equipment, teachers, and doctors to Nicaragua. Cuba was to be the big loser in this proxy struggle with the United States. After President Reagan came to power, Grenada was invaded and pro-U.S. governments came to power in Central America.

The Mood in Havana

The Cuba of 1981, while not like that of Graham Greene's *Our Man in Havana*, had its saints, sinners, ideologues, camp followers, and unconcerned. The saints and ideologues were the young revolutionaries from El Salvador and Guatemala, in Cuba for training and indoctrination; the thousands of young students, from places as disparate as Nicaragua and Angola, red-scarfed in honour of the Communist Party and receiving free education and compulsory indoctrination; the European intellectuals attracted by left-wing causes on pilgrimages to a functioning revolutionary state; and Latin American artists and writers seeking political inspiration for their creative impulses. There was also a procession of Third World leaders coming to seek inspiration, guidance, and material help. Almost every month, the resident ambassadors would be summoned to the airport to stand on the hot tarmac to greet these leaders. Occasionally, Marie-Jeanne and I would be invited to dine with the president and his brother Raul with a guest of distinction, such as Samora Machel of Mozambique, who wanted me to lobby the Canadian government to launch a major aid program in his country.

The sinners and the unconcerned were concentrated among the resident ambassadors, our closest contacts in the highly controlled society. A few, like me, were inexperienced, on our first postings and learning the ropes, and (I hope) still too young to be blasé. Others were on their last postings, full of stories about exotic assignments in their long careers, now killing time before retirement. Few were destined for the top ranks of their diplomatic services; most had been sent to a place that excited little interest in their capitals, and they knew it. One, who came drunk to every reception or dinner, was formerly an ambassador to Idi Amin's Uganda; he was psychologically scarred, damaged to the core by the screams of torture victims coming from the central prison behind his official residence in Kampala. Another, previously marked for early and rapid promotion in his foreign service, was lying low in Havana, hoping the political leadership in his country would forget his ill-fated involvement in some dubious activities that had recently come to light. Despite his apparent sophistication, he believed in the evil eye; he was always nervous about being targeted by the voodoo gods so cherished by adherents of Cuba's underground Santeria. Another dozen or more African heads of post, forgotten and unpaid by their impoverished governments, made ends meet by selling goods to Cubans on the black market and buying cars from their diplomatic colleagues to ship home to sell illicitly at high prices. Corruption even extended to the Soviet and East European comrades. The spouses of communist diplomats and technical staff conducted a thriving illegal business at the exit doors of duty-free shops selling bluejeans, food, and Cuban rum at inflated prices to Cubans, for whom such goods were unavailable.

El Commandante en Jefe

The main preoccupation of everyone – Cubans, visiting sympathizers, and diplomats alike – was Castro-watching. For Cuba was a one-man country in 1981, just as it had been ever since Fidel Castro, sporting a long black beard, a cigar clenched in his teeth, and with his favourite rifle cradled in his arms, led his Twenty-Sixth of July Movement out of the mountains to power. Castro dominated everything. His every utterance received lead coverage in the state-controlled newspapers, and on radio and television; when he was not featured making speeches, he was shown watching baseball games or visiting factories or farms. His picture, most often accompanied by a text daring the United States to do its worst, was on display provocatively on huge billboards set up at the main intersections and at the square in front of the old United States embassy building.

In 1981, at fifty-seven, Castro had been "maximum leader" for twenty-two years and was at the height of his physical and oratorical powers. His hair was still black and he continued to wear out crowds with marathon speeches during which he quoted at great length the most detailed and arcane statistics to bolster whatever case he was making. He cultivated a revolutionary-chic style. His military uniforms with one star on the shoulder were always impeccably pressed. Cohibas were his cigars of preference, Chivas Regal his whisky of choice, and an Uzi machine gun his personal weapon.

Our first contact with the president occurred within two weeks of our arrival. The Inter-Parliamentary Union, the world's most important and representative organization of parliamentarians, was holding its annual meeting that year in Havana. A senior group of Canadian members of Parliament and senators led by Senator Gildas Molgat was in town. Most were predisposed to like Cuba and its president. At the opening ceremony, however, President Castro made a virulent speech attacking the United States for being an imperialist exploiter of the disinherited of the earth and the United Kingdom for oppressing the Catholics of Northern Ireland. Castro's romantic image was destroyed for the Canadians, who had never heard anything like this before. Several started to make plans to leave Havana in protest.

I decided to force a face-to-face meeting between Castro and the Canadian delegation to allow a dialogue in the hope of heading off the premature departure of key delegates. The president had already been invited to a reception at our residence that evening. Realizing there was little hope that he would visit the Canadians when he was invited to receptions at more than one hundred other missions, I resolved to pass a message indirectly to the president via the Cuban Ministry of the Interior, to make my point.

It was common knowledge that the telephone lines of all diplomats were tapped by the Ministry of the Interior and that the president was an avid reader of this form of raw intelligence. I therefore made a series of telephone calls to diplomatic colleagues on the open line loudly telling them that the Canadian delegation was on the point of departing Cuba to protest the president's speech; only a personal appearance by Castro that evening at my residence would prevent a walkout. Within thirty minutes, I received a call from a flustered Foreign Affairs official to tell me the president was coming, and to ensure that the Canadian delegation did not leave beforehand. Within another thirty minutes, a dozen tough, heavily armed Ministry of Interior agents in civilian clothes arrived to search our residence for terrorists and weapons. Marie-Jeanne and I had a temporary fright when an agent unearthed four-year Laurent's toy pistol. Before another thirty minutes had passed, technicians had arrived to install new telephone equipment and a full medical team were occupying a spare bedroom.

Fifteen minutes later, the president himself was at the door. After mingling for a few minutes with the other guests, Castro joined the Canadian parliamentarians in the library and the charm offensive began. He told the group that he held Canada in great esteem. Canada had stood by Cuba during its darkest hours, resisting pressure from Washington to cut relations and restrict trade. Cuba considered Canada a special friend despite differences in our social systems. He considered himself to be a friend of Prime Minister Trudeau and had developed close ties with him during his visit to Cuba several years earlier. The monologue continued with the president allowing that he may have been somewhat harsh on the United States and the United Kingdom. However, Cuba was under threat from the United States. He was the target of repeated CIA assassination attempts. Anyhow, Cuba had a duty to help revolutionaries everywhere. With a smile, he said that he had not realized that so many Canadians had Irish roots. He laced his intervention with statistics quoting per capita incomes, levels of education, numbers of doctors, and, of course, the sugar crop. The session ended with a description of Cuba before and after the "triumph of the Revolution."

The Canadian delegation, with one or two exceptions, was awestruck. To my surprise, after having vehemently criticized Cuba and Castro among themselves, they did not challenge the president when faced with him in the flesh. After three hours and the taking of numerous photographs – delivered to delegation members before they departed – the president took his leave. This scenario was repeated over the two years of our posting whenever Castro met visitors from Canada. The Cuban president would reduce even the most critical visitor to the status of an admirer with the strength of his personality, the depth of his knowledge, his imposing physical presence, and the revolutionary mystique of his person. He would then send them expensive gifts of the finest cigars and rum, allowing his guests to return to Canada to boast about their links of privilege and intimacy with one of the world's great first-generation revolutionary figures. Former foreign minister Flora MacDonald was the only visitor out of the dozens I brought to see Castro who had the guts to ask him directly about the thousands of political prisoners in his jails. She didn't get a straight answer.

Personal Relations

For reasons best known to himself, President Castro maintained a close but ambivalent relationship with me. At the time, I flattered myself into thinking that this was because he valued my views on the situation in Central America, where he was supporting revolution and wanted contact with someone who did not form part of his immediate stable of yes-men. I had to abandon this ego-enhancing theory when I noted that he never, ever, asked my opinion on anything, and while he would visit for hours, the dialogue was confined to the president talking and me listening. The thought crossed my mind that perhaps the president believed he could overwhelm me with the force of his personality and turn me into an uncompromising supporter of Cuban policies. My body language probably did nothing to discourage this impression. I was genuinely impressed by Castro at the time, relishing the opportunity to make my mark as a newly minted ambassador by transmitting to headquarters the latest pearls of revolutionary insight obtained in tête-à-tête conversations, between equals, of course, around the dinner table. The real

reason was probably that he wanted to send a signal to Prime
Minister Trudeau, whose funeral he would attend almost two
decades later, that he valued their friendship and wanted closer
ties with Canada.

The president took a close personal interest in our housing
situation and made the renovation of the Canadian official
residence – which looked remarkably like a dilapidated Southern
mansion from *Gone With the Wind* – virtually a Cuban national
priority. The walls were black from mould and the roof was so
rotten that twenty-gallon garbage pails had to be placed at
strategic locations throughout the house to catch rainwater.
Headquarters did not have a budget to cover the costs of the renovations, but Castro took matters in hand, sending a construction
brigade to carry out the work at a price that I personally set. When
I told him some months later that the quality of the work was
not high and little progress was being made, he became furious,
thundering, "My orders are always obeyed!" He appointed the
president of the National Assembly, Flavio Bravo, to supervise
the workers and to provide him with regular updates. The residence was then completely redone at minimal cost to the
Canadian taxpayer. In the process, the Cuban security and intelligence service probably filled the walls with the latest generation
of listening devices, but neither I nor headquarters was concerned,
since we assumed the building was bugged anyway.

The president became a regular visitor to our residence,
coming to dinners and remaining until the small hours of the
morning, reminiscing about his days as a student revolutionary
in Colombia and elsewhere in Latin America and about his years
as a guerrilla leader in the Cuban mountains. For security
reasons, his office rarely confirmed his acceptance of invitations
before he appeared at our door. It did not take a genius, however,
to read his intentions. Ministry of the Interior troops would seal
off the neighbourhood, guards would materialize in the garden,
the president's personal food taster would take up his position

beside the cook in the kitchen, and technicians would hurriedly install new telephone lines. The president would then roll up in his big, black Soviet Ziv limousine, leave his Uzi pistol machine gun on the back seat, and come in to spend the evening with the Bartlemans, wearing, as always, a bulletproof vest under his well-pressed military shirt. I was principally interested in his views on the situation in Central America and on relations with the United States.

I also gained an inside look at the life of the Cuban elite. Orders were apparently given that every effort should be made to receive the Canadian ambassador and to accept his invitations. In contrast to my colleagues from the British embassy and the American-interest section of the Swiss embassy (the unofficial U.S. diplomatic presence in Cuba), who were denied access to anyone above the level of director, I could see anyone at any level at almost any time. Once, a dozen deputy ministers came to lunch with one hour's notice when a visitor appeared unexpectedly from Canada. My wife and I were invited to the homes of senior officials and to restaurants and cultural performances. We saw that there was an enormous disparity between the mass of the people who lived an austere revolutionary life and the privileged at the top who formed the hard-core supporters of the system. The homes of the elite were well appointed and special stores, not open to the public, existed to serve their needs. Milovan Djilas's classic description of life in Yugoslavia under Tito in *The New Class* could have been written about Cuba under Castro.

Marie-Jeanne and I had one inside glimpse of Castro's personal lifestyle when he arranged for the minister of fisheries to take us and my brother Bob, visiting from Muskoka, to spend a weekend at the presidential retreat on an island in the Bay of Pigs. The president told me that he had entertained Prime Minister Trudeau at this very spot. A Council of State vehicle driven by a Ministry of the Interior driver took us at top speed to a secret base manned by a special detachment of elite bodyguard troops. The minister of fisheries then escorted us to a large, luxurious yacht, which had a machine gun strapped to the deck. Two gunboats flanked us and a helicopter gunship flew overhead as we raced some twenty kilometres across the Bay of Pigs to the island. Heavy security was required, we were told, to deal with CIA attempts on the lives of the president and his guests.

At the island itself, three military half-track vehicles waited at the dock to conduct us to palatial lodgings. Various attendants provided for our every need: we fished from a large custom-built barge complete with a mahogany bar; seamen in white gloves baited the hooks, dropped the lines into the water to the correct depth, and removed the fish once caught. Since the area was out of bounds to the public, the waters were swarming with fish eager to take our bait. Our hosts also took care to ensure that we enjoyed ourselves swimming and snorkelling. I once found myself having difficulty with my equipment. A Cuban frogman, assigned to ensure that the guests did not drown, appeared from nowhere to lift me out of the water, holding me aloft while I removed excess water from my mask. In the evening, Castro telephoned to ensure that we were comfortable. It was evident that there was little difference between the lives of those at the top in either the capitalist or communist systems.

Dirty Tricks

The attention would have been flattering if the Cubans had not at the same time subjected my family and me to constant harassment. Shortly after I arrived in Cuba, a general in the Ministry of the Interior, whose cover was that of a senior official in the tourism department, asked me to override Ottawa's objections and issue him a visa to visit Canada as a favour. This I refused to do. He was furious, as was his boss. I introduced myself to the Minister of Interior at a function at the president's some time later. "I know who you are," he said, and turned his back on me.

The first attempt to compromise me was farcical. One evening, the telephone rang. Still unused to ambassadorial conduct, I answered it, rather than wait for the butler to do so. A woman with a sultry voice was on the line. She had seen me at an official function, and wanted to get to know me better. Could we not arrange a discreet meeting? I would not be disappointed. My wife need never know.

The next evening the telephone rang again and I answered. The caller had a large supply of gold. He had no means of getting it out of the country. I could become a very rich person if only I would meet him quietly and take it off his hands for a modest price.

The third call, the following evening, was from a man. He had seen me, and I was so handsome. He had fallen in love with me and we just had to meet. I gave up answering the telephone, although I often wondered what would have been on offer in a fourth call.

In the coming year there were reminders that the Ministry of the Interior was watching, but nothing particularly serious occurred, other than the case of the cat with the possible ear for espionage. Loving animals, I welcomed a stray tabby into the embassy and offered it treats. After the cat had thus been graced with ambassadorial favour, the Canadian security guards and employees allowed it to roam at will through the most heavily protected areas of the mission, including my office, where it became a fixture on the sofa. One day, however, the quiet of my office was broken by a sharp whistling sound coming from one of the cat's ears. No one on my staff had ever heard of such a thing. Was it a natural phenomenon? Or was it a transmitter inserted by the clever Cubans that had gone haywire and was sending rather than receiving? I should have cut off the head to have a look or at least send it to Ottawa for analysis. Convinced that my friend the cat would not have been a willing accomplice to spying and would not, in any case, approve the removal of its head, I merely shooed him out the door, leaving it to the Cuban Ministry of the Interior, if they were really responsible, to decipher the sounds of the great outdoors at its leisure.

Ten years later, reading the memoirs of a retired CIA agent, I discovered that I may have been somewhat hasty in discounting the possibly that my feline companion was a spy. The retired spook recounted how the CIA spent twenty-three million dollars in a top-secret project to turn cats into eavesdropping devices. The mad scientists apparently cut open cats to insert batteries in their abdomens and ran antennas up their tails. The first cat was hit by a taxi on the way to its first "intelligence operation," and subsequent "agents" displayed more interest in garbage cans than enemy targets before the Americans abandoned the whole idea. The Cubans were perhaps more successful with their program.

At the beginning of the second year things became truly nasty. One morning, all the Cuban cooks and cleaners employed personally by the ten other Canadian families at the embassy were either thrown into jail or resigned without warning. Someone nailed a dead rat to the door of the commercial officer's house. My colleagues at the embassy were besieged by telephone threats and insults. The first secretary called to say that his dog had been poisoned and was dead. Marie-Jeanne and I checked our dog, Zaka, a member of our family who had been with us for six years. She too had been poisoned and was dying. We rushed her to a veterinarian, who pumped out her stomach and kept her alive for the time being. I then raced to the Foreign Ministry and demanded to see the director for North America, a former ambassador to Canada.

My message was blunt: "Call off your goons!" He was taken by surprise and grumbled that someone was trying to destroy Canada's relations with Cuba. Within minutes of my return home, a Cuban government veterinarian was at the door to provide follow-up care. I shipped Zaka to my parents in Canada in the hope that Canadian veterinarians could restore her to health. My father, who met her at Toronto airport, was shocked and saddened by what he saw. Her hair had fallen off in large patches, her kidneys were damaged, and she could barely walk. Within six months she was dead, and our family was devastated.

The Cuban staff were released from jail and reported for work later the same day. The harassing calls to my staff stopped on cue. I never learned why the Ministry of the Interior acted that day as it did. Perhaps a Cuban diplomat in Canada had been roughly handled in a Canadian counter-intelligence operation? Perhaps I had inadvertently given offence to someone high up in the Cuban hierarchy? Perhaps someone believed it was time to repay me for securing the freedom of the Cuban passenger at Gander? Whatever the reason, poisoning animals is a despicable act unworthy of agents of a government that claimed to be defending the principles of an enlightened revolution.

The incident was not to be the last, however. Another deeply disturbing operation was mounted against us, affecting all four members of our family. To protect individuals still alive in Cuba from the Cuban secret police, I cannot provide details, even now, more than two decades later.

After these incidents, Marie-Jeanne and I were relieved when I was called back early to take up an assignment as director-general of security and intelligence in Foreign Affairs. With regret we prepared to leave, despite the dirty tricks of the Ministry of the Interior, which were not unusual in communist countries during the Cold War. The Cuban people were warm-hearted, friendly, and genuine, as long as politics were not discussed. Our children acquired an extended family in the form of a household staff who loved children. They attended school for the first time, learned to speak Spanish, and spent countless hours on the beaches and in the swimming pool. For them it had been a happy time.

Punishment, This Time from Canada

But before we left, punishment, this time from Canada, was visited upon us. We at the embassy were used to receiving eminent Canadians from the government, the private sector, and the artistic world coming to Cuba to do business, promote trade, enjoy a holiday, shoot a movie, or perform in cultural events. Headquarters would advise us of the impending visit and work with us to arrange appropriate programs. The visits, such as one by the famous Canadian classical guitarist Liona Boyd, who came to film a show (and put on a gala performance at our residence for President Castro), usually took place without a hitch.

One week before our departure, however, Eugene Whelan, Canada's minister of agriculture, accompanied by his wife and a bevy of aides, arrived to break the mould. I was happy at first when I received a cryptic message informing me that the minister was including Cuba in a business trip to Latin America. I was aware of his reputation as a self-made man who had risen from childhood poverty to become a successful farmer and politician. Like other Canadians, I was aware of his friendship with the rising star of Soviet politics, Mikhail Gorbachev, who had made a highly publicized tour of Canada some months earlier. The minister had done an excellent job in showing the Soviet leader the success of Canada's market-economic agricultural sector and made a firm and influential friend for Canada in the process. His visit, I was sure, could only deepen our relations with Cuba. True, he had made it clear during his travels that he was not fond of Canadian diplomats. I had not yet met him, however, and was unaware that he relished blowing his stack and some years earlier may even have made Prime Minister Pearson afraid of him, as he later revealed in his autobiography. I was thus not unduly worried. I myself was from a humble background and in my years in the foreign service, I had always established good relations with visiting firemen, relying on hard work and meticulous preparation to ensure the success of their missions.

There is a first for everything. Waiting at the airport for the minister to arrive, I had a premonition that I would soon face one of the most trying times of my career. The sky was overcast, the air heavy, and the heat oppressive. It was so humid, my shirt was glued to my body and salty perspiration flowed into my eyes. In my imagination, it could have been the opening scene of an old Boris Karloff horror movie. Or perhaps, I sensed, my aboriginal ancestors were sending me a message to flee before disaster struck.

The aircraft was one hour late. Marie-Jeanne and I stood on the melting tarmac with the Cuban minister of agriculture as the small Canadian government plane circled the airport and came in for a landing. A scowling minister, his trademark green cowboy hat tilted aggressively forward on his head, his wife, and a glum-looking group of aides clambered out, giving the impression they had been sent against their will to carry out some disagreeable task. There were no apologies to the welcoming minister and protocol officers for the tardy arrival, and the party departed for the official guest house put at their disposal as a courtesy by the Cuban government.

The house, the same one used by Gerald Regan and his del-egation in the spring of 1981, while fairly spartan, was clean and comfortable. The minister, however, emerged from his suite one hour after arrival screaming: "I never have been put in such a dump! There is no cold water! What sort of useless ambassador are you anyway? You so-called diplomats are just a bunch of cookie-pushing idiots!"

The tirade continued for ten minutes with much unprintable language. He had seen a dead fly in his bathroom and the cold water had run out when the other members of the delegation had taken showers. As he yelled at me, I stood, open-jawed, thinking how I could possibly have gone wrong. I clearly remembered inspecting his quarters the day before. Either through gross incompetence I had missed the dead fly, or the fly had thought-lessly died after I left. Either way, it was my fault.

To my shame, I also realized that I had not turned on all the taps in the building before I had checked the availability of cold water in his bathroom. Gerald Regan had not complained when he stayed there two years before. Then again, I thought, perhaps his aides had not taken showers. More likely, however, the minister had turned on the tap marked *C* thinking it meant *cold*, when in fact it meant *caliente*, or *hot* in Spanish. It did not matter; I was still to blame for not being in his bathroom to guide his hand to the right tap.

In the circumstances, I wanted to follow the golden rule adopted by all public servants who wish eventual promotion when confronted with enraged politicians: contritely accept the blame and hope the offended one will forgive and move on. Unfortunately, I did not have time to apologize. The minister stormed out the door. He did not even wait for the briefing in which I had intended to tell him not to drink the water from the taps, which could cause diarrhea, but to use the bottled water set aside for the purpose.

We then departed to call on a senior representative of the Cuban government. The conversation was frosty. The minister was still furious and in no mood to talk business. The Cuban minister hesitantly noted that Cuba had been importing five hundred million dollars of Canadian products each year and paying cash. Could the minister use his influence in Ottawa to persuade the Canadian government to extend a fifty-million-dollar line of credit to facilitate this healthy trade?

The minister ignored the question. The only thing on his mind was the fly in his bathroom and the lack of cold water. He gave the hapless Cuban a severe dressing-down and we exited to prepare for our next event – the welcoming dinner at the government convention centre. My wife and I left in our car and the minister and his spouse followed behind in another.

More disaster awaited. The Cuban Ministry of the Interior, in a fit of pique, had arrested my driver on a trumped-up charge just days before the visit and sent a member of its own service to replace him. I had rejected their man, obviously a spy, but had been forced to find a replacement from among my existing staff. I was to discover in short order that my new driver, promoted from his job as a gardener, was actually blind in one eye. In retrospect, I don't think the sight in the other eye was very good, either.

Approaching the convention centre with the minister following behind, the gardener/chauffeur misjudged the entrance to the driveway, rolled over the lawn, hit a low-lying concrete barrier, tore out the muffler, and impaled the radiator on an iron post. The minister glanced at us with disgust as he was driven past. My wife and I abandoned our car, steam pouring from its radiator, and slunk into the building wondering what would happen next. The minister's mood improved as the evening progressed, and I learned from a sympathetic aide why he was determined to make me suffer. It seemed that during the delegation's just-completed visit to Colombia, the embassy in Bogotá had rented two aircraft to fly the party to a remote part of the country. When the visit was over, the embassy officers boarded their aircraft and departed. The minister and his party boarded their aircraft, which broke down. The remaining Canadians spoke no Spanish and none of the Colombians spoke English. It was some time before they could leave, and the minister was determined to wreak his revenge on the first member of Foreign Affairs he found; I was the sacrificial lamb.

This insight did not comfort me. I was similarly made uneasy by the minister's insistence that I join him in drinking a large glass of fiery Cuban liqueur after the meal. I declined because I have little tolerance for alcohol and the Cuban brew was deadly. He lifted his glass, downed the concoction in one swallow, looked me in the eye and said, "This will separate the men from the boys."

I barely slept that night and presented myself early the next morning at the guest house to prepare for the full day ahead. When the minister staggered into the dining room, his face was as green as his hat. Now, I thought, we will see who was the boy and who was the man. Having drunk copious quantities of water from the tap and been sick all night, he asked whether the water from the tap was fit to drink. I dodged the question. He started to berate me but his wife told him to calm down. A senior aide then took over, urging me with a liberal use of four-letter words to get my act together, *or else!*

We departed in a convoy of ten vehicles for a tour of a giant showcase dairy farm deep in the countryside. Three of the cars provided by the Cubans, all in poor mechanical condition, broke down en route, stranding members of the delegation on the side of the road – for which I was, of course, blamed. We visited the cows, made the usual appreciative noises to indicate our admiration for this agricultural triumph of the revolution, and proceeded to Varadero, where we were joined by the members of the party abandoned en route.

I had a private talk with the aide, who apologized to my wife but not to me for using foul language in her presence. He continued to complain, however, refusing to accept the accommodation arrangements made by the Cubans and saying that his room was too small for a man of his status. My wife and I gave him our room and moved in with our Cuban escort officers in a nearby guest house. The next day, when we rejoined the Canadian group, a junior aide sidled up to me to say quietly, "There is a god." The room we had given up to keep the peace had been infested with fleas. The aide who had taken our room had suffered all night, was covered in welts, and whimpered throughout breakfast. Fortunately, another aide was an expert bird-caller. He kept everyone amused with an impressive display of cooing, whistling, and chirping that drowned out the snivelling of his colleague.

Returning to Havana, Marie-Jeanne and I hosted a reception for the minister but Castro, obviously unhappy with all the complaining, did not put in an appearance. Around eleven at night, however, he changed his mind and sent word that he would call on his official visitor at the Cuban guest house. Despite his unhappiness at having to receive the president so late in the evening, the minister could not say no. An unsmiling Castro greeted him at the entrance and looked around to confirm that all was in order.

Cuba, he said, tried to do its best to treat its visitors well. A developing country, however, could not offer the same facilities to its guests as a Canada could. The minister responded by noting that if he had known how poorly equipped his accommodations would be, he would have brought his (expletives deleted) tools. Castro was not amused. He gently stroked his beard and stared at the ceiling as he thought of his response. He then asked, "How many dairy cattle are there in Canada?"

Canada's minister of agriculture did not know. Priding himself on remembering as much arcane detail on the Canadian economy as Castro did on Cuba's, he was mortified and demanded the answer from his aides. No one spoke. The responsible person with the book of Canadian facts, obtaining his revenge for rough treatment, pretended that he had mislaid his documentation. Everyone now joined me in the doghouse. The minister fumed and snorted before chewing out aides, the defiant, the sycophantic, the loyal, the flea-bitten, and the bird-caller – as well as Canada's ambassador, of course – for our ignorance of the vital piece of Canadian economic data. Castro watched the spectacle with satisfaction before providing the exact answer, which he had looked up in preparation for this verbal duel, down to the last cow. He then left in triumph, leaving the minister to ponder the dangers of locking horns with one of the world's master dialecticians.

The luncheon on the final day at our residence was a sullen, silent affair. The minister and his wife sat at one end of the pool and everyone else – the disgraced – at the other. Only Anne-Pascale and Laurent, unaware of the tensions, had fun, gambolling in the water and climbing on the shoulders of our visitor who, it turned out, loved children. The minister and his party boarded the aircraft with a visible sense of relief. They had not enjoyed their sojourn in Fidel's socialist paradise any more than I had enjoyed receiving them. With a bleak smile, the minister promised that he would write a letter of complaint to Foreign Affairs about my poor performance, adding thoughtfully that this was only to help me do a better job next time.

He was a man of his word, sending a letter to the foreign minister about the lack of cold water and the dead fly in the washroom of the Cuban guest house, saying I was to blame for these great hardships that had ruined his visit. The matter was not mentioned to me when I returned to headquarters. Whelan and I were both, of course, too polite to mention the subject when we met again many years later.

My family and I left Cuba within the week to start a new chapter in our lives. On the day of our departure, the first news reports of the killing of Prime Minister Maurice Bishop of Grenada began to come in. It would not be long before the marines would land in that country, chase out the Cubans, and end Castro's dream of spreading his version of socialism in the Caribbean.

9

Israel in Crisis

Israelis and Palestinians who genuinely wanted peace were the exception in the passionate mood of the times.

Laurent and Anne-Pascale, just eight and nine years old, were inconsolable, crying buckets of tears when told they would have to leave their friends and the cozy setting of the small elementary school in Chelsea, Quebec, in the middle of the school year. It was October 1985 and I had just accepted an offer to move to Tel Aviv by the first week of January to be ambassador to Israel. As a secondary responsibility, I was also named high commissioner to Cyprus, mainly to maintain liaison contacts with a battalion of Canadian peacekeepers manning the line of confrontation between Greek and Turkish Cypriots.

I had just completed my headquarters assignment and was ready to move on. Marie-Jeanne and I looked forward to living in one of the world's most dynamic societies, linked closely to Canada's Jewish community, and to the opportunity to explore first-hand the area that had given birth to three of the great monotheistic religions. The children were unhappy, it was true, but like foreign-service parents everywhere in similar circumstances, we crossed our fingers and told ourselves their horizons would be expanded by exposure to life abroad.

A Regional Hot Spot

Developments in Israel had made a vivid impression on me both before and after joining Foreign Affairs. As a child, I had been steeped in biblical lore at my village Sunday school and was familiar with many of the Old Testament place names, which had been resurrected in modern Israel. Like millions of others, my knowledge of Israel at that time was derived almost exclusively from the popular novel *Exodus*, which outlined in heroic terms the story of the creation of the twentieth-century state. As a teenager in 1956, I had followed on our black-and-white television set the fortunes of Israel's defence forces as they made their lightning strike on the Suez Canal in an attack coordinated with France and Britain against Egypt. France and Britain emerged with bloody noses when the United States disowned their conduct and insisted that they withdraw their forces, but Israel was largely excused on the grounds that it was fighting for its survival.

After joining Foreign Affairs in 1966, I had access to classified cable traffic and thus was able to follow the passionate messages sent by Canada's ambassadors in Cairo and Tel Aviv on the deteriorating Middle East situation. In those days, before the Internet and twenty-four-hour television news channels, the Canadian government accorded much greater weight to reports from Canadian embassies for basic information on developments and for policy advice. In contrast to the diplomatic practice of today, officers spent an enormous amount of time drafting and polishing articulate and erudite political reports to headquarters. Whereas today's diplomats are admonished to interpret events from as close to a Canadian perspective as possible, at that time long messages lauding the merits of the country to which one was accredited and criticizing the policies of that country's adversaries were tolerated and even encouraged.

The debate between Cairo and Tel Aviv was fierce. Rival camps of supporters developed in Ottawa. But when the Six Day

War began in 1967, most members of Foreign Affairs (and the public at large) reacted emotionally and strongly in favour of Israel. That small country had stunned the world and surprised itself by destroying the air and ground forces of Egypt, Syria, and Jordan in record time and seizing control of the Sinai, the Golan Heights, and the West Bank. Most Canadians, however, were puzzled when Israel did not return the conquered territories, despite appeals from the U.N., and began to implant settlements throughout these areas, and even in overcrowded Gaza.

In 1970, I was assigned responsibility for covering the Arab-Israeli dispute as part of the package of duties handed to me as an analyst in the Intelligence Analysis division. What I saw was alarming. Secret intelligence reports from the Americans and British indicated that the dispute, in particular Israel's deteriorating relations with Egypt, constituted an even greater threat to world peace and security than Cold War confrontation in Europe. Egypt started an undeclared war of attrition to regain control of the Sinai, raining artillery shells down on Israeli positions along the Suez Canal. Israel replied in kind, but was less able to sustain losses of life.

Israel started deep-penetration air raids into Egypt. The U.S.S.R. became involved, providing Egypt with advanced radar systems, surface-to-air missiles, and twelve thousand of its own troops dug in close to the canal. The Israelis attacked the sites. Moscow sent in advanced fighter aircraft and Soviet pilots. Israel shot down five fighters. By late 1970, the intelligence services were reporting that a risk of war existed between the U.S. and the U.S.S.R., the champions of Israel and the Arab world respectively. All sides backed down, if only temporarily, and by the summer of 1972, when I left my analyst job for Bangladesh, an uneasy calm prevailed on the line of confrontation. Egypt and Syria then attacked Israel in the 1973 Yom Kippur War. Israel was the winner but the losses were heavy, the victory Pyrrhic, and the dynamic of Arab-Israeli relations changed forever.

Rescuing Marie-Jeanne

My first direct encounter with Israel was personal, dramatic, and difficult. As I have already related, in the fall of 1974, on my initial posting to NATO in Brussels, I met and proposed marriage to Marie-Jeanne. The wedding date was set for September 12, 1975. All went well until one week before the wedding when I received an urgent telephone call in my tiny office at the Canadian delegation. Marie-Jeanne, a stewardess on Sabena airlines, had been struck on the head by a bulkhead door that came loose on a flight to Israel, aggravating a hairline fracture of her skull that she had sustained in a car accident some months earlier. She was at the brain-injury section of the Tel Hashimir military hospital in Tel Aviv. Could I go to Israel and sort matters out?

I flew at once to Israel, arriving at the international airport late on a Friday evening. Barricaded behind sandbagged counters as protection after a series of suicide terrorist attacks, the customs and immigration officials were nervous and suspicious of all incoming passengers. Emerging from the terminal building into the searing evening air, I joined a throng of people jostling and pushing to get on the bus to Tel Aviv. It was a mix of the Middle East, Eastern Europe, and New York City that greeted me when I got off at the Central Bus Station. Young men and women in uniform carrying assault rifles mingled with pale figures dressed in black who could have come from the movie *Fiddler on the Roof.* The salty, humid Mediterranean air smelled strongly of overripe fruit and vegetables. The trash littering the road and sidewalks and the dogs scavenging from the overflowing garbage cans added atmosphere and vitality to the Levantine setting. Young entrepreneurs dipped into cauldrons of boiling water to fish out corn on the cob to sell to a peripatetic clientele hurrying to catch buses. I bought a steaming ear of corn and smothered it in butter and salt; standing on the street corner, I savoured the most succulent food I had ever tasted.

Michael Bell, an old friend, who was first secretary to the Canadian embassy in Tel Aviv, and his wife met me the next morning and drove me to the hospital. Marie-Jeanne was in pain but desperate to leave. The ward for head injuries was filled with soldiers wounded two years earlier in the Yom Kippur War and there was much shouting and moaning. Crammed into a small room at the back that was used to store oxygen bottles, Marie-Jeanne said that a series of tests had been conducted but she had received no feedback. A doctor had walked into her cubbyhole, pinched her hard on the foot to check the state of her central nervous system, and walked away with a satisfied air when she screamed. I tracked him down and persuaded him to release Marie-Jeanne into my care. It was then a simple matter to arrange medical evacuation for her on a flight out the next day.

Having arranged for Marie-Jeanne's release, I turned into a tourist, heading for Jerusalem to see whether the image I held of the City of David conformed to reality. The taxi driver, an immigrant from New York, regaled me on the two-hour trip with stories of his participation in four wars. He pointed out battlefield sites, such as the monastery at Latrum, and drew attention to the wrecks of vehicles destroyed in the efforts to relieve the siege of Jerusalem in 1948. We picked up two hitchhiking soldiers, encumbered with rifles and kit bags. Forbidden under Israeli military regulations to talk to strangers, they remained silent throughout the journey.

Jerusalem made an impression on me rivalled only by my first sight of the Taj Mahal and of the Parthenon. It was dry and clear that September day, and the light shimmered on the sixteenth-century city walls constructed by Suleiman the Magnificent. Situated on the heights between the Judean desert and Dead Sea to the east and the relatively well-watered Judean hills sloping down to the Mediterranean to the west, Jerusalem's location and the special translucent, almost ethereal quality of its air, I was later told, had attracted mystics and hermits over the ages. I spent the day wandering the Christian, Jewish, Muslim, and Armenian quarters. Most of the religious sites were as depicted in our old family Bible – printed in Philadelphia in 1874 and proudly proclaiming, "The Whole Embellished with Nine Hundred Illustrations, On Steel, Wood, and in Colours."

Entering the Old City by the Jaffa Gate, I made my way on foot through narrow passageways past hot ovens baking honey, pistachio, pine-nut, and almond-paste delicacies; open-air fruit, vegetable, and butcher shops selling foodstuffs to Arab housewives; coffee and tea stands frequented by old men playing dominoes; restaurants wafting out a mix of garlic and spices from shwarma, falafel, hummus, and other delicious local dishes; and souvenir stores with tacky wares side by side with elegant boutiques offering expensive glassware, Jerusalem pottery, and pots and oil lamps two thousand years old. My first stop was the Church of the Holy Sepulchre, the traditional site of Jesus' tomb. Despite its state of disrepair and its cacophonic mix of competing religious caretakers, it was an ecclesiastical refuge of shadows, flickering candles, cool humid air, incense, priests and nuns in traditional garb, Latin, Greek, and Coptic chapels, tombs, icons, wall hangings, and tourists – both the curious and the devout. Standing under the main cupola, I tried to imagine the scene on this spot in July 1099 when fervent conquering crusader knights prayed in blood up to their ankles after slaughtering the thirty thousand Muslim and Jewish occupants of Jerusalem. Christ's tomb – the chapel of the Holy Sepulchre – I entered with awe. An impecunious Ethiopian monk, crouching in the gloom, extended his hand in a silent quest for alms.

I then made my way through the Jewish quarter, largely destroyed in the fighting in 1948 and reconstructed in Jerusalem stone when the city was retaken in 1967. The boutiques and shops were upmarket, selling expensive glassware, clothing, menorahs, and antiquities. Jewish tourists from around the world mingled with Israelis at the entrances to museums, synagogues, and on the exposed ruins of the old Roman city of Aelia Capitalina, built in 132 on the site of old Jewish Jerusalem. I then descended steep steps to the Western Wall, where Jews have worshipped since the destruction of the Temple by Titus almost two thousand years ago. Then it was up again to the Haram ash-Sharif, the compound enclosing the Dome of the Rock and al-Aqsa Mosque. I followed the instructions of the attendants, removing my shoes to pay my respects before entering these shrines, the third-most-holy to Muslims after Mecca and Medina. I then returned to my taxi via the Armenian and Muslim Quarters, passing the spot where, fourteen years later, as ambassador to Israel, I would be struck by a stone hurled from a rooftop during the first intifada, or Palestinian uprising, of the 1980s.

The next morning, I signed the release papers and accompanied Marie-Jeanne as she was driven to the airport, bouncing around in the back of a pickup truck converted into a makeshift ambulance. A security official pulled me aside at the entrance to the tarmac to subject me to a severe grilling before I was allowed onto the aircraft. My diplomatic passport counted for nothing and neither did the presence of the embassy first secretary, who confirmed my identity. My suitcase was roughly searched and the reasons for my visit disputed. There was, of course, nothing personal in any of this; the official simply wanted to be certain that I did not harbour some hidden terrorist intent.

Return to Israel
Now, a decade later, I was returning with my family. The two children soon overcame their distress, caught up in the excitement of preparing for yet another posting, and reassured by the fact that our two household dogs and cat would share the experience. Marie-Jeanne threw herself into the preparations for the move and I launched myself on a program of pre-posting training. The month of December 1985 I spent reading files in the Middle

Eastern division, calling on cabinet ministers and parliamentarians with a special interest in Middle Eastern affairs and introducing myself to members of the Jewish and Arab communities in Canada. The meetings were difficult. Most of my interlocutors were fair-minded, but a vocal minority on each side insisted that it was our duty to support its side and its side only in the Arab-Israeli dispute. They would be watching, they warned me, to ensure that my support did not falter. Each side asserted, of course, that it was well plugged in politically; my career, they threatened, would be ruined if I did not toe their mutually exclusive lines.

The family then spent New Year's Eve skating on the Rideau Canal in minus-thirty temperatures and watching the fireworks on Parliament Hill, not knowing that it would be nine years before we would return again to live in the Ottawa area. One week later, with some trepidation and much anticipation, the Bartleman family and menagerie landed in the soft, warm air of the Israeli winter. There was much to get used to. My chauffeur was overly helpful. He kept up a constant chatter and continually interrupted our private conversations. We tried switching to French and then to Spanish to retain some privacy. He knew both – plus Arabic, Greek, and several other languages. He was infuriating, adding his unwanted opinions on the political situation in Israel and the Arab-Israeli conflict whenever a visitor from Canada accompanied me on official calls. He tagged along uninvited when Marie-Jeanne and I tried to shop, offering gratuitous advice on the wares on offer.

The official residence in Ramat Hasharon, a Tel Aviv suburb, had seen better days. A small house located on a huge lot, it had been rented by the Canadian government for some thirty years. In that period, the landlord collected exorbitant rents, reaching the level of five thousand American dollars monthly, while doing no maintenance work. To make matters worse, he had just advised the embassy that the rent would be doubled when the lease expired in September. Financial constraints had made it difficult for the Canadian government to keep the building in good order. True, the nest of large poisonous snakes, whose slithering around in the attic just above the master bedroom had disturbed the sleep of one of our predecessors, was gone. But the house was cold in winter and hot in summer. Little attention had been paid to the grounds since the time several years before when an overzealous administrative officer had covered the lawns with several large truckloads of pig manure, stinking out the neighbourhood and arousing the ire of the neighbours.

The gardener, a Palestinian, made the daily trip from Gaza to the residence, rising at three in the morning to be at work at seven. Alas, he was so tired from his journey, and from selling Gaza oranges to a clientele built over the years in the neighbourhood, that he spent his time sleeping in the tool shed rather then tending the grounds. The maid, of rural Yemenite origin, had come to Israel in the 1950s under Operation Flying Carpet, during which Yemen's Jewish population was clandestinely moved into Israel by Mossad, the Israeli security agency, to escape persecution. She spoke no English, French, or Hebrew, and the operation of a vacuum cleaner remained a mystery to her. The Colombian cook lived in a separate house on the grounds, which she kept in such a slovenly state that it looked as if it had been transported from the slums of Bogotá, her home city. She was sullen and uncommunicative. She knew how to make only one dish – roast chicken, which was invariably delivered to the table partially raw. She produced a husky nine-year-old son, whom she had kept concealed from the previous ambassador and brazenly said that the embassy had given authority for him to live in her staff quarters. We would have had no objection, except that his favourite sport was tormenting our son, Laurent.

Marie-Jeanne broke down in tears and said she was returning with the kids to Chelsea. Then, her anger aroused, she did battle. A place was found for our chauffeur elsewhere in the driver's pool.

He was replaced by another driver, just as chatty but lacking a knowledge of French and Spanish and not inclined to follow us into every store. After much prodding, headquarters agreed to allow us to sign a lease on a less expensive but magnificent home on the cliff overlooking the Mediterranean in the Tel Aviv suburb of Herzliya Pituah. The cook met and married an American marine and left. The maid and the gardener were compensated for their years of service and departed. A Filipino couple, Angelita and Florencio, who were to become our close friends, took their place.

The large community of dual Israeli-Canadian citizens who lived in Israel embraced us with enthusiasm. We were invited to their homes, ate countless gefilte fish Sabbath dinners, and were welcomed to Jewish festivities. Most invitations were straight-forward. Canadian Jewish groups were heavily involved in aiding Israel through contributions to Israeli charities, for which they received tax credits in Canada. Almost every week, Marie-Jeanne and I were received warmly at the openings of libraries, sports complexes, and other facilities funded from Canada.

There were sometimes surprises.

At one meeting, a rabbi, asked to introduce us to the audience, delivered an impassioned speech about the Bartlemans and their commitment to Israel. Confusing the accident Marie-Jeanne had in 1975 as an employee of Sabena with another incident at roughly the same time in which terrorists had seized a Sabena air-craft en route to Israel and shot crew members, he ended his speech with passionate praise, saying Marie-Jeanne had suffered and almost died for Israel. Breaking down in tears, members of the audience rushed to embrace her. I rose to my feet and tried to explain that the rabbi had confused Marie-Jeanne with someone else. No one paid any heed and Marie-Jeanne's reputa-tion was born.

Marie-Jeanne and I prided ourselves in accepting as many invitations from Israelis and visiting Canadians as possible. Sometimes, however, the purpose of the event was not clear until after it was over. We were once invited by an ultra-orthodox group to visit their community, which was heavily subsidized by Canadian supporters. We arrived early one afternoon at the entrance to the community to be greeted by its entire population, at least three hundred strong. They were waving Canadian flags. The Canadian national anthem followed. A poem composed in our honour was recited and we were taken on a tour of the town. We inspected houses and apartments, as well as the school and medical clinic. The final event involved a ceremony with local Arab notables involving exchanges of documents, speeches, and many cups of tea. The language was Hebrew but no one would translate for us. We were then conducted to our car for a final ceremonial goodbye. At that point we realized that the entire venture had been staged to permit a film crew to do a documentary film for use in fundraising in Canada. We never heard from the community again.

Our children, in the meantime, were accepted into the American School at Kfar Shmaryahu. Both received a rich exposure to the life of the area, accompanying us on frequent walks in the Old City of Jerusalem, picnics among Greek and Roman ruins in both Israel and the occupied territories, visits to crusader castles, antiquities-buying expeditions to our favourite shops, holidays on the Dead and Red Seas, and travel in the region, especially to Petra in Jordan, to Cairo and the Valley of the Kings in Egypt, and to Nicosia and Larnaca in Cyprus. They also once witnessed Middle Eastern passion first-hand when I made a wrong turn into a demonstration, driving through a hail of stones and a fog of tear gas that permeated our car, provoking coughing and crying fits.

The embassy, located on the seafront, was in a dilapidated building converted some years before from a modest hotel to an office. There was an oversupply of bathrooms and kitchens. The elevator often did not work and the air conditioning was temperamental. Staff did not return home for lunch and usually ate in one of the myriad hole-in-the-wall establishments around the office. No one was perturbed at the dog excrement, empty soft-drink bottles, and paper that littered the poorly repaired sidewalks. It was part of the local colour, as was the rough friendliness of Tel Avivians.

The Canada-based staff were all top-notch, experienced foreign-service professionals, including, at different times, Rod Bell, Michael Mace, John McNee, and Michel de Salaberry, most of whom had volunteered to be sent to Israel and all of whom would later be given their own posts as ambassadors. Ottawa voraciously consumed our daily reporting, anxious to provide the foreign minister with our views on breaking developments prior to question period in the House of Commons, and to prepare our mission to the United Nations in New York for crucial votes affecting Israel. To keep up with the demand, I met every morning with the small political-economic section and with the military advisor and his team to review overnight developments, and coordinate our daily activities.

The Strategic Environment
The first two years of our posting coincided with a relatively quiet period in Israel's frenetic history. The country was still licking its wounds after the reverses suffered more than a decade previously in the 1973 war, and more recently from the bloody losses sustained in the killing fields of Lebanon following its invasion in 1982. But Israel was under no external threat. To the south, a cold peace had existed with Egypt since diplomatic relations had been established following Egyptian president Anwar Sadat's visit to Jerusalem in December 1977. To the east, Jordan remained a large, weak, and compliant buffer state. To the north, Lebanon was a no man's land of competing religious and political factions. It had long ago lost any ability to threaten Israel but provided bases from which Iranian-sponsored Hezbollah groups conducted periodic terrorist attacks on Israeli troops, now confined to a so-called security zone just inside the Lebanese

border. Syria, which wanted to recover the Golan Heights lost in the 1967 war, remained the most serious threat, but was careful not to provoke Israel. Some three billion dollars in military aid received each year from Washington ensured that Israel maintained the best-equipped armed forces in the region.

Internally, there were major divisions. Israeli Arabs constituted some 15 per cent of the population and had the right to vote, but they were an uneasy minority. Jewish Israelis in turn were heavily split into religious and non-religious worlds and between Ashkenazi (European), Oriental (Middle Eastern), and Ethiopian backgrounds. How to deal with the Palestinians living in the West Bank and Gaza, who were governed under old British mandate laws, were a source of further division. Roughly half the population was prepared to concede some land to Jordan if the Hashemite Kingdom would take on responsibility for exercising authority over the Palestinians. The other half was led by the sizable contingent of settlers whose homes were implanted throughout the occupied territories and whose position in the debate was clear. There was, however, a national consensus that Jerusalem would never be relinquished.

By the time we arrived, these multiple divisions meant that forming a government had become an almost impossible task. Labour Party dominance, as had existed in the early years of Israel, was a thing of the past. Likud, which became the main party of the right after winning several elections, could no longer rally sufficient support to govern alone. The solution adopted was to form a national-unity government in which the prime ministership alternated between Likud and Labour.

I developed contacts with the key political players, in particular with Shimon Peres, Yitzhak Rabin, and Yossi Beilin from Labour, and Yitzhak Shamir, Mose Arens, and Ariel Sharon from Likud, as well as with President Chaim Herzog, who was above politics. The embassy maintained links with Israeli mayors, journalists, academics, and the business community.

Responsible for Canadian interests in the West Bank and Gaza, we also cultivated a network of ties with the Palestinian community. A generous aid program gave us the flexibility to undertake a wide range of small development projects affecting the daily life of the people as well as privileged access to Palestinians from all walks of life. We maintained close ties and a relationship of confidence with the International Committee of the Red Cross and the United Nations Relief and Works Agency. They, in return, shared with us their internal reports on conditions within prisons and refugee camps.

Leaders such as Shimon Peres, who was prime minister when we arrived in Israel, Yitzhak Rabin, who was defence minister throughout most of our posting, and Ezer Weizman, leader of a small centrist party and destined to be president, recognized the danger facing Israel. Peres, born in Poland, had moved to Israel at an early age and became a protegé of David Ben-Gurion, the legendary first leader of the new state. Rabin had made his mark as a soldier, chief of staff in 1967 when Jerusalem was taken and later became Israel's first native-born prime minister. Weizman was the nephew of Israel's first president and a famous swash-buckling head of Israel's air force in his younger days. They were heroes of the 1948, 1956, and 1967 wars who had been hawks until they confronted the carnage of the 1973 war.

Their attitudes had changed with age. They recognized that Israel would have to give up part of the occupied territories in exchange for peace. They were always accessible to me. Israel, they said, had a date with destiny. The dream of its founders, they explained, was that Israel be Jewish and democratic. Incompatible choices were now required. To remain a democracy, Israel would either have to relinquish control over the 1.5 million Palestinians in the West Bank and Gaza, or keep the territories but accord its inhabitants the same rights as Jews.

The former course, they said, could undermine Israel's security and would be violently opposed by the settlers. The latter option would mean that the Arabs, whose population growth rate was greater than that of the Jews, would eventually outnumber Jews in Israel, and Israel would no longer be a Jewish state. The solution of these leaders was to find a way to give the heavily populated Arab areas of the West Bank and Gaza to Jordan, and to retain control over the areas deemed to be of vital security interest. But neither the Palestinian people nor the Arab states wanted Jordan to fulfill this role. Jordan rejected the responsibility and called upon Israel to negotiate with the PLO. No serious political leader at that time would dare upset the Israeli public by choosing such an unpopular option. The policy approach of the mainstream peace camp was therefore at a dead end at this point.

Canadian Policy

As for Canada, our policy was to give strong support to the security, well-being, and independence of Israel. Lester Pearson and Supreme Court Justice Ivan Rand had played pivotal roles in the United Nations in 1947 in helping pave the way for the General Assembly vote legitimizing the establishment of the state of Israel. Canada did not, however, recognize permanent Israeli control over the West Bank and Gaza, and was adamantly opposed to settlements there. Canada supported the concept of Palestinian self-determination, but in 1986 had not yet accepted, unlike the Europeans, the PLO as representing "the sole legitimate representative of the Palestinian people." In an international community generally hostile to Israel, Canada was regarded as more friendly than the Europeans and somewhat less sympathetic than the Americans. In terms of influence over Israeli actions, we had little or none; only the Americans counted. But this reality had not stopped Canadian governments in the past from speaking out on the Arab-Israeli dispute and would not deter an activist approach during the coming intifada.

The Intifada

In the fall of 1987, the first secretary, the military advisor, and I made dozens of visits to the West Bank and Gaza, meeting teachers, doctors, businessmen, politicians, and many ordinary Palestinians, being hosted in the homes of notables and feted with meals of lamb and other Arabic dishes. Everyone told us the same thing: pressure for change had reached intolerable levels. We became convinced at the embassy that it would only be a matter of time before an explosion of popular rage would occur in the occupied territories. When it came, the intifada nevertheless surprised us in its intensity and duration, dragging on and overshadowing other developments for most of our remaining time in Israel.

On December 8, 1987, an Israeli trucker hit a car filled with Palestinian workers, killing four. The last straw had broken the camel's back. Virtually the entire population of Gaza and the West Bank went out into the streets to confront Israeli soldiers and police. In response, the Israelis closed their borders to the occupied territories, placed the areas under curfew, and moved in reinforcements. Defence Minister Rabin, on a fundraising drive in the United States, thought it would soon be over and did not return to take control of the armed forces until December 21. By that time, the fire was out of control. The world press congregated at flashpoints to watch the confrontations. The new year arrived and the unequal conflict continued unabated. Raw emotion became the stuff of everyday life.

My wife and I often went to Yad Vashem, the museum to the Holocaust in Jerusalem – it was an essential stop for Canadian visitors to Israel. The piles of shoes and clothing from death chambers, the ashes of thousands under a slab of black stone, and the memorials to millions of slaughtered Jewish children expressed a message no words could convey about the roots of the Israeli psychology. Many of our neighbours were Holocaust survivors. All had lived through a succession of wars with their Arab neighbours. Many had fought in these conflicts. Some had lost loved ones. Even those who recognized logically that the violence of the intifada was confined largely to stone-throwing in the occupied territories instinctively looked upon it as another existential threat to their survival.

This period marked the low point for me personally in an emotionally draining posting. I listened, fascinated by the fanaticism of Palestinians and Israelis alike as they insisted that God, history, and justice were on their side and on their side only. My efforts to host meals to which I invited Israelis and Palestinians were complete fiascos, with supposedly moderate individuals shouting abuse at each other over the dinner table. In Hebron, Nablus, and a dozen other Palestinian communities, I saw young Palestinians, some as young as five or six, dare Israeli soldiers to shoot them as their parents applauded. Israelis and Palestinians who genuinely wanted peace were the exception amid the passionate mood of the times.

My visits to the occupied territories became hazardous. The Palestinians vowed to punish anyone, diplomats included, who violated their self-imposed strikes; Israeli soldiers fingered their weapons as we passed through their roadblocks. Young Palestinians, perhaps frustrated at the response of the international community to their plight, stoned me in a refugee camp despite the presence by my side of Palestinian elders; I escaped with minor abrasions thanks to my heavy winter coat. Another time, someone heaved a boulder at me from a rooftop in Jerusalem. It would have killed me had it hit me in the head; it hit my leg, leaving bruises but inflicting no major damage.

I had become accustomed to Palestinians throwing stones that always missed at the official car. My luck, however, changed. One Sunday afternoon, entering East Jerusalem with Marie-Jeanne, a gang of masked youths ambushed us, hurling rocks the size of grapefruit, caving in the side of the vehicle with thunderous blows. By some miracle they missed the windows and we were not injured. On the same weekend, the back windows of my military advisor's Jeep were smashed as he travelled in Gaza. Alarmed, headquarters shipped us an old armoured car from its storage site at the Canadian embassy in Ankara, Turkey. It came armed with a launcher for smoke grenades fixed to the rear, a case of grenades in the trunk, windows that would not open and glass so thick that the view outside was like peering through the bottom of an empty Coca-Cola bottle. It did, however, give us yeoman service, allowing us to drive through riots with impunity. The sound of rocks bouncing off armour became, in my imagination, no more worrying than gravel hitting the old car of my youth on Muskoka's dirt roads.

Controversy broke out in Canada and elsewhere on the Israeli handling of intifada. There were demonstrations by supporters on both sides, editorial pronouncements in the major newspapers, and questions in the House of Commons. Prime Minister Mulroney and Foreign Minister Joe Clark squared off, the former saying he believed the Israeli armed forces were acting with restraint and the latter condemning Israeli tactics. Every visitor from Canada – ministers of the Crown, journalists, tourists, businesspeople and religious leaders – had strong opinions on the confrontation that they expected me to share. Few Canadian ambassadors, I believe, were ever exposed to such pressures to take sides on an issue that polarized Canadian public opinion. I acted as conscientiously as possible, coordinating the flow of information to Ottawa from all sides while providing my own views and those of my team. Israeli and Palestinian journalists, other diplomats, senior Israeli military officers, members of the Israeli Knesset, senior figures such as former foreign minister Abba Eban and Jerusalem mayor Teddy Koleck, and the head of the International Committee of the Red Cross, whose staff had access to the prisons, provided us with their perspectives, complementing our visits to the conflict zone.

On instructions from headquarters, I called on Defence Minister Rabin, who was directly responsible for the policy, to complain about Israel's tactics. Rabin glowered and said Canada's concerns were of no interest to him. He then showed me the door.

Unwilling to give up, I approached him at a dinner party where we were both guests. We knew each other socially from our common membership in a local tennis club, where I was occasionally pressed into service by his wife, Leah, when really desperate, as her tennis partner. My expectation that I would be welcome was, however, short-lived. The defence minister was sitting, nursing a glass of Scotch, with Thomas Friedman, the famous *New York Times* foreign correspondent, future Pulitzer Prize winner, and chief diplomatic correspondent of his newspaper.

It was quickly made clear to me that I was not welcome. Neither replied to my greetings when I sat down. I should have taken the hint and gone elsewhere, since they obviously wanted to talk about the intifada without interruption. Instead, I stupidly dug myself in deeper. Smiling thinly, I searched desperately for something to say.

I blurted out, "Uh, how would you describe the state of Canadian-Israeli relations?" Talk about shooting oneself in the foot! In most countries, such a question from an ambassador would have elicited a polite, perhaps noncommittal response, even if relations were terrible. National leaders from all 185 countries on the globe were used to diplomats accredited to their countries asking this type of question. It was a standard ice-breaking, conversation-opening gambit. Protocol dictated that the leader would reply, "I love your beautiful country. My wife's brother [or cousin, grandmother, sister-in-law] is married to a Canadian. Our countries may have their little differences from time to time, but relations are fundamentally solid and will not

be damaged by difficulties such as they are now encountering."
Or words to this effect.

Too late, I remembered that I was in Israel, where straight
talking was a national art. After all, the term *sabra*, used to describe
Israelis born and raised in Israel, meaning "prickly on the outside
and sweet on the inside," had not become the national label for
nothing. Rabin did not reply for two or three long minutes. He
puffed on his cigarette, slouched back in his chair and began.

"Mr. Ambassador, let me tell you something. Israel's relations
with the United States are superb. They could not possibly be
better. They would be on the thirty-fifth floor of a thirty-five-
storey building. Now I come to the countries of Central America.
They may be small but their ties with Israel I would place on the
twentieth floor. And do you know why? Their leaders do not
criticize our handling of the intifada and they buy arms from us.
Canada I would put on the ground floor. Your leaders criticize
our handling of the intifada and refuse to buy our weapons."

I had no comeback. Rabin and Friedman sat quietly waiting
for me to get up and leave. Joe Clark had announced some weeks
before that Canada would no longer purchase arms from Israel
or sell to them. I was now paying the price. I left the table in
silence as Rabin looked on remorselessly and Friedman stared at
me with cold pity. For weeks afterwards, I tried to think of what
I should have said to save face. But even in retrospect, nothing
came to mind.

Parliamentary Visits

Delegations of Canadian parliamentarians arrived to assess the
situation for themselves. The first, in February 1987, was a
fact-finding mission from the House of Commons Standing
Committee on Foreign Affairs, determined to come up with
objective truth on a difficult, complex, and controversial matter.
The Israelis co-operated in arranging a series of briefings in Israel,

and the embassy arranged a tour of refugee camps in Gaza and the West Bank under the auspices of the United Nations. The final session with senior Israeli officials at the Foreign Ministry was a stormy affair. The Canadians returned from the camps filled with indignation and ready to criticize the tactics of the Israeli defence forces and Mossad. The Foreign Ministry staff robustly defended their security institutions and the debate degenerated into a yelling match.

Delegations whose expenses were paid by Arab- or Israeli-backed organizations had no obligation to try to be objective. Sometimes parliamentarians from such groups broke the unwritten rule that he or she who pays the expenses sets the conditions for the visit and approached the embassy to set up appointments with spokespersons from the other side to obtain a balanced picture. We would then inevitably find ourselves involved in controversy, criticized by one side or the other for interfering in the public-relations efforts of the sponsors.

One delegation broke all the bounds of propriety. I met the group at the Allenby Bridge at the Jordanian-Israeli border. The leading parliamentarian insisted on calling me "Your Highness" when "Jim" would have sufficed. At a briefing session later in the day at the Israeli Foreign Ministry, this distinguished visitor broke in two the plastic spoon used to stir his coffee and used the handle part to clean the wax out of his ears. Our briefer, the mild-mannered deputy foreign minister, Yossi Beilin, gazed at the senator in fascination as first one ear and then the other was fastidiously harvested. I was relieved that he did not then stick the spoon up his nose; we Canadians had standards to uphold!

Determined to witness Israeli-Palestinian confrontations first-hand, the visitors seemed overly interested in the novelty of watching an actual violent conflict and seeing the resulting human suffering. I was ill at ease, acutely aware that a fine line could be drawn between visiting victims for the purpose of bearing witness and engaging in disaster tourism – sightseeing to obtain thrills from seeing what live ammunition and rubber bullets could do to human flesh. After all, they had officials from the Canadian embassy as guides and were in no physical danger from either Palestinians or Israelis. Visiting refugee camps, they watched from a safe distance the daily deadly ritual of young boys throwing stones at soldiers who shot rubber bullets at them in return. One parliamentarian even remained overnight in a camp hoping that he would catch an Israeli patrol abusing Palestinians. In Gaza, visiting a clinic filled with the wounded, another parliamentarian publicly berated a young Palestinian doctor, who had taken a break from his duties to brief us, for smoking a cigarette. In a patronizing tone, she told the young man – who was working twenty-four-hour shifts for little or no pay caring for the injured – that he was a poor example for his people.

Several spent the entire visit drunk or half-drunk, consuming enormous quantities of beer and whisky in a hospitality suite I had unwisely set up for them in their hotel. I was breathing a sigh of relief as their bus pulled out of the driveway to return them to the Allenby Bridge to cross to Jordan when the vehicle lurched to a stop. Members of the delegation piled out and ran by me without a word, returning several minutes later with all the remaining booze from the hospitality suite. "It's a long drive to the border," they cried as they boarded the bus.

Return to Normal

In September 1990 the undersecretary telephoned to discuss with me the position of head of mission to the North Atlantic Council of NATO. I accepted before he offered me the job. It was time to move on and the new posting was an ideal one. Professionally, the assignment would allow me to participate in the end-game as the Cold War came to a close. On a personal level, Marie-Jeanne, whose stepmother was gravely ill in Brussels, was grateful for the chance to be closer to her. I looked forward to renewing my acquaintance with a country and people I had come to know so well during my posting to NATO in the mid-1970s.

Despite my sometimes rocky relations with the Israeli government, the Foreign Ministry hosted an elaborate farewell luncheon for me, assembling the key figures with whom I had worked. The Israelis, it seemed, respected individuals who defended their country's positions strongly. The five Bartlemans and their household pets then took their leave of Israel, closing another chapter in our lives. True to form, Israel was once again caught up in a crisis. It was three months after Iraq's invasion of Kuwait, allied preparations to push the Iraqis back were well advanced, and we had already been issued gas masks. No one doubted that when the fighting started, Iraq would hit Israel hard with its arsenal of missiles.

On the flight to Brussels, relief mixed with regret as we escaped the emotional roller coaster. My memories were a collage of chaotic images: blood-red azaleas growing wild on Mount Carmel in the early spring; white blossoms on almond trees on the Judean hills; Jerusalem in the early morning seen from the Mount of Olives; the Muslim call to prayer resounding throughout the old city; empty highways and full synagogues on Yom Kippur; fierce, exhilarating Mediterranean winter storms lashing our cliffside home; fishing with the children at a kibbutz in northern Israel with the dull thud of artillery firing into Lebanon off in the distance; the smell of tear gas; traffic jams in Tel Aviv; an offer of ten camels for our daughter; Passover dinners; feasts of lamb; little old ladies barging into grocery-store lineups ahead of me; oranges in Gaza; injured children from both sides in their hospital beds; and the eyes – the eyes of the fanatics, the eternally optimistic, the duplicitous, the fearful, the cynics, the saints, the resolute, and the dying.

Five years later, while serving as foreign-policy advisor to the prime minister, I met Yitzhak Rabin over dinner at 24 Sussex Drive in Ottawa and again a year later in New York, just two weeks before his assassination. He had aged perceptibly but had become a tenacious fighter for peace. His raspy voice was unchanged but he had a smile on his face and was confident that the Israeli public would support him as he moved to implement the groundbreaking Oslo accords. His death would end the best chance for peace with the Palestinians since the establishment of the state of Israel in 1948.

10

Return to NATO

No one, however, foresaw the Soviet collapse, not even Fidel Castro.

It was with a sense of trepidation that I presented my letter of introduction from Prime Minister Mulroney to Secretary-General Manfred Woerner on October 22, 1990, formally advising him that I was Canada's new permanent representative and ambassador to NATO. Having served on the Canadian delegation some years before, I knew that I had enormous shoes to fill. The eyes of my predecessors – George Ignatieff, Jules Léger, Charles Ritchie, Arthur Menzies, Gerry Hardy, John Halstead, James (Si) Taylor, and Gordon Smith – a who's who of the senior foreign service, followed me inquisitively from their framed photographs along the corridor walls as I returned to the office many of them had occupied in past decades. They were, in my imagination, wondering if I would be up to the job. In the ambassador's office, it seemed that nothing had changed in thirteen years. The desk, the bookshelves, the sofas, the picture of a much younger Queen – even the dust – seemed to be exactly as they were when I last ventured into this room in the summer of 1977, summoned by the ambassador of the day to explain some esoteric aspect of arms-control negotiations.

The mission, I was well aware, had been without an ambassador for more than four months. The chargé d'affaires and the head of the political section gave me a rough welcome, greeting my arrival with scarcely concealed skepticism. My predecessor, they pointed out with a touch of nostalgia, had been one of the out-standing members of the NATO council. My knowledge of NATO, they made clear, dated from another era – that of the Cold War – and was of little relevance to the security challenges of the 1990s. My new ambassadorial colleagues received me indifferently. Busy preparing for the annual meetings of the alliance's foreign and defence ministers, they had little time to spare for a new colleague who had been out of the mainstream for five years and who came from a member state whose interest in NATO had been in decline for years.

The Cold War and Its Demise

My new colleagues on the delegation and on the council were right. While I did not join Foreign Affairs in 1966 to fight the communists, with two assignments in the security and intelli-gence world at headquarters and postings to NATO and to Cuba at the height of the Cold War, I had been a metaphorical foot soldier in the Manichean struggle between East and West that had been raging since the end of the Second World War. The villains in the comic books I devoured as a child who had been evil Nazis during the war changed to nefarious "commies" in the late 1940s. Little Orphan Annie and Daddy Warbucks fought the Cominform to defend capitalism. By the early 1950s, there were air-raid drills in my school, so certain in the consciousness of the villagers was the likelihood of war. One better-off neighbour even constructed a fallout shelter in his backyard and kept it stocked with fresh water, canned goods, and a rifle (to ward off the desperate hordes who were likely, in his imagination, to seek to share his refuge when the time of crisis occurred). By the late 1950s, the sons of Second World War veterans were joining up and being sent to NATO bases in remote corners of France as Canada's armed forces were rebuilt, strengthened, and redeployed to help defend our European allies who were threatened by communist aggression.

From Containment to Détente

Throughout this period until about 1969, the United States followed a policy of seeking to contain the expansion of communism; the Soviet Union's priority was to seek parity with its rival in nuclear weapons and gaining advantage in the new countries in Third World that were emerging from decolonization. The 1970s, which coincided with my first posting to NATO headquarters, was one of uneasy détente. President Reagan then changed American policy in the early 1980s, seeking to roll back communism in the Third World and to defeat it in Europe. Moscow tried to compete with the United States in this new titanic struggle, and bankrupted itself in the process. The Soviets' war in Afghanistan, during which the CIA provided decisive support to the rebels, then demoralized their armed forces and ruined the finances of the U.S.S.R. The coming to power of Mikhail Gorbachev in 1985, following the deaths in succession of three worn-out elderly leaders – Leonid Brezhnev, Yuri Andropov, and Konstantin Chernenko – brought onto the scene a leader forced to play with a weak hand and who was obliged to back down in every major confrontation with the United States and NATO.

President George Bush, Sr., who assumed office in 1988, was faced with managing the collapse of the post-war order as Hungary, Poland, Czechoslovakia, Bulgaria, and Romania shook themselves free of communist rule, and East Germany was incorporated into a unified Germany. British prime minister Margaret Thatcher and French president François Mitterrand almost turned this massive victory for the West into a disaster with their reluctance to accept the reunification of Germany. Fortunately the American president saved the situation by throwing the weight of the United States behind German chancellor Helmut Kohl's drive to reunify his country. By this time, the United States had won the struggle for control of Central America, the Cubans had pulled out of Africa, and wars in the Third World had lost their East-West character.

Strategic Miscalculations

No one, however, foresaw the Soviet collapse, not even Fidel Castro. In my last meeting as ambassador to his country with the Cuban president in the fall of 1983, he was at the height of his global influence and confident that history was on the side of the "Revolution." At that time Washington, London, and Ottawa were concerned that there was a better-than-even chance that other countries would follow the lead of Grenada under the Marxist New Jewel Movement, and Nicaragua under the Sandinistas, and go communist. But the next time I met the Cuban leader, some twelve years later, the Soviet subsidy had long since been cut off and he was a sick old man. His influence was by then confined to ruling one of the few remaining communist outposts in the world, and he spent his time bitterly reminiscing about the good old days.

As director-general of the Foreign Affairs bureau of security and intelligence in the mid-1980s, I was responsible for managing the production of political intelligence for the Canadian Intelligence Advisory Committee, the body responsible for providing intelligence assessments to the Canadian government. Our bureau included a unit of Russian-speaking specialists who were world experts on Soviet economic matters. Another was staffed by polyglot officers who systematically interviewed refugees and immigrants from the countries of the Warsaw Pact for useful data. Information from electronic-intercept stations monitoring the airwaves over the Soviet Union was available to our analysts. Top Kremlinologists from the United States and the United Kingdom shared their secrets with members of our team. And no one suspected that the deep freeze was about to turn into rapid thaw.

We did appreciate, however, that the world had become a much more dangerous place as a result of President Reagan's early efforts to roll back communism. The high-risk areas were not in the Third World, where Reagan's muscular efforts had quickly borne fruit. The flashpoint was in Europe. The intelligence community did not know that the Soviets were being compelled to spend a crippling proportion of their national income on defence in a futile effort to catch up to the United States militarily. It was concerned, however, that the Soviet armed forces were becoming increasingly edgy. The shooting down of civilian Korean Airlines flight KAL-007 when it strayed over Sakhalin Island in 1983 was an indication of heightened nervousness.

The Soviet reaction to NATO exercise ABLE ARCHER 83 was, however, a revelation. It was no different from the war-game exercises I had participated in during the 1970s at NATO headquarters. Yet the Soviets were suspicious of the heavy classified-message traffic they detected between the war-games players in NATO capitals and the major NATO commands. Alarmed by President Reagan's speeches about the "evil empire," the Soviets were prepared to believe that this exercise was really the prelude to a pre-emptive attack by NATO on Warsaw Pact forces in Central Europe. They accordingly readied their forces, including those with nuclear weapons, for action. Fortunately, the NATO exercise ended without mishap, but the world had come perilously close to nuclear war through miscalculation. Only the most-senior leaders in key allied countries were told what had happened and they were shaken. The incident may have played a part in persuading President Reagan to launch his subsequent initiatives to reduce dramatically the NATO and Warsaw Pact nuclear arsenals. It may also have encouraged Prime Minister Trudeau in his seemingly quixotic solo mission to try to persuade the superpowers to make drastic cuts in their nuclear inventories.

Clandestine Wars

Given the incalculable damage that would be caused were nuclear war to start, hostilities between NATO and the Warsaw Pact were confined to proxy wars in the Third World and to quiet but deadly running engagements between their security and intelligence services. Clandestine agencies played major roles in overthrowing governments considered overly friendly with "the other side." The CIA was involved in many Third World coups, including "regime changes" in Guatemala in 1954 and in South Vietnam in 1963. It also provided the support that allowed the Taliban to drive the Soviets from Afghanistan in the late 1980s – creating a monster that came back to haunt the United States on September 11, 2001. The CIA's effort to overthrow Castro by supporting Cuban exiles in the Bay of Pigs operation was, however, a failure, as were early attempts to overthrow the government of Salvador Allende in Chile. The Soviet security and intelligence services were instrumental in keeping communist control over Central and Eastern Europe, in helping to overthrow the government of Afghanistan in 1979, and in supporting wars of national liberation throughout the Third World.

The Cold War was also a time of intense cat-and-mouse games between the security and intelligence services themselves. On the one side was the Soviet Union, supported by the covert organizations of its Warsaw Pact allies and Cuba. On the other was the United States, supported by its allies, in particular the United Kingdom, Canada, Australia, and New Zealand, all linked by international agreements to work together, dating from the end of the Second World War. Both sides shared similar objectives: to gain secret information that could be useful in the waging of the Cold War and to weaken the opposing secret services. To achieve those ends, any means were deemed acceptable – planting double agents, co-opting members of rival services, blackmail, intimidation, the paying of bribes, and eavesdropping on telephone and cable traffic. Marie-Jeanne was happy when I left this job and no longer had to meet grim-faced intelligence and counter-intelligence officers visiting Canada under diplomatic cover.

Lacking an offensive spy agency, Canada was not a major player in this secret war. Our attention was focused on defending ourselves against repeated efforts by the Soviet Union and its allies to compromise our diplomats and military personnel, to intercept our secret communications, and to steal or purchase technology that could be useful to the Soviet armed forces. Most efforts that I witnessed both as a diplomat serving abroad and as an official in the Ottawa security and intelligence world were sordid, if occasionally humorous, affairs. While often dramatic and portrayed as romantic in the movies, these Le Carré world activities were really sideshows during the Cold War. The allied services did not even detect the extent of the rot in the Soviet system.

Protecting Canada's Foreign Service

The security division in Foreign Affairs made great efforts to prevent our employees from falling into the clutches of the KGB and its sister services. Briefing officers, usually former members of the RCMP Security Service, warned employees that the other side would try to tempt them by providing prostitutes, money, and illicit goods, secretly filming the encounters to catch the gullible and blackmail them. They used dramatic methods, providing case studies of employees who had fallen into the Soviet net. The subsidiary message was that if someone was foolish enough to behave badly and be subject to blackmail, the best policy was always to report the matter to headquarters, which would invariably show leniency (even if one's spouse might not).

Sometimes they overdid the drama – adopting accents when speaking English that made them resemble KGB agents in James Bond movies; when speaking French, they sounded like Peter Sellers playing the role of the bumbling detective in a *Pink Panther* movie. They put on display a wide variety of KGB listening devices removed from Canadian embassies to make the point that foreign-service employees at all levels should expect that their every word and action, even in their bedrooms, was being monitored. An enormous amount of time was devoted to the mysteries of keys and locks. The specialist on the subject, a locksmith (aptly named Mr. Keys), performed Houdini-like demonstrations for generations of recruits to beat into their heads that there was not a lock that could not be picked by a cunning Soviet agent.

By far the greatest danger they warned about was homosexuality. This – if they were to be believed – was a fatal
"character flaw" as defined in the Official Secrets Act; if unde-
tected, it would surely lead to treason. The briefers assumed in
those days that homosexuality was confined to males only. It may
be hard to believe today, but in the 1950s and 1960s homosexuals
were subject to government-mandated witch hunts. Up to the
1980s, Canadian government policy forbade their employment in
the public service. The RCMP Security Service was responsible for
implementing the policy and amassed thousands of files on suspected homosexuals. The service was even supposed to have
invented a machine with wires that attached to particular body
parts that was to determine "scientifically" whether someone
harboured homosexual tendencies. It apparently failed. But for
generations, the hunt for homosexuals was pressed with vigour.

When I became director-general in this world on my return
from Cuba in 1983, I managed to end the ban on the recruitment
of gays and the firing of those who were outed. The long-standing
policy, I pointed out in a report to the undersecretary, was illegal
under the then new Charter of Rights and Freedoms, and from
my review of the matter it was not justified on security grounds.
The report was returned to me with no notation other than "I
agree." The policy that had ruined the careers of so many foreign-
service employees and led hundreds of loyal, hard-working public
servants over the years to lead lives of deception thus ended with
a stroke of a pen and with no debate.

I myself was targeted twice in the course of my career. I have
described elsewhere the efforts of the Cuban security service
(itself trained by the East German security service) initially to
suborn me and later to punish me and my family. The other incident, a minor one, occurred during my posting to Bangladesh
in the early 1970s. A Soviet diplomat, a member of the KGB,
came to a reception I was hosting after a golf tournament organized for the diplomatic corps. Golf, he said, was about to be

introduced as a new sport in the U.S.S.R. and he wanted to pick up a few pointers from his capitalist friends. He then proceeded to invite me and diplomats from the United Kingdom and Australia to accompany him as his guests to his favourite brothel. With my diplomatic colleagues, I laughed at his brazenness, but as soon as he departed my residence we stampeded to our cipher rooms to send reports to our security officers at headquarters to assure them that we had not fallen into the trap.

Not only Western diplomats were afraid of being compromised by contacts with the other side. I was invited once by the Indian high commissioner to a dinner at his residence in Dhaka. The other guests were from Eastern Bloc countries. The host assigned me a seat at the dinner table between the wives of Bulgarian and Romanian diplomats; their husbands were seated at opposite ends of the table. Both women spoke English and were professionals in their own right.

Trying to make conversation, I turned to the woman on my right and banally said, "How are you?"

It was as if I had asked her to be my mistress and report to me all the secrets of her country. Before she could reply, her husband yelled in an indignant voice, "She is fine!" – stopping the conversation around the table in its tracks.

I turned to the other and asked the same question. The loud voice of her husband provided the answer: "She likewise is fine!"

I decided to persist. "And what is your profession?"

"She is a medical doctor," shouted her husband.

I suppose that I should have given up, but I perversely continued, seeking to conduct the type of inane conversation common at dinner parties around the world. This time, however, the dialogue at least had the virtue of being animated as the Bulgarian and Romanian shouted points of conversation at me to pre-empt my dialogue with their wives. The next day, in accordance with Government of Canada security regulations, I duly filed a report to the departmental security officer detailing my social contacts with the communist diplomats and their spouses. The Eastern Bloc diplomats, I am certain, filed similar reports to their security officers. The Bulgarian and the Romanian would have been able to reassure their headquarters that Jim Bartleman, representative of a hostile power, had not succeeded in compromising their wives, even if a dinner party had been ruined.

Post–Cold War NATO

As a Cold War veteran acutely aware that a sword of Damocles had hung over the heads of civilization for many long years, I was not surprised that the prevailing mood at NATO headquarters in October 1990 was euphoric. There was a sense that history was at a turning point. Communism, which had threatened the West since 1917, had been vanquished. The threat of Soviet expansion in Europe, which had prompted the creation of NATO in 1949, had disappeared. On November 19, 1990, at a Conference on Security and Cooperation in Europe in Paris, leaders of NATO and the Warsaw Pact signed the most comprehensive arms-limitation agreement since the Treaty of Versailles ending the First World War. The Soviets agreed to cut their armed forces in Europe (including European Russia) by 50 per cent and Germany accepted a ceiling on its forces of 370,000 military personnel. The arms-control talks on which I had spent so many thankless years in the mid-1970s, had at last been met with success. The Cold War was officially over.

But there was no peace treaty, and many questions remained. NATO leaders directed that the permanent representatives prepare new aims and a new strategic doctrine to replace those developed during the forty years of Cold War. We then gathered informally in "brainstorming" sessions to debate the issues, meeting in a cramped conference room around a table so small that the knees of the participants pressed up against those of colleagues on either side. I became more intimate with the Belgian and Danish permanent representatives than either they or I would ever have wished.

We met twice a week and every permanent representative felt obliged to speak whether or not he had anything to say. The already dim lighting turned blue from the smoke of the Gauloises cigarettes favoured by the French permanent representative, and the air grew foul from the stink of the pipe of the Dane and the sickeningly sweet odour of the cigarettes of the secretary-general, which would eventually kill him. The Italian and I asked that smoking not be permitted, but we were ignored. He then installed a small battery-powered fan on his table to blow the smoke from his neighbours back at them, but they did not take the hint.

The debate progressed in fits and starts from fall 1990 to fall 1991. Although we were supposed to speak personally to facilitate the building of consensus on the big issues, it was an open secret that delegations received instructions from our capitals prior to each session. We exerted whatever leverage our countries possessed. Countries were organized in descending order of importance, like the concentric circles of the underworld in Dante's Inferno. The United States, in splendid glory, occupied the first circle. France, Germany, and the United Kingdom were grouped together at the next level. Canada and Italy shared the third level, with the other countries spread out below. National cliques existed. Britain and the United States were inseparable. Germany and France maintained a discreet love affair. The United States caucused privately with the United Kingdom and Germany on all major issues to try to obtain agreement before they were debated in the North Atlantic Council.

Canada's Highest Priority
Canada's priority at this time was NATO's relationship with the countries of Central and Eastern Europe. More than a million Canadians could trace their roots to Ukraine, some five hundred

thousand were of Polish origin, and tens of thousands had come
to Canada as refugees following the abortive uprising in Hungary
in 1956 and the failure of the Prague Spring in 1968. For Canada,
Europe did not stop at the eastern borders of NATO or the geographic confines of the European Community. At the Canadian
delegation, we took literally the assumption, prevalent during the
Cold War, that these "captive nations" would be welcomed back
into the mainstream of Western life once they had been freed
from communist rule. We were acutely aware that for much of
the twentieth century they had existed in a security vacuum
without allies, making them easy prey to Hitler and victims of
Stalin. In our view, the international community had a moral
responsibility to ensure that they were not left in a security limbo
once again.

Our European allies did not share Canada's enthusiasm. They
nevertheless supported the issuance of an invitation to the former
satellite states to establish liaison relations with NATO and for the
leaders of their Eastern European neighbours to come to Brussels
to address the North Atlantic Council. They agreed after a vigorous debate, in which Canada and France occupied the extreme
ends of the spectrum of views, to announce a series of measures
designed to strengthen ties between NATO and its new neighbours, such as intensified military and political contacts. After
some pushing by Canada and strong resistance by France, they
were even prepared to agree to establish NATO information offices
– located in the embassies of NATO countries – in Central and
Eastern capitals.

Our European NATO allies did not want to go any further.
They wanted a breathing spell to absorb change; it was not given.
Soon Presidents Lech Walesa of Poland and Václav Havel of
Czechoslovakia came to Brussels at separate times but on the same
mission. Walesa was an electrician by training and a trade union-
ist by instinct. He was like a working-class fish out of water with
the snobbish, hyper-sophisticated European ambassadors. His

electric-blue suit, his sparkling white and freshly pressed shirt, and his somewhat loud tie contrasted with the elegant and subdued tailoring of NATO's senior diplomats. His speech was embarrassingly earnest to the ears of those used to subtle doses of irony and sarcasm. The Polish president, their body language seemed to say, was a member of a lower class meeting the middle and upper classes, a man of limited education and world view among the educated and well travelled, a deeply religious man from a country of believers encountering skeptics, and the leader of a poor, backward country seeking admission to their exclusive club. He may have been one of the great figures of the struggle for freedom in the post-war era, but he took himself a little too seriously for the taste of most.

With Havel, it was different. The Czechoslovak president was a bourgeois among the bourgeois, a postmodern sophisticate among his fellows, and a playwright among intellectuals. His shirt, tie, and suit were fashionably rumpled, and ash on his lapels from the cigarette dangling from his lips gave just the right touch of bohemian insouciance to his overall appearance. He was, moreover, not earnest. His face betrayed ennui as the ambassadors, myself included, vied with one another to praise the velvet revolution and his central role in it. I thought I could trump the others, announcing in my intervention that Canada was establishing a scholarship program for deserving Central European scholars in honour of the visit of one of the great heroes of modern Europe to NATO headquarters. Havel glanced at me indifferently, took another pull on his cigarette, and waited for the next acolyte to make his offer.

Appearances aside, both men were courageous, natural leaders who had suffered imprisonment. Had they launched their campaigns of civil disobedience earlier in the Cold War – in the time of Stalin, or even Khrushchev – they would have been executed by the KGB. Their good fortune was to appear on the scene after the signature of the Conference on Security Cooperation in

Europe Final Act in 1975 which set out human-rights norms to which their governments were supposed to adhere. They both said the same thing: the end of the Cold War had left a security void and economic uncertainty in the centre of Europe; unless they were admitted into NATO and integrated into the European Community, their countries would remain vulnerable to Soviet influence and to takeover by undemocratic forces. The message was one the European members of the alliance did not want to hear. They drew the line at the establishment of institutional links between NATO and former Warsaw Pact countries and at any movement in the direction of extending a security blanket eastward.

The European members had spent forty years in an alliance with a membership that monopolized the American security guarantee in Europe. Reluctant to share the protective umbrella of the United States with their rediscovered neighbours, they also wanted to avoid putting themselves in the position of having to come to the defence of countries that had unresolved ethnic and border problems. They felt overwhelmed by the pace of nasty events occurring in their near neighbourhood, the former Yugoslavia. They were demoralized by their internal problems of low economic growth, rising unemployment, growing criminality, and rising public resentment against the inflow of immigrants from North Africa and Central Europe. Most important, they did not want NATO to take any steps that could upset the process of reform and rapprochement with the West in the Soviet Union. Eventually, however, they were forced to bow to the pressure from their newly democratic neighbours to the east. Closer institutional links were established, which were to lead in the coming decade to NATO membership.

Championing Ukraine
Given the large number of Canadians of Ukrainian origin, Ukraine was a special priority. I hosted dinners and receptions at my residence in Brussels to introduce Ukrainian military and

political leaders to their NATO counterparts. In a dramatic step, we blocked other NATO members from delaying recognition of Kiev (after Ukraine declared independence in December 1991) until it undertook to destroy its nuclear arms inherited from the former U.S.S.R. This caused deep unhappiness in other delegations that thought we were taking our support for Ukraine too far.

They were appalled, for example, when I told them that the Canadian delegation was hosting young diplomatic interns from Ukraine, exposing them to the day-to-day workings of a NATO delegation. Proper security procedures were in effect to protect confidential documents, but, without exception, the other ambassadors took me to task, saying that only nationals of the member states should have access to the offices of the NATO delegations. One ambassador even said that becoming a member of the council was akin to taking holy orders and that my actions were equivalent to heresy. But once the old ways of thinking were challenged, the others followed suit, however reluctantly. Within two months, the American and German delegations were welcoming interns from other former Warsaw Pact countries into their offices.

I pressed on as unofficial champion of Ukraine, successfully lobbying to be sent as a NATO representative to brief key figures in Kiev and Odessa on the advantages of drawing closer to the alliance. Accompanied by a NATO admiral and a senior official from the international staff, I arrived in Kiev on a cold late-October day after a direct flight from Brussels. Ukraine had gained its independence almost a year earlier, but the immigration and police officials still wore their Soviet-era uniforms and were brusque and unsmiling. We were met by representatives of the Foreign Ministry, who expedited entry procedures and whisked us to the largest and most modern hotel in the city. The avenues were broad and lined with trees in the final phases of fall colours. The late-autumn sun glistened off gilt-ornamented churches and monasteries.

The beauty of the city masked private hardship and despair. Ukraine's leadership was weak and corruption was widespread. Relations with Russia, with which it was disputing the ownership of the Black Sea fleet, were at a crisis point. The standard of living had declined drastically after the collapse of communism and had fallen even more following Ukraine's declaration of independence. Inflation was at astronomical levels and the value of the local currency was derisory. The most expensive seat at the opera was less than five cents in Canadian money. Food was expensive and difficult to obtain, and it was a struggle for the people to pay their heating bills. Old women stood at street corners selling their meagre possessions in an attempt to make ends meet.

We were not spared at the hotel. Although the outside temperatures fell below freezing at night, the heat had not been turned on and I shivered in my room. When I complained, the hotel manager told me to go to bed. Since it was only five in the afternoon, I visited the dollar shop, ubiquitous in all communist or former communist countries, which sold imported luxury goods for foreign currency, and bought a gigantic hair dryer. Taking it to my room, I set the controls to maximum, but found that as much heat was escaping the poorly fitted windows as the dryer was generating. I tried directing the flow of air at a fixed spot on the bed and lying carefully in its path. I gave up and crawled under the covers when it became apparent that while part of my body was being warmed, the rest was becoming glacially cold.

The warmth of the welcome from ministers, senior officials, leaders of the military, the press, and even the Ukrainian KGB, several of whom I had hosted during their visits to Brussels, more than made up for freezing in my room. They greeted us enthusiastically, eager for our support to establish closer ties with NATO. We were then supposed to be whisked by plane to Odessa on the Black Sea to meet the political and military leadership in this militarily sensitive area. All internal flights had been cancelled for lack of aviation fuel, and it was decided that we would take the night train. It was a return to the past, a journey that would have been familiar to Boris Pasternak, the Nobel Prize–winning author whose accounts of rail traffic in First World War Russia were among the most poignant in his novel *Doctor Zhivago*.

With electricity supplies low, the city was dark as the liaison officers drove us to the railway station, itself plunged in darkness. Thousands of shabbily attired people with shawls or blankets over their shoulders waited in the obscurity, clutching cheap suitcases and waiting impassively for trains that would take them to destinations around the country. Our guides led us by flashlight through a maze of corridors to the train for Odessa in which two compartments, one for the NATO team and one for our escorts ("minders" from the Ukrainian version of the KGB), had been reserved. A female attendant lit a fire, stuffing newspaper and wood into a stove at one end of the railway car to heat a boiler that would warm radiators in our compartments.

As the train crawled out of the city, we ate sausages, herrings, and black bread washed down with vodka as we looked out at the dreary, desolate, and phantasmagorical scene. Derelict factories and rusty machinery were faintly visible in a desert landscape, testifying to the disintegration of Ukraine's industrial base, which had collapsed with the communist dream. As dawn approached, collective farms, the pride of the old Soviet Union, came into view, but all I could see was abandoned farm equipment lying amidst high grass and weeds.

We arrived, however, in another world. Odessa, with its wide esplanade and rich store of pre-revolutionary architecture, including one of the world's finest opera houses, proved to be a remarkable jewel on the Black Sea. The same messages conveyed to us by the elites of Kiev were repeated. The commander of the Odessa military district said that he and his men were prepared to fight to the death to defend their new country. I noticed, however, that he and his fellow generals were more comfortable speaking Russian than Ukrainian and spent much time describing in proud detail the heroic struggle of the Red Army against the Nazis in the Crimea during the Second World War. They were, moreover, uncomfortable receiving a delegation from NATO, their sworn enemy throughout the Cold War. The officer-training establishment where they received us reeked of the urine of six thousand cadets and gave the impression of being in terminal decline, with windows broken and paint peeling from the walls. The glory days of the military were over.

Seeking to obtain a sense of what life was like in the days before the 1917 revolution, I visited a local monastery. Long-bearded monks, rubber boots deep in the oozing manure and cassocks brown around the bottoms where cloth met dirt, were shovelling the ripe fertilizer onto the fields from horse-drawn wagons. The chapel was crowded with the faithful – old ladies dressed in black were in the majority amid a sprinkling of younger people. The air was filled with smoke from burning tapers and the devotions were interspersed with frequent signs of the cross. It was as if I had stepped into a scene of rural life in old Russia described by Tolstoy himself. I sensed the spiritual resurrection of a people who had survived seventy-five years of communist persecution and who now had no idea what to do with their new freedom.

Crises in the New NATO

Even without instructions from our governments, we had to prevent a return to the Cold War.

"**P**resident Gorbachev is ill and has been replaced by a state committee." It was early morning on August 19, 1991, and I was watching CNN at home in Brussels. The announcer added that the head of the KGB, the prime minister, and the defence minister had taken over in Moscow. Despite the reassuring words, it was obvious that a coup was being mounted that might push the Soviet Union back to hardline communism and return the world to the Cold War. NATO was facing its most serious crisis in years. I needed guidance from the Canadian government on what to do.

The Collapse of the Soviet Union
What relationship NATO should establish with the Soviet Union following the collapse of its empire in Central Europe had been the most important issue facing the alliance since the fall of the Berlin Wall in 1989. Was it too early to take at face value Gorbachev's protestations that the Soviet Union would never again threaten the West? In NATO debates, Canada's position was that the alliance response should be based on the future capabilities and not on the intentions of the Soviet Union. While the Soviet Union would remain powerful in the future, just as it had been in the past, the withdrawal of Soviet forces from Central Europe, then underway, had changed the military balance irrevocably and for the better.

Old habits die hard, and other permanent representatives did not accept the view I espoused. Despite their rhetoric about the new world order and Francis Fukuyama's widely quoted thesis in *The End of History and the Last Man* that the universal principles of Western liberalism would soon dominate a world in peace, it was difficult for my colleagues to imagine a European security landscape devoid of a Soviet threat. They maintained that the Soviet implosion could not continue indefinitely. Moscow had acquiesced without a whimper in the freeing of the satellite states; it had meekly accepted the reunification of Germany, reversing its single most important foreign-policy goal since the time of Stalin; its economy was collapsing; and its constituent republics were restive. Common sense, they maintained, dictated that the tide would eventually turn and there would be a reassertion of Soviet power on the European scene.

Now the hardliners were taking over – or so it seemed. I telephoned Ottawa for instructions. Those colleagues at the Pearson Building headquarters not on vacation had no more information than I had and were in no position to help. The secretary-general then called an emergency meeting of the North Atlantic Council. I hurried to NATO to take my place in the council chamber to discover that I was not alone in having no guidance from my capital. Throughout the countries of the alliance, senior officials and ministers were on holiday. Even without instructions from our governments, we had to prevent a return to the Cold War. We issued a press release warning the coup leaders of "serious consequences" if the Soviet Union abandoned reform. Our communiqué was a bluff, since it would have been inconceivable for NATO to take military measures against even a weakened Soviet Union that retained such an awesome nuclear capacity. The most we could have done would have been to cut off our diplomatic contacts with Soviet liaison officers at NATO headquarters. The coup leaders, we gambled, would not know this.

We then scheduled a special meeting of North Atlantic Council foreign ministers to take over the management of the crisis. Foreign Minister Barbara McDougall arrived on an early flight from Montreal on August 21. She had been briefed before her departure from Ottawa that the coup was likely to succeed and that NATO would have to find a way to accommodate itself to the new reality. Having already spoken to the press in Canada to this effect, she was angry when I told her that the prevailing view at NATO headquarters was to do everything possible to assist Boris Yeltsin, the president of the Russian Federation (one of the fifteen constituent republics of the old U.S.S.R.), in restoring the situation. The minister was a quick study, however, enjoyed the respect of her colleagues, and was thus able to weigh in on the debate.

Shortly after the meeting began, Secretary-General Woerner was pulled out of the room to speak on the telephone to Yeltsin, calling from his command post in Moscow. The Russian leader, the secretary-general told us on his return, had been heartened by our communiqué the day before and appealed to NATO to stand firm. He needed our help, he was reported to have said, to support his efforts to force the coup leaders to back down. Later, while the ministerial meeting was still in session, Woerner announced that the Soviet president had been released and the coup attempt was over. Yeltsin was the hero of the hour. A democratic Russia and fourteen other newly independent countries would emerge from the ruins of the Soviet Union, and NATO would be an institution in search of a role.

Closing the Bases

It did not take long for Canada to draw its own conclusions about the change in the European strategic situation. On February 24, 1992, headquarters advised me that the Department of Finance had taken the decision to close the Canadian bases at Lahr and Baden-Baden in Germany, with a 1994 deadline for the departure of the troops. It was the most important development in

Canada's relations with NATO since Prime Minister Trudeau's decision to slash Canada's troop levels in Europe in 1969. Since the announcement in Canada would be made in the context of a budget report to Parliament on February 26, I was instructed not to question the decision or even to let the secretary-general or other members of the alliance know ahead of time.

Early on the morning of February 26, I called on Manfred Woerner to give him the news and to request that a special meeting of the North Atlantic Council be held to allow me to convey Canada's decision. Jeremy Kinsman, the assistant deputy minister for international security matters in Foreign Affairs, came along to provide moral support. Woerner was bitter. He said that Canada had betrayed the alliance, which had not even been given the chance to comment on our plans before the decision had been taken. He expected the United States to follow Canada's lead and make further cuts in the size of its forces stationed in Europe. To my protestations that Canada would remain heavily involved on the ground in European security affairs through the provision of peacekeepers in the former Yugoslavia, he said that our peacekeeping efforts were mere eyewash to cover the shirking of our responsibility to NATO.

To the session of the North Atlantic Council I pointed out that Canada was not unique in the alliance in acting to cash in on the peace dividend. Belgium and the Netherlands had already closed their military bases in Germany. It also made no sense for Canada to maintain a military presence in Europe designed to help stop a Warsaw Pact attack across the German central plain when Russia no longer constituted a threat, the Warsaw Pact no longer existed, and Germany was reunified. Continuance of Canadian bases in Germany therefore would be of token value only. Canada could not afford to indulge in symbolism when its troops were required for peacekeeping in the vortex of conflict in the Balkans, which was to replace implosion in the former Soviet Union as Europe's most pressing security problem in the coming decade.

The Collapse of Yugoslavia

In the spring of 1991, the Swedish ambassador and his wife invited Marie-Jeanne and me to dinner at their elegant Brussels residence. There were perhaps eighteen of us around the table, drawn largely from countries where our hosts had served in the past, including Yugoslavia. The conversation was animated and our hosts regaled us with funny stories of their diplomatic experiences in our capitals. When the ambassador turned to Yugoslavia, no amusing anecdote came readily to mind. Instead, he toasted the Yugoslav people and expressed a pious hope that the warfare just starting in that country would soon end. Everyone, except the Yugoslav envoy and his wife, raised their glasses.

"You don't understand," the wife said. "You just don't understand – the first blood has been shed; no one can now stop the killing." After a momentary pause, the cheery conversation resumed around the table. But I never forgot her stricken face. I would see it before me in the coming years each time I participated in ineffectual NATO debates on the deteriorating situation in the Balkans, in which we erroneously assumed that the warring parties would eventually respond to appeals to stop slaughtering each other.

The burgeoning crisis in Yugoslavia in 1989 and 1990 had initially been overshadowed by momentous events occurring elsewhere in the region. It was assumed that Yugoslavia would follow the path of Poland, Hungary, and other communist-led countries and opt for liberal democracy. The renaming of the Serbian Communist Party as the Serbian Socialist Party by the Yugoslav leader Slobodan Milosevic in 1989 was seen as a step in the right direction. Milosevic's suppression of the rights of the two largest minority populations in Serbia, the Hungarians of Vojvodina and the Albanians of Kosovo, passed almost unnoticed. This was possibly because the Albanians, the larger of the two minorities, were Muslim and not regarded by many Western Europeans as authentically European.

By 1991, the nationalist forces tearing Yugoslavia apart had become uncontrollable. Slovenia, followed closely by Croatia, reacted strongly against Milosevic's efforts to impose Serbian hegemony over the Yugoslav Federation. Slovenia acted first, declaring independence and driving the Yugoslav army from its territory in June. This was not a major setback for Milosevic since there were few ethnic Serbs resident in Slovenia. Croatia's declaration of independence, however, was another matter. Full-scale fighting immediately broke out between Croatians and the sizable Serbian minority, supported by the Yugoslav army now reduced to its Serbian rump. Seizing the heavy weapons stored at the various military garrisons in the area, the Serb side inflicted severe punishment on the Croats, reducing villages and towns to rubble and occupying all areas where the Serbs were a local majority. In a foretaste of what was to come, both sides engaged in massive human-rights violations, including the indiscriminate killing of civilians.

Meanwhile, at NATO headquarters, we exchanged views on the deteriorating situation in the Balkans at our weekly meetings of the North Atlantic Council but avoided engagement. Civil war in Yugoslavia constituted no direct threat to the security of member states. The issues were, moreover, simply too hot to touch since they raised old animosities among the allies. France, in the early days of the crisis, was strongly sympathetic to the Serbs, recalling its special links to Serbia dating back to the First World War. Greece, sharing a common religion with the Serbs and having historically close ties to Belgrade, felt that Serbia could do no wrong. Germany, on the other hand, recalling its bloody conflict with Tito's partisans during the Second World War, was hostile to Serbia; it also had a long memory, unable to forget its First World War alliances with the Austro-Hungarian Empire, and strongly supported the independence aspirations of Slovenia and Croatia, which had been part of that empire.

The United Kingdom, with many of its front-line troops tied down in Northern Ireland, was afraid of finding itself caught in an insoluble Balkan quagmire and did not even want to discuss the matter. The United States, in the words of Secretary of State James Baker, "didn't have a dog in this fight." Washington, suffering from Gulf War fatigue, was of the view that the Europeans should shoulder the responsibility for managing and resolving the Yugoslav crisis. Italy, a long-standing rival of the former Yugoslavia for influence in the Mediterranean, and still resentful over the outcome of its post–Second World War disputes with Tito over Trieste, was suspicious of all the warring parties in the former Yugoslavia.

With NATO unwilling to act, the problem of Yugoslavia, by default, came to rest on the shoulders of the European Community. The Europeans were initially hopeful that they could handle the crisis without NATO and the United States; some countries even looked forward to the challenge as a means of demonstrating to their publics and to the world that Europe had come of age. Negotiations were well advanced among its members in that summer of 1991 to transform the European Community, with its focus on economic integration and political co-operation, into the European Union, with a single currency, full economic and monetary union, and foreign- and defence-policy integration; it was expected that the text codifying these gains would be incorporated in a treaty to be approved at a summit meeting of European leaders at Maastricht in the Netherlands before the end of the year.

President Mitterrand of France and Chancellor Kohl of Germany provided the leadership to drive ahead the construction of Europe. They and many European leaders assumed that, with the collapse of communism, the evolving European structures would be able to handle the crises afflicting their neighbourhood, including in the former Yugoslavia. It was their belief, for example, that if moral suasion did not work, they could always mount a peacekeeping mission to keep order under the auspices of the Western European Union. They could not have been more mistaken.

On July 1, the Netherlands assumed the presidency of the European Council, the supreme political body of the new Europe, whose leadership rotated among member states every six months, and was responsible, *inter alia*, for coordinating European foreign-policy initiatives. The Dutch foreign minister, Hans Van den Broek, representing the presidency, visited Belgrade and Zagreb to urge the warring parties to negotiate a peaceful settlement to their dispute, telling them that their chances for closer association with the European Community would be compromised if they did not behave in a civilized manner. He obtained agreement for a three-month ceasefire and for the deployment of a European Commission Monitoring Mission, composed of several hundred unarmed observers, to supervise the truce. The Dutch were soon disillusioned; nationalist passion outweighed any economic incentive to compromise, and fierce fighting resumed. Henry Wynaendts, a senior Dutch diplomat, who had been entrusted by the European Community to supervise the ceasefire, came to brief us at NATO, still shaken from a close brush with death when Croatian gunners had opened fire on his aircraft, paying no attention to its markings. His mission was in ruins.

Lord Carrington, former British foreign secretary and secretary-general of NATO, was brought out of retirement and thrown into the breach. He organized a meeting in Geneva with the leaders of the opposing sides, who agreed to a ceasefire; it was never implemented. The United Nations Security Council became involved for the first time, calling for an embargo on the delivery of weapons and military equipment, but it had no means of enforcing its decree. Finally, U.N. secretary-general Javier Perez de Cuellar appointed Cyrus Vance, the former American secretary of state, as his personal envoy to work with Lord Carrington.

The European Community and the United Nations, backed up by the crisis-management facilities of the Conference on Security and Cooperation in Europe, were now involved, yet the situation continued to degenerate. NATO, for its part, stood aloof, taking no action other than to issue press releases, metaphorically wringing its hands, condemning the violence, and calling for a negotiated solution. I recall listening to the perfunctory debate on Yugoslavia at the November 1991 NATO summit in Rome; as we met, the Serbs were bombarding Dubrovnik, a UNESCO heritage site, less than two hours away by air, and could not have cared less for the toothless communiqués issued by Presidents Bush and Mitterrand and the other leaders of the most powerful alliance in world history.

The conflict then spread to Bosnia. German Foreign Minister Hans-Dietrich Genscher precipitated the descent into the abyss by threatening to take unilateral action and recognize Slovenia and Croatia by Christmas 1991 if the European Community did not do so itself. Unwilling to upset Germany in the wake of the signature of the Maastricht Treaty, the countries of the European Community fell into line. Canada and the United States, with sizable Croatian immigrant populations, followed suit. President Itzebegovic of Bosnia had no choice but to declare his constituent republic independent following a referendum boycotted by the Serb minority. A civil war was then ignited among the Serbs, Croats, and Muslims of the new country that would eventually end in December 1995, when a peace agreement brokered by the Americans at Dayton, Ohio came into force. In the interim, hundreds of thousands of people would be killed, millions would be driven into exile, and the confidence of Europeans in themselves and the strength of their institutions would be cast into doubt.

The New Europe Drops the Ball

Canada adopted a low profile in the discussions at NATO in the fall of 1991, torn between a natural reluctance to endorse any outcome that could legitimize the breakup of a federation, and a desire to support the right of exploited states to choose democratic, albeit separate, futures. We were, however, prepared to assist in a practical way. Canadians with Serbo-Croat language skills were assigned to the European Commission Monitoring Mission. Minister McDougall arranged directly with German Foreign Minister Genscher, president of the Western European Union, to have me attend a key meeting of foreign and defence ministers that was to decide whether to send a peacekeeping force to Croatia. I was empowered to offer a battle group of twelve hundred Canadian troops to serve with the Europeans if the decision was to proceed.

The meeting, attended by the foreign and defence ministers of all Western European Union countries, was one of the most important in the post–Cold War period for what it failed to accomplish. Having announced to the world that the new Europe was ready and willing to assume greater responsibility for security problems on its borders, the Europeans got cold feet when faced with a virulent war without the comforting presence and leadership of the United States, and decided to do nothing. As I found in the ensuing debate, the divisions among countries that hindered action in NATO were just as strong in this entirely European framework. The Greeks argued with the Dutch over who was more guilty for the mess in the area; the Italians said that they had special interests in the region but were unable to offer any troops because of their role as an invader in the Balkans under Mussolini in the Second World War; the Germans called for urgent action by the others but said that they would not be able to offer troops for constitutional and historical reasons; and the British said that all their available forces were tied up in Northern Ireland. They added that no one should forget the fate of the German troops who found themselves bogged down for years during the Second World War fighting "incredibly fierce Serbian troops."

This failure of European resolve would so badly damage the movement for a greater European security and defence identity that it took the shortcomings in American leadership during the Kosovo air campaign in the latter part of the 1990s for it to revive in a serious way. The ball, having been passed from NATO to the European institutions, was now dumped into the lap of a reluctant United Nations.

I left the Western European Union meeting with Canada's offer to provide a battle group still in my pocket. The Canadian government, determined to act whether or not the Europeans moved, then pushed the United Nations to authorize the dispatch of a peacekeeping mission, and was one of the first to make available a major peacekeeping force deployed in early 1992 into Croatia. To facilitate agreement, the Security Council approved a Chapter Six (classic peacekeeping action) rather than a Chapter Seven (military-intervention operation). The difference between the two was of critical importance: lightly armed troops with a mandate to negotiate rather than impose their will were authorized, rather than forces equipped and mandated to fight to impose a settlement.

With the benefit of hindsight, it is difficult to understand why the Canadian government would send lightly armed troops into a hornet's nest. Like the other members of the peacekeeping community that had provided troops to hot spots over the decades, however, it did not yet understand that traditional peacekeeping was outdated in the post–Cold War world. Our troops had no hope of fulfilling their mandates with armaments and equipment suited to patrolling the ceasefire lines of relatively peaceful dispute zones in the past. Cyprus was not Bosnia. Once committed, however, it would prove impossible politically and difficult logistically to pull the troops out. Canadian soldiers in the former Yugoslavia would henceforth be made virtual hostages of the peoples they had ostensibly come to protect, and the

Canadian government would be stuck for years trying to extricate them honourably from almost hopeless conditions.

From Brussels, my colleagues and I watched the United Nations stumble time and again as it attempted to fulfill its "mission impossible." The original mandate was to provide a force for a peacekeeping mission in Croatia only. Incredibly, the United Nations located the headquarters for this force (United Nations Protection Force, or UNPROFOR) in Sarajevo, capital of neighbouring Bosnia. By the time the full force was deployed into Croatia in April 1992, Bosnia was itself in flames. UNPROFOR headquarters staff, including Canadian Brigadier-General (later Major-General) Lewis MacKenzie, found themselves trying to direct operations in Croatia, protect themselves from sniper and mortar attack, and dampen the conflict around them in Bosnia.

Although only the third-ranking officer in the UNPROFOR hierarchy, MacKenzie had a gift for media relations and was adopted by the international press. He became well known for his Joseph Heller *Catch 22*–style comments that exposed the hypocrisy of the international community's commitment to the peoples of what was by then the former Yugoslavia as well as the cynicism of the media. In one sally, in July 1992, he said, "If I could convince both sides to stop killing their own people for CNN, perhaps we could have a ceasefire."

Reassigned in the summer of 1992, he set up Sector Sarajevo with the Canadian battalion sent from Croatia and a French marine infantry contingent, and opened the Sarajevo airport for humanitarian-aid flights. MacKenzie was present to greet French president François Mitterrand, who paid a surprise visit to the Bosnian capital that captured the attention of the world. When MacKenzie stepped down from his UNPROFOR role, he came to my residence in Brussels to brief the NATO permanent representatives. Our eyes were opened by what he had to say about conditions in Sarajevo and about Bosnia's slide into anarchy, which in his view the United Nations would not be able to stop. Accustomed to more dispassionate briefings, we were ill at ease when he described how his men routinely killed snipers in self-defence.

In the meantime, the United Nations Security Council assigned ever-increasing responsibilities to UNPROFOR. In 1992 it was successively ordered to dispatch observers to Bosnia, to assume control of the Sarajevo airport, to provide protection to United Nations High Commissioner for Refugees aid convoys, and to control the borders of Bosnia. In 1993 it was directed to provide protection to six "safe" areas (Sarajevo, Tuzla, Zepa, Gorazde, Bihac, and the ill-fated Srebrenica) and to use force in response to any attack on these zones. But UNPROFOR never received the resources to carry out these roles properly. Hence it often found itself forced to hand over humanitarian supplies to drunken trigger-happy militia thugs in order to pass through roadblocks. Its soldiers, lightly armed and not authorized to intervene in the fighting, became ineffectual witnesses to the daily killing and mistreatment of civilians, earning the scorn and eventually the contempt of all sides.

NATO, as the only organization in Europe with the military muscle to make a difference, was drawn slowly and reluctantly into Bosnia in support of the United Nations. The old suspicions and disdain that had characterized relations between the two organizations during forty years of Cold War faded away as it became apparent that they needed each other to cope with Bosnia. Canada, together with the Netherlands, Denmark, and Norway, worked hard to dispel the preconception, rife among members of the international staff and the delegations of the larger European members and the United States, that the United Nations was run by Third World technocrats interested only in Third World problems. In New York, Canadian diplomats had to fight against a bias that Boutros Boutros-Ghali, who replaced Javier Perez de Cuellar as secretary-general in January 1992, did not try to conceal, that NATO was a remnant of the Cold War and a symbol of a world in an alignment that no longer existed. These tensions never entirely disappeared and complicated efforts in the coming years to deal with the crisis in Bosnia.

Pushed hard by Manfred Woerner, who believed passionately that NATO had a moral obligation to help, the North Atlantic Council sent warships to the Adriatic in August 1992 to work with a small flotilla dispatched by the Western European Union. Their mission was to enforce the United Nations Security Council resolution banning the supply of arms to Serbia, Montenegro, Croatia, and Bosnia. In October, it provided early-warning aircraft to monitor the airspace over Bosnia, which had been declared out of bounds for military flights by the United Nations Security Council (the no-fly zone). In November, NATO provided UNPROFOR with an operational headquarters deployed into Bosnia with one hundred personnel, and equipment and supplies. In April 1993, it agreed to authorize NATO fighter aircraft to shoot down aircraft violating the no-fly zone. In June, NATO foreign ministers meeting in Athens authorized the use of alliance air power to protect the safe areas. However, authority to commit the aircraft to action was left in the hands of Boutros-Ghali, who was reluctant to exercise it. It was also unclear whether NATO air power was to be confined to protecting the UNPROFOR troops against attack, or whether it was also to be used to protect the civilians in the safe areas.

Throughout this period, the North Atlantic Council and NATO military planners sought to draw lessons from the failures of traditional peacekeeping in Bosnia as we prepared quietly for the call, expected to come eventually, for the alliance to intervene with ground forces. Initially, Canada was regarded as the repository of wisdom on the subject and we played a major role in the debates. Manfred Woerner's remarks to me in February 1992 that Canadian peacekeeping activities in the former Yugoslavia were eyewash to cover the closing of bases in Germany did not reflect his opinion later in the year. The edge we held in peacekeeping expertise, however, disappeared as UNPROFOR confronted circumstances that peacekeepers of the past never had to face. The rule book had to be rewritten as peacekeepers found themselves trying to keep a peace that did not exist, becoming unwitting accomplices to ethnic cleansing and being dragged into the conflict itself on the side of the Muslims. The Americans, who dominated NATO's military planning cells, vowed that they would never allow NATO to become involved in traditional peacekeeping operations where lightly armed troops sought to interpose themselves between warring factions. Planning for intervention in Bosnia therefore was based on the principle that the environment would be non–permissive, the troops equipped for war, the rules of engagement robust, and the forces of a size sufficient to overwhelm any potential enemy in the field.

Canada had participated in more operations than any other country during the Cold War era, when traditional peacekeeping (separating warring parties with their consent) was the norm. Now we had relinquished that role in the new security environment of ethnic civil war, taking a back seat to countries such as Pakistan and Bangladesh which, attracted by U.N. financial subsidies, willingly sent large contingents into harm's way in global hot spots.

Lift and Strike

In the summer of 1993, CNN and other major news organizations provided continuous coverage of the war in Bosnia, including on–the-spot reporting of atrocities on a scale not seen in Europe since the Second World War. Aroused citizens demanded that their governments act to alleviate the suffering and to bring the war to an end. The Muslims, Croats, and Serbs continued to butcher each other – men, women, and children – indiscriminately. Warlords and criminals on all sides preyed on the weak, even extorting protection money from members of their own sides. In the most outrageous case, a Muslim warlord in the Sarajevo area combined fighting Serbs with running a smuggling operation and charging exorbitant fees for the safe passage of aid supplies to his own people. Dirty tricks, such as the shelling of one's own civilians by the Muslim leadership in Sarajevo and blaming the Serbs before the world press, became commonplace. But by this time, the Serbs were clearly branded in the public mind as the aggressors and there was growing support for having the international community intervene in the war on the side of the Muslims. Within NATO, opinion had also shifted. France was no longer on the side of Belgrade and only Greece was prepared to defend unconditionally Serbia's actions.

The United States, unwilling to commit ground forces in a war in which humanitarian rather than national-security interests were at stake, was prodded by its public to take action. Washington began advocating lifting the United Nations sanctions that prevented the parties to the conflict from arming themselves, and even argued for providing large-scale assistance to the Muslims, and intervening by using air power against the Serbs. Those countries in NATO that were contributing troops to UNPROFOR (Canada, France, Britain, Spain, the Netherlands, Belgium, and Luxembourg), had blocked an American effort to have the alliance adopt such an approach in April. There was little confidence that air power by itself could stop the Serbs from attacking the safe areas, and the lives of peacekeepers would be placed at risk. Canada took the leading role in these debates, putting me in the spotlight. The stage was thus set for a major clash between Canada and the United States when the tightening of the siege of Sarajevo by the Serbs in July 1993 led Washington to launch a major effort to get its way.

On July 30, I left Brussels with Marie-Jeanne and the three children to spend our summer vacation at my sister's home in Muskoka. Early in the morning on August 1, the telephone rang. The Americans had called an emergency meeting of the North Atlantic Council for Monday afternoon, August 2, to seek approval for a plan to allow NATO aircraft to intervene decisively in the civil war with heavy bombing of Serb positions throughout Bosnia to relieve the siege of Sarajevo and to ease the pressure on other safe areas. Prime Minister Kim Campbell, Foreign Minister Perrin Beatty and Defence Minister Thomas Siddon had been consulted. Canada had decided to block the American action to prevent the Serbs from taking retaliation against the lightly armed UNPROFOR troops, including more than one thousand Canadian peacekeepers stationed in vulnerable positions in Bosnia. Glen Shortliffe, secretary to the Cabinet, directed that I return immediately to Brussels to defend the Canadian position.

After a difficult journey back to Brussels, marred by a long delay in the departure of my flight from Toronto to Amsterdam, and a high-speed road trip from Schipol Airport to NATO headquarters, I arrived tired and dishevelled at my office one hour before the meeting. A senior general from National Defence headquarters was there to greet me, having flown directly from Ottawa in the comfort of a Challenger jet and arriving in time to get a good rest before the critical meeting. It turned out that his mission was to keep an eye on me to ensure that I obeyed the instructions from Ottawa. Although I had, I thought, excellent relations with the senior Canadian military, I was a mere civilian and thus, it seemed, not to be fully trusted to protect its interests.

After receiving a quick briefing from my staff, I called on Manfred Woerner to say that Canada would not join any consensus in favour of the American proposal. Prime Minister Campbell (who had visited the Canadian delegation to NATO some months earlier as defence minister and was thus familiar with the issues) would be monitoring the debate and had given instructions that the safety of our peacekeepers was not to be endangered by its outcome. Manfred, who favoured the American initiative, was not happy but was prepared for what was to come.

At the council meeting, former U.S. ambassador Reginald Bartholomew, who had been recalled from his position at NATO earlier in the year to attempt to put some coherence into Washington's approach to Bosnia, was the principal American spokesman. He sought to railroad the proposals through, asking for an early decision to put air power at the service of diplomacy. The NATO commander in the region, he said, should be empowered to act at times and places of his choosing without having to seek the approval of the United Nations. The air campaign should not be limited to protecting UNPROFOR personnel, but should be used to protect civilians and to attack Serb targets anywhere in Bosnia. The German, Turkish, and Dutch permanent representatives strongly supported the American position. The others, after expressing initial misgivings, fell silent, indicating that they would probably be able to go along with Bartholomew's proposals.

It was left to me to say no. I pointed out that some three hundred Canadian peacekeepers were located in Srebrenica, an enclave surrounded by Serb fighters. Another seven hundred were in Visoko, twenty-five kilometres from Sarajevo and within reach of Serbian artillery located on the surrounding heights. Canada had no intention of putting its soldiers' lives at risk by acceding to the American plan. Moreover, we could not endorse any initiative that would lead NATO to intervene in the war on the side of one of the parties or to undermine the role of the United Nations. Finally, if the United States got its way, Canada would take steps to pull all of its forces immediately out of the former Yugoslavia and would work to have the entire UNPROFOR mission ended.

Bartholomew was furious. In the ensuing marathon meeting, which lasted until early in the morning the next day, he tried to corner me and show that no other country shared Canada's approach. I responded that, with no troops at risk on the ground in Bosnia, the United States was in no position to question the credibility of a UNPROFOR participant like Canada. At critical moments, the French permanent representative intervened to lend support. The other permanent representatives generally remained

Foreign Minister Joe Clark
visits the ambassador to Israel
with the Dome of the Rock
and the Old City of Jerusalem
in the background.

James Bartleman, Joe Clark, and Israeli prime minister Shimon Peres,
March 1986.

Paying our respects at Yad Vashem
Holocaust Museum, 1986.
(*Zvi Reiter*)

James Bartleman and Marie-Jeanne visit Ethiopian Jews in hospital, 1986.

1987. Tel Aviv banquet with James Bartleman beside Ariel Sharon, then Israeli
trade minister. (*Uzi Keren*)

James Bartleman (Canadian permanent representative to NATO), Assistant Deputy Minister Ken Calder, aide, and Defence Minister Kim Campbell in discussions, Brussels, 1992. (NATO photo)

Flanked by representatives from Belgium and Bulgaria, Foreign Minister Barbara McDougall consults with James Bartleman at Foreign Ministers Meeting in Brussels, 1993. (NATO photo)

James Bartleman, Prime Minister Jean Chrétien, and NATO Secretary-General Manfred Woerner in Brussels, 1994. (*J.M. Carisse*)

Former prime minister Pierre Trudeau visits his old haunts at 24 Sussex Drive, June 1994. From left: James Bartleman, André Ouellet, Jean Chrétien, two European guests, Pierre Trudeau, and Jacques Delors of the E.U. (*J.M. Carisse*)

James Bartleman meets the Pope, 1994 ... (*A. Mari*, L'Osservatore Romano)

... and President Clinton, 1997, while Eddie Goldenberg waits his turn. (*J.M. Carisse*)

Five Continents. September 1998. James Bartleman presents his letters and credentials as high commissioner to South Africa to President Nelson Mandela, as Marie-Jeanne looks on.

Making a presentation at an OXFAM aid project in Namibia, 1999, as young Alain watches.

January 1999. Alain and his father enjoy an encounter with a bushman friend before the arrival of the tour bus.

The Sixth Continent. James Bartleman presents his letters and credentials as Canada's high commissioner to Australia to Prime Minister John Howard, October 1999. (*Michael Jensen*)

James Bartleman in his role as diplomatic advisor to the prime minister with Jean Chrétien in his office. Later, in 2002, the prime minister appointed him Lieutenant-Governor of Ontario. (*J.M. Carisse*)

silent. By arguing over every comma, by inserting conditions that safeguarded Canada's position, and by simply sitting in my chair and outwaiting the opposition, I eventually got my way. The secretary-general then called a recess in the proceedings to permit me to telephone the Privy Council Office. Prime Minister Campbell, who was standing by, quickly gave her assent and I returned to give the news to a relieved council. The text I accepted stipulated that the United Nations commander in Bosnia would be consulted in drawing up plans for the use of air power and would have a veto on the choice of targets and the commitment of aircraft to action.

I had known in advance from a report by a senior Canadian military officer in Bosnia who was a personal friend that the UNPROFOR commander would never authorize air strikes that would put the lives of peacekeepers in danger. In fact, all the senior officers of UNPROFOR in Bosnia were prepared to ask to be pulled out of the field in protest if the American initiative had succeeded. Hence the "compromise" that I had come up with meant that, in effect, NATO air power would only be used to defend the lives of peacekeepers through the provision of close air support, and would not be used to intervene in the war on the side of the Muslims. Canadian soldiers would thus not be killed in Bosnia as a result of the decisions taken by the North Atlantic Council that night. But neither was the war any closer to solution.

The Canada–United States confrontation at NATO left the Americans with a sour taste in their mouths. They made strong representations both from the National Security Council and the State Department to the Canadian embassy in Washington, complaining that I had been too unyielding. Washington was most unhappy that I had watered down the original NATO declaration. They reminded the embassy that President Clinton had gone out of his way to help Prime Minister Campbell at her first G7 meeting in Tokyo on trade issues. The U.S. administration had

expected Canada to be more accommodating to strongly held
American national-security positions; they hoped that Canada
would not repeat its heroics when NATO next discussed the use
of air power in Bosnia.

We learned later that Madeline Albright, then American
ambassador to the United Nations, had consulted her British and
French colleagues on the initiative. Secretary of State Warren
Christopher had personally spoken to key NATO foreign ministers
and obtained grudging support from most of them. Neither,
however, had thought to consult their Canadian opposite numbers
and had paid the price. I was personally happy that our minister
had not been included in this inner circle. We were as a result able
to fight for a decision that best served our national interest.

Resumption of Fighting

Sarajevo was given a temporary reprieve from bombardment in
the wake of the August 2 decisions and the Serbs abandoned their
most forward artillery position on Mount Igman. However, the
fighting flared up again in the fall of 1993 and winter of 1994.
France and Britain increased the size of their contingents to four
thousand and three thousand respectively. Canada maintained
more than two thousand troops in the field, half in Croatia and
half in Bosnia. A sizable force was cut off in Srebrenica, with Serb
forces preventing the Canadians from leaving. This would precipitate another confrontation between Canada and its allies – this
time with France and Britain as well as with the United States.

In early January 1994, NATO leaders gathered in Brussels to
discuss an American initiative to strengthen ties with the countries
of Central and Eastern Europe. It was the first NATO summit that
Jean Chrétien attended and he was blindsided on Bosnia by
the other leaders. The evening before the start of the summit, the
prime minister and I attended a dinner for NATO leaders hosted by
Belgian prime minister Jean-Luc Dehaene. Prime Minister John
Major of the United Kingdom, without consulting us, circulated

the text of a draft declaration that he wanted to release the next day. It threatened air strikes against the Serbs if they did not allow the Canadian troops in Srebrenica to depart and let a Dutch force come in to replace them. The proposal was warmly received, particularly by Presidents Clinton and Mitterrand, with whom Major had probably consulted beforehand. The dinner ended before Prime Minister Chrétien could register Canada's views.

As the leaders filed into the drawing room for coffee and liqueurs, the prime minister grabbed me by the arm and approached Major and Clinton one after the other to say that Canada had reservations about the British proposals, which he intended to spell out at the summit discussions the next day. Major earnestly tried to explain and justify the initiative. Clinton turned on the charm, putting his arm around the prime ministers's shoulders and saying, "Jean, this will really work. Don't worry."

Canada's prime minister refused the soft soap and we left for the residence of the Canadian ambassador to Belgium to discuss how to proceed. I pointed out that the Canadian troops in Srebrenica were in no particular danger, although their rotation out was long overdue. They would, however, be put at great risk if they were to attempt to fight their way through the Serb lines, even if supported by fighter aircraft providing close support. Our peacekeepers had been in situations like this many times in the past; they would eventually negotiate their way out. The prime minister was satisfied with this approach and went to bed.

During the night, the British briefed the international press on their initiative, to put pressure on Canada to agree. The Canadian media contingent was incensed that the Canadian delegation had not briefed them first and filed reports complaining about the inexperience of the new Chrétien team. The next day, the prime minister reminded his summit partners that UNPROFOR had been given the impossible task of serving as a "Red Cross with guns." Canada, he said, would be the judge of the best way to extricate its troops from Srebrenica; we would not agree to language in a NATO communiqué that served public-relations purposes only and endangered our soldiers. He then faced the Canadian press contingent to explain the Canadian position, calming them down.

The frustration that led Britain and France, supported by the United States, to take the lead at the Brussels summit to seek action against the Serbs then came to a head. On February 4, nine Muslims were killed and twenty were wounded in a mortar attack in Sarajevo. The next day, the toll was sixty-six dead and 197 wounded from a follow-up attack. It was time to make good on NATO's promise, made at the August 2 North Atlantic Council meeting and reaffirmed at the January summit in Brussels, to prevent the strangulation of Sarajevo.

The United Nations secretary-general wrote to Manfred Woerner on February 6 to request that the North Atlantic Council authorize the senior NATO commander in the alliance's southern command to launch air strikes "against artillery or mortar positions in and around Sarajevo which are determined by UNPROFOR to be responsible for attacks against civilian targets in that city." France, which by that time had two thousand troops in Sarajevo, proposed that an ultimatum be given to the Serbs to withdraw their forces from the Bosnian capital and place all their heavy weapons under United Nations control. Foreign Affairs, supported by Defence, instructed me to oppose the French initiative on the grounds that the peacekeepers could be endangered. The prime minister, however, shared the general revulsion at the Serbian action and intervened, giving orders that Canada should lend its support, provided the double-key decision-making procedure worked out the previous August was followed. The North Atlantic Council Agreement then issued an ultimatum to the Serbs to withdraw their heavy weapons twenty kilometres from the centre of Sarajevo within ten days or face NATO air attack. The Serbs blinked, complying at the last minute.

The siege of Sarajevo was over, but only temporarily. Later in the year, and again in 1995, the Serbs would call NATO's bluff, renewing their assault on Sarajevo and other safe areas. They shrugged off NATO air strikes, and carried through with their threats to seize UNPROFOR peacekeepers as hostages. UNPROFOR and NATO would be humiliated in the same way time and again in the coming eighteen months. But in the end, the Serbs would be the losers. Their outrageous behaviour would lead NATO to intervene in the war against them in a massive air campaign in the fall of 1995, helping precipitate the imposed peace of Dayton in November of that year. I would find myself involved in this file again, this time as the crisis manager in Ottawa during my next assignment to headquarters.

12

Parallel Lives

A divisive quarrel on morality then broke out.

The NATO ambassadors and their spouses saw too much of
each other. Individually, they made friends among themselves in the normal way, based on personal chemistry and shared
interests. However, individual relationships took second place to
the tyranny of the group. Almost every day, the sixteen heads of
mission met formally for protracted debates in the council
chamber. Each Tuesday, they met again for a lengthy working
lunch to review matters too sensitive to be raised in an official
setting. Every week, an ambassador would host a dinner where
the majority of the guests would be fellow ambassadors and their
spouses. The spouses maintained similar incestuous contacts.

On the rare occasion when a diplomat not from NATO issued
an invitation, Marie-Jeanne and I were certain to meet a bevy of
NATO ambassadors and their spouses at the dinner. We became too
familiar with each other's jokes. We ran out of positive things to
say. We became involved in each other's personal lives.

A divisive quarrel on morality then broke out. The marriage
of an ambassador collapsed, and his wife departed and someone
else moved in. One group of ambassadors and their spouses
declared that this was scandalous. Never would they speak to the
sinful ambassador and "his mistress," much less allow them to
darken the doors of their residences. Another group sprang up
to defend the cause of true love, vowing that they would not

speak to those who would not speak to the errant ambassador, nor would they invite them to their homes. Voices were raised. Tears were shed. Every ambassador and his spouse was pressed to take a position. It was like a rerun of the Cold War and its dictum: "Your enemy is my enemy and your friend is my friend." Neutrality was not an option. Marie-Jeanne and I laughed, incurring the hostility of both camps.

Finally, foreign ministers stepped in to call the ambassadors to order. The ambassadors reluctantly fell into line, leaving their spouses to carry on the combat behind the scenes. To preserve our sanity, Marie-Jeanne and I in desperation sought social contacts elsewhere in the military and in the surrounding Belgian community.

Cultivating the Military

It was easy to develop close personal ties with our NATO military partners. They invited us to their homes. They inundated us with invitations to tour military bases, to observe military exercises, to participate in seminars at major NATO commands at Norfolk, Virginia, and Naples, Italy, on maritime matters, to dine with the Supreme Allied Commander at his château at Casteau, and to participate in annual air shows in England and France. Transport and most other expenses were, of course, paid by the military establishment. Spouses were invited to accompany their husbands on most trips, though they did not participate in the classified briefing sessions.

There was no hidden agenda. The military were interested in cultivating the members of the North Atlantic Council and their spouses both to get to know the local civilian heads of the alliance better and to obtain the benefit of our views on a range of strategic issues. Hence they exposed to us their latest thinking on the strategic environment of the future and welcomed our criticisms, however frank. The permanent representatives, for their part, gained insights into the latest in military thinking, saw the most modern military hardware, and observed troops in action. Sometimes, however, hospitality offered with the best of intentions can have painful consequences.

Such was my fate when I accepted an invitation from Canada's military to return to Canada to go fishing and discuss strategy and other weighty military-political matters with a group of senior American and Canadian generals. I was delighted to accept the offer, even if on this occasion spouses were not included. From my stint as director-general of security and intelligence and from my time as high commissioner to Cyprus accredited from Tel Aviv, when I often visited Canada's peacekeepers, I knew and respected Canada's military. However, I might have been better off if relations had been a little less friendly. Perhaps then the military would not have taken me to their salmon-fishing camp in Labrador for the bit of fishing that nearly killed me.

The camp had been operated by the Canadian Forces for over a generation to host NATO defence ministers, senior American military officers, and Ottawa mandarins. Off to a poor start, we were grounded for two days by heavy rain in Goose Bay, Labrador, and arrived late at our destination. The guides, anxious to make up for lost time, handed fly rods to me and another victim and immediately took us to the river. It was already evening, but the salmon, they assured us, were more active at that time of day. A guide led the two of us on foot to the top of magnificent rapids that tumbled down in a torrent of white water over rocks and the debris of fallen trees and logs for more than a kilometre. Settling us in a boat equipped with a powerful outboard motor, he propelled it through the heavy current and tied it to a buoy located fifteen metres from shore. Turning off the motor, he gave us a brief lesson on casting with a fly rod and told us to start fishing. We cast. We cast again. And again. There were no bites other than from blackflies and mosquitos. After sitting for an hour in the massive flow of silent water gliding by before beginning its downward plunge, the guide grunted that we should try somewhere else. He started the motor, untied the boat, and the fun began.

The motor died and the current swept the boat towards the head of the falls. Panic in his eyes, the guide screamed for someone to throw out the anchor. That was poor advice. As the boat lurched into the rapids, my colleague in the rear fumbled around trying to execute the order. I scrambled to the back, pushed him aside, picked up the anchor and heaved it into the foaming water. A bad move. The anchor bit the bottom, the boat came to a sudden stop, the stern disappeared under the onrushing flow, and we were swept out of the boat into the torrent. The guide washed up on the shore but his guests had no such luck.

The next few minutes were an eternity. The water at this spot was not deep but the current was strong. I tried to stand, but as my feet hit bottom the surging water pitched me head over heels down the slope, slamming me into submerged rocks and logs, and dropping me into deep pools. My life jacket saved me, pulling me back to the surface time and again before the torrent would grab me once more to restart the wild ride. Everything happened in slow motion. I could see the darkening evening sky, hear the cries of the guides as they shouted the alarm, and feel all-consuming pain each time I hit a rock or submerged log. Exiting one whirlpool, my eyes met those of a fisherman standing on a small island. His gaze was completely blank, as if it were normal to see someone being swept down rapids in Labrador. When I last saw him, he was lifting his rod to begin another cast. Nothing was going to keep him from his fishing.

About eight hundred metres from the start, I clawed my way onto a large boulder ten metres from shore. My colleague, I saw, was clinging to a tiny rock a short distance upriver from me, his chin but not his nose under the water, looking like a lost crocodile awaiting his prey. A guide on the shore called out for us to let go and allow ourselves to be carried to the calm waters below the rapids where we could easily be fished out. I yelled back to tell him what I thought of his proposal, using choice phrases not employed since my youth in Muskoka. Meanwhile, the current tore my companion's hands from his rock. As he went by, I grabbed him and hauled him up beside me. After the guides finally dragged us to shore with ropes, I could hardly walk, so badly bruised were my legs and torso. My colleague was in no better shape.

We had, however, landed on the shore opposite to our camp. The nervous guides hustled us to a boat, anxious to get us back to treat our wounds and to provide dry and warm clothing to prevent hypothermia. In their anxiety, they promptly ran their craft onto a sandbar in the middle of the river where it stuck, obliging us to ease our aching bodies back into the freezing water to lighten the load to free the boat. When we eventually reached the camp, there was complete confusion. Never before had they almost drowned their guests. Our clothes were stripped off, blankets piled on, and rum poured down our throats. My colleague and I played down the incident. We did not want to spoil the atmosphere. Besides, we were with the military and felt that we had to conform to what we imagined to be a macho code.

The rest of the week was torture. My legs were racked with the pain of cramps and I could not bend my knees. Nevertheless, every morning at four I felt obliged to join the others to return to the river, usually in the rain and always in clouds of mosquitos. We would then fish non-stop for fourteen hours with short breaks for breakfast and lunch. No one caught a fish. It was an exercise in masochism, but everyone said they were having fun. In the evenings, we were obliged to drink Newfoundland's national drink, a foul-tasting concoction made from a mixture of raw alcohol and the residue of rum barrels and called, with good reason, screech.

I returned to Brussels black and blue, limping, with no salmon, an enormous headache, and determined to think twice before accepting further invitations, however well-intentioned, from Canada's military.

But then it was not only Canada's military that offered "free hospitality" that could be hazardous. The Norwegian armed forces invited me for a flight in an air-force plane to Narvik above the Arctic circle to observe a monster military exercise. Guests were offered the opportunity to watch British and Dutch marines conduct a mock amphibious assault, followed by transport to an American aircraft carrier for lunch and a briefing.

I accepted, assuming the trip would be similar to the one I took in my NATO days in the 1970s, when I had accompanied Canadian ambassador Hardy for a naval exercise off the coast of Norfolk, Virginia. At that time, the American hosts had indulged every whim of the ambassadors. Each representative had as liaison officer a white-uniformed American admiral. Transport to the fleet some 110 kilometres offshore was by luxury helicopter. The landing on the deck of the *Lexington*, the flagship of the battle group, was smooth. The meals and briefings were of the highest quality, and the ensuing firepower display, in which guns were shot off, missiles launched, aircraft catapulted into the sky, and air-to-air and air-to-ground missiles fired, was a magnificent show.

I should have known better. The Norwegians, not being a superpower, had neither the resources nor the inclination to mollycoddle their ambassadorial guests. After a short night at Narvik, they roused us at three in the morning for a four-hour bus ride northwards to the exercise site, where we huddled in near-freezing temperatures at dawn to watch the marines come ashore in the rain – which was about as exciting as it sounds. The journey to the carrier was not by comfortable helicopter and there were no pleasant admirals serving as liaison officers. Instead, we were outfitted with life jackets, crammed like sardines in a can into a small, windowless fixed-wing utility aircraft – short, squat, and beetle-like – and briefed on how to try to escape in the event it ditched in the sea. The bad news, the briefer told us with a sadistic smile, was that it was not unheard-of for this type of aircraft to flip off the carrier flight deck and end up in the water upside down. The good news was that the aircraft should float. All we had to do was to free ourselves from our safety belts – not always easy, he admitted, since we would be hanging upside down in a pitching sea – and follow the simple instructions to the exit.

The pilot then took off into the storm and steered his aircraft, buffeted by the high winds, to a rough landing on the flight deck, where it was caught by tailhook before it could plunge off the end into the ocean. On departure, we faced backwards in our seats as a catapult flung our little aircraft into the sky as from a child's slingshot. Our bodies strained against the safety straps and our heads were almost torn from our torsos by gravitational force. My children, fans of midway rides, would have enjoyed this experience; I did not.

Our next adventure was not so bad – the mere failure of landing gear and the subsequent emergency landing of our aircraft. Marie-Jeanne and I had joined the other ambassadors and their spouses for a trip to the United States, courtesy of the American and the German military. The Luftwaffe provided the transport in one of its VIP aircraft. We were barely aloft when an embarrassed pilot informed the passengers that there was a problem with the landing gear. After asking for our indulgence, he flew to a major German air-force base for an emergency landing. After dumping fuel, he then brought the aircraft safely down in a mighty shower of sparks to be welcomed by a dozen fire trucks.

We paid little attention. After all, the same problem, we assumed, could happen on any civilian flight. The next incident was much more serious and I began to wonder about the quality of maintenance on military aircraft. General George Joulwan, Supreme Allied Commander Europe, was our host when I accompanied my NATO colleagues on a trip to Italy to visit a NATO air base. Our local means of transport was a British helicopter. We piled in, General Joulwan and six ambassadors, and we were off over the Italian Alps. Thirty minutes into the flight and three hundred metres up, a red light warning of engine failure started to flash. The engine stopped and the helicopter dropped like a stone. A pilot calmly pushed a button, throwing the rotor blades into the emergency automatic-reverse-rotation mode, breaking the descent. Fortunately, we ploughed into moist, deep, and recently tilled earth in a mountain pasture rather than into the surrounding rocks. No one was hurt, although everyone was shaken up. The general, a much-decorated Vietnam veteran, shrugged it off, saying that he had been in many helicopter crashes in the course of his combat career with no lasting injuries.

I was secretly pleased with these adventures, for I, unlike General Joulwan, had no war stories to tell my children. I would now be able to brag about surviving the hospitality of the Canadian Forces, the Norwegian armed forces, the Luftwaffe, and the Royal Air Force.

Four Years Not in Provence

Determined not to let our official duties and contacts overwhelm us, Marie-Jeanne and I tried to live as normal a life as possible within the Belgian community. Having maintained close contacts with Marie-Jeanne's Brussels family over the years, it was easy to reinsert ourselves into the world we had left in 1977. The two older children spent their high-school years in Brussels and graduated with bilingual international baccalaureate degrees, equipping them for early entry to Canadian universities. Alain, only one year old on arrival in Brussels, was spoiled by Angelita and Florencio, the Filipino couple who had accompanied us from the Canadian embassy in Israel, where they had been cook and butler, to fulfill similar roles at our NATO residence.

Freed from the myriad hospitality duties incumbent on the spouse of an in-country ambassador of a bilateral mission, Marie-Jeanne indulged a dream to take a rigorous full-time two-year course at a Belgian institution of higher learning to become a licensed Belgian antique dealer – not to open a business but to obtain a thorough education on European furniture, paintings, silver, crystal, and lace. In a fit of enthusiasm, we then decided to purchase a period house to renovate on the weekends and holidays, using the expertise Marie-Jeanne had acquired to furnish it. Ancient farmhouses close to Brussels, we soon discovered, were prohibitively expensive. We had better luck when we ventured deep into the Belgian Ardennes.

Driving through the hamlet of Livarchamps, some twelve kilometres from Bastogne of Battle of the Bulge fame, we stumbled on exactly what we wanted. The farmhouse, which combined living quarters, stable, and barn in one mid-eighteenth-century stone structure, was in poor shape, although it had recently been occupied. Rusted sheets of galvanized tin covered holes blown in the roof by German artillery in December 1944. The interior walls and wooden staircase were pockmarked by splinters from artillery shells. The drainpipes were welded Second World War American shell casings, the second-storey floors were rotten, the wiring was antique, the toilet was a noxious hole in one of the stables, and the water supply came from a tap in the ancient diary.

The setting, however, was spectacular. Nestled in a small valley one kilometre from the Luxembourg border, the village was bisected by a picturesque stream, adorned with an eighteenth-century chapel, and surrounded by wheat fields and pine forests. There were wild boar, deer, badgers, and immense numbers of birds. Walking trails, through a profusion of wildflowers, plum trees, gooseberry and raspberry bushes, and apple trees, radiated out in all directions. In the village itself, there were but five households: two families were actively engaged in farming the surrounding fields, a schoolmaster made the daily trip to Bastogne, another neighbour was a retired farmer; and in the last household was an older couple who had inherited the property and were seeking to sell. All the houses were made of stone and all, except the one for sale, were in impeccable shape and displayed great pride of ownership with pots of geraniums hanging from windows.

Rejecting a higher offer from a scrap-metal dealer who wanted to convert the barn and grounds into a junkyard, the owners sold us the property at a bargain price. Every available weekend and holiday thereafter we devoted to restoring the property to its eighteenth-century glory. Dispensing with the services of an architect, Marie-Jeanne drew up the plans and we went to work. Fulfilling a handyman's dream, I purchased hand tools, grinders, power saws, a cement mixer, axes, a sledgehammer, a table saw, a plane, shovels, chisels, a chainsaw, wheelbarrows (one for Marie-Jeanne and one for me) and dozens of other tools. Sand blaster, pneumatic drill, power nailer, and other tools I rented as necessary for short-term jobs.

There were surprises. The original fireplace, two metres high, one metre deep, and one and a half metres wide, used for cooking and heating two hundred years previous, we uncovered in the old kitchen. The barn floors proved to be eighteenth-century oak planking in perfect condition. The beams in the living quarters, we discovered after we scraped off a dozen coats of paint, were of oak so ancient they were a deep chocolate brown. Under the grime of the centuries we found two-hundred-year-old cabinets, doors, and window frames. Less welcome was the discovery that the roof needed to be replaced in its entirety and an exterior wall redone before it collapsed, taking the building down with it.

Restoration became a family enterprise. Laurent and Anne-Pascale helped with the nailing and laying of floors. Alain took rides in the wheelbarrow. My brother-in-law pitched in to help. Angelita and Florencio occasionally lent a hand in their free time.

A nephew from Canada came to assist with the heavy lifting. Taking her turn shovelling sand, aggregate, and cement into the mixer, Marie-Jeanne wheeled the liquid mess to where I worked restoring the ninety-centimetre-thick stone walls. Walkways we constructed from flat pieces of stone, acquired free of charge at a disused local quarry. The stone walls separating two stables we removed to make room for a living room and kitchen, wheeling the stone out of doors to construct a retaining wall fifteen metres long by two metres high. We then dumped rubble behind the walls for fill and obtained the help of a local farmer to cut down scrub trees, pull out stumps, and spread topsoil to make a lawn. Pine beams and planks for the ceiling over our new kitchen and dining room we obtained from a local sawmill. To refinish the interior we used antique staircases, mouldings, doors, and flooring from dealers specializing in the sale of these items recovered from demolished châteaus and churches. Surprising myself, I was able to frame and finish new bedrooms, the bathroom, the kitchen, and the living room. Tackling the exterior, we repaired the stucco and applied heavy water-resistant paint to the walls. Contractors did the specialized work, replacing the roof and installing central heating, Thermopane windows, modern plumbing, and electrical wiring.

To furnish our new acquisition, we haunted country *brocantes* (Belgium's version of garage sales, where local farmers often put antique furniture on the curbside to sell). We then took to visiting the Place du Jeu de Balle, the flea market in old Brussels, where entrepreneurs specializing in estate lots of furniture, books, art, and appliances from houses of the recently deceased came at three in the morning to sell their holdings at wholesale prices to antique dealers. With her newly acquired expertise, Marie-Jeanne knew fake from authentic. Flashlight in hand, she would poke through the trucks as they arrived with their wares to obtain the best bargains.

The building was thus transformed from the ugly duckling of the village to a comfortable country home at minimal cost. Livarchamps became our family retreat – the place to spend Christmas, Easter, and summer holidays. Friends came on weekends, joining us on long walks through the Ardennes forests and for country-style luncheons of local specialties. We invited the villagers and they reciprocated, receiving us in their homes for family meals and helping out with advice and occasionally with their muscles and brains when my renovation skills were not up to the task at hand.

In time, we developed close friendships with the villagers, coming to know them more intimately than any of our diplomatic colleagues. Marie-Jeanne, with her Belgian roots and her residual memory of Walloon, the distinct local language learned from her mother as a child, was quickly accepted. After initially being suspicious of me – *un étranger* – and after overcoming their initial difficulties with my North American French accent, they embraced me as well. After all, *les braves canadiens* had helped free Belgium in both world wars. Our new neighbours were soon sharing with us the local gossip: whose potato field had been ravaged by wild boars; who had shot a deer out of season; who was not being faithful to her husband; whose daughter was soon to be married; and whose son was not doing as well as he should at school.

They then gradually unburdened themselves of angst fifty years old. The heavy fighting in the village in December 1944 was alive in their memories as if it were yesterday. Each in his or her own way described how they had welcomed American troops in September 1944, only to see their liberators driven out in December in the last great German offensive on the Western Front of the war. The village changed hands several times in fighting lasting three weeks. The house we had purchased had been headquarters alternately of the Germans, the Americans, the

Germans, and finally of the Americans. Particularly horrifying was an incident when allied aircraft strafed a German horse-drawn supply column passing through the village, leaving dozens of dead and dying men and animals in their wake. The villagers had to sleep in the fields as artillery exploded around them. Homes had been destroyed and farm animals killed. At the end, trucks piled high with American war dead had passed through the village, pigs feasted on German corpses, and rough justice was meted out to surrendering Germans by the victors.

As a result, the people were passionately pro-American and anxious about their security. Only the Americans, they repeated, could protect them from the Germans, whom they had never forgiven despite the movement for European unity, and from the Russians, for whom fifty years of Cold War had bred in them a visceral fear. Most kept extra stocks of basic provisions in their cellars in case of another war.

Enamoured with the village and our house, Marie-Jeanne and I decided we would eventually retire there. However, after we finished the renovations, the allure of life in a small Belgian village began to fade. What we had loved in Livarchamps was the challenge of restoring a building to its original state, not the pleasure of sitting before our eighteenth-century fireplace, a glass of wine in one hand and a plate of local *charcuterie* in the other, listening to the Belgian rain and reliving the Battle of the Bulge. We were ready to move on when the call came for us to return to Ottawa in March 1994. In 2000, two months before we learned that we were being posted back to Belgium, we sold our dream house. The friends we had made in the village, however, would be friends for life.

13

Changing Skies

They change their sky, not their soul, who run across the sea.
— Horace

My distinguished predecessors at NATO, staring at me from their framed photographs on the walls of the Canadian delegation, were now smiling ironically as I passed them on my way to my final council meeting on March 18, 1994. I had been recalled to Ottawa on short notice to take up other responsibilities. The official dinner parties to bid farewell were over. My colleagues had said polite things in obligatory speeches about my role as Canada's representative to NATO over the previous four years, but they were holding something back. My willingness to question ingrained attitudes towards Russia, Central Europe, Ukraine, and most dramatically American leadership on Bosnia had shaken up the establishment. They were hoping, I think, for a less iconoclastic successor. I would learn the truth when the secretary-general spoke formally to say goodbye before the ambassadors, members of the international staff, and high military representatives.

It could have been worse. Manfred Woerner made his farewell pronouncement: "With the benefit of hindsight, it is fair to say that what . . . appeared to be Jim's unorthodoxy has become a model." However, he added, "he is as unconventional as a diplomat can be without risking unemployment or a lifetime assignment to the North Pole." I think he meant to pay me a compliment, but I am not sure.

Ottawa 1994-1998

My new position, foreign-policy advisor to the prime minister and assistant secretary to the Cabinet for foreign and defence affairs in the Privy Council Office, would be the most senior one I would hold in my public-service career. My betters would promote me to the top ranks of the foreign service and then to a position equivalent to that of deputy minister. I would love my work. But just as it seemed that things could not get any better, my depression would start.

It would, however, be two years before I would begin the downward slide. Meanwhile, I started my new job by abandoning Marie-Jeanne, Anne-Pascale, and Alain in Brussels until the end of the school year. There was nothing unusual in this. It was part of the corporate culture at Foreign Affairs for personnel to leave their families on other continents when operational requirements so demanded. I was actually one of the lucky ones. Informed of my new position shortly after the federal election of October 1993, I was commanded to report for duty by the beginning of January at the latest. The new prime minister, Jean Chrétien, intervened to say I could start whenever I wanted; family, he said, took priority over my new responsibilities. I was thus able to cut the time of separation in half, leaving for Ottawa in mid-March accompanied by Laurent, who was prepared to take his chances in a local school partway through the academic year. We did the best we could as bachelors: he cooked for me on the weekends and I spent the rest of the week cleaning the kitchen. We both rejoiced when the other members of the family joined us at the end of June.

The mood in the nation's capital was grim that spring of 1994. The worst recession in years was deepening and tens of thousands of public servants were being given their walking papers in an effort to cut a massive government deficit. The country's foreign-policy agenda was overloaded and the staff in Foreign Affairs were struggling to cope. Their morale was poor for understandable reasons. Record numbers of political appointees had been para-chuted into choice jobs as heads-of-mission in the late 1980s and early 1990s, closing off opportunities for advancement for the professionals. Their place of work, the Pearson Building, was overcrowded and showing signs of two decades of wear and tear. Salaries had been frozen for years, junior officers were grossly underpaid, promotions were few, and middle-ranking officers were resigning in droves.

Foreign Affairs remained mired in decades-old jurisdictional disputes with other government departments. No one knew who was in charge at the top. Leadership at the political level was exercised by a confusing triumvirate of ministers responsible for general affairs, trade, and aid, backed up by another layer of ministers. And the real power and often the day-to-day management of foreign-policy issues was shifting from the ministers at Foreign Affairs to the prime minister, increasing an already crushing workload for the officers who had to serve the Privy Council Office as well as their own department.

The rank-and-file foreign service officers who joined in the 1980s and 1990s were keeping the ship afloat. Despite aspersions cast their way by people nostalgic for an era that looked better with the passage of time, they were as good as and sometimes better than those who had come before, including my generation. Often more highly educated than their predecessors on entry, they benefited from training at a foreign-policy institute before starting work. Many had seen the world, some were older and more mature, a number (if not enough) were visible minorities, and a group of outstanding women had assumed positions of senior responsibility. Contrary to assertions that they were narrow technocratic specialists lacking humanist attributes, there was more than their fair share of authors, philosophers, and original thinkers in their ranks, including Émile Martel for literature, Rob McCrae for philosophy, and Jill Sinclair for outlawing anti-personnel land mines.

I already knew dozens of these excellent colleagues and would extend my circle of contacts even more in the coming years. Some of the issues, for instance those concerning human-security initiatives such as the creation of the International Criminal Court and the banning of child soldiers taken by Foreign Minister Lloyd Axworthy, were ones that would only rarely call for the participation of my team in the Privy Council Office. Others that demanded close attention by the prime minister I was familiar with from previous postings: conflict in the former Yugoslavia, enlargement of NATO, the peace process in the Middle East, political and economic change in Latin America, the evolving role of the United Nations, and relations with many of the countries where I had served over the years.

However, many subjects on the common agenda of the prime minister and his foreign minister would be completely new. The campaign to ban anti-personnel land mines, which would take up so much of the prime minister's time, especially in the critical last six months before the treaty was signed, was only the most visible of the topics on the new foreign-policy agenda. Another one, of greater intrinsic importance since it was central to the economic health of the country, was the prime minister's unprecedented crusade to pull Canada out of recession by export-led growth through free-trade initiatives and Team Canada trade missions. Other new issues included contending with modern globalization, with its emphasis on the pursuit of wealth in a digital world, with the mistaken assumption that the security of Canada and its allies would never again be threatened as it was during the Cold War, with the rise in importance of the Asia-Pacific and Latin American regions, with humanitarian crises in the failed states of Africa, with confrontation over fish with Spain, with reform of the international finance institutions, with global warming and the Kyoto Accord, and with the emergence of the anti-globalization movement.

Much was accomplished in these years, which corresponded to the first half of Prime Minister Chrétien's time in office. By the summer of 1998, the recession was a thing of the past, banished in large measure by a spectacular growth in Canada's exports (aided by a weak dollar as much as by trade promotion). Relations between 24 Sussex Drive and the White House were better balanced than they had been for a generation and were marked by mutual respect between President Clinton and the prime minister; it did not hurt that Anthony Lake, the president's national security advisor, and I had become friends. Canada had made a name for itself by insisting that the G7 nations address the issue of reforming the international financial institutions at the 1995 Halifax summit, even if the organizations proved resistant to change. We had saved the turbot fishery by staring down the Spanish navy in March and April 1995 in a high-risk operation unprecedented outside of wartime in Canada's history. With the vigorous efforts of Canadian diplomacy, NATO relented and accepted Central European states as members at its summit of July 1997. And of course, there was the anti-personnel land mines treaty of December of the same year.

These successes, however, masked an erosion of Canada's place in the world that had been in progress for years, largely outside the control of whatever government was in power. Economically, Canada's relative position was falling as countries with larger populations, such as Mexico, Brazil, and India, caught up. Politically, crucial fundamentals of our foreign policy that had conveyed prestige and support for our sovereignty in the Cold War era were also changing. Old-fashioned peacekeeping, at which Canada had excelled for more than a generation, was being discredited and buried in the charnel house of Bosnia. Our traditional alliances were shifting. Canada was drifting economically and militarily away from the new Europe. We would seek new partnerships in Latin America and Asia and attempt to maintain our independence as our country was drawn even more closely into the economic orbit of the United States. Our international influence and economic prosperity would henceforth be a function of our special relationship with Washington – for good or ill.

The Onset of Illness and South Africa

I first became aware that something was wrong in late November 1995. Thinking that it was a simple stomach upset, I paid a visit to our family doctor seeking a quick fix. Asked to describe my work schedule, I proudly related all the "important" things that I had been doing recently, saying that I kept up a similar pace year-round. The doctor ordered an extensive series of tests that indicated that I had no physical problems. "But your body," he told me, "is trying to tell you to change your job."

This was advice I did not want to hear. I loved what I was doing, embracing stress, working twelve hours daily from Monday to Friday, spending the weekends on the telephone, and regularly forgoing statutory holidays and annual vacations. By the spring of 1998, however, I had become so ill that carrying on was no longer an option. I asked to return to Foreign Affairs. The prime minister respected my choice and wished me godspeed.

In August 1998, I left with Marie-Jeanne, eight-year-old Alain, and Stella, our lovable mutt from the Gatineau Hills of Quebec, to take up a posting as high commissioner to South Africa with accreditation to Namibia, Mauritius, and Swaziland. Anne-Pascale and Laurent had by then left home to pursue their studies in science and law respectively at universities in Ontario and Saskatchewan. We picked South Africa because Marie-Jeanne wanted to return to the continent of her birth and I was interested in the country of Nelson Mandela. The posting, we thought, would last four years, after which we would return to Canada and I would retire. We would, in fact, remain abroad four years but would serve in three posts on three separate continents, not getting to know any one in the depth they deserved.

As if by magic, the debilitating psychosomatic pain stopped on our flight to South Africa. I was elated. Life was once again worth living. Once settled in Pretoria, my professional instincts were aroused by a country with a rich white society living side by side with an impoverished black one, with millions of uneducated and unemployed black youth, with levels of crime that would put a Colombia to shame, with a staggering proportion of its population infected with HIV/AIDS, and with a people nevertheless optimistic about the future. Marie-Jeanne rediscovered immense daytime skies, starlit heavens, fierce thunderstorms, red earth, eucalyptus and acacia trees, birds with gorgeous plumage, and the flowers of her youth. Alain loved his school, made many friends, and bonded with the household staff. We did things as a family for the first time in years, visiting the game parks in South Africa, exploring the cold deserts of Namibia, and swimming in the Indian Ocean off Mauritius.

My depression, however, was lurking under the surface, revealing itself in terrifying nightmares that left me shaken every morning. I sought escape by immersing myself in the task of managing a multi-purpose mission with trade, immigration, consular, and aid functions, as well as general political relations. The ties between Canada and South Africa, I quickly found, were more emotional than substantial. Canada's role in the anti-apartheid struggle was genuinely appreciated by the South Africans. However, that fight had been over for years when I arrived and South Africa's main focus of commercial and political interest was in the neighbouring African states, Europe, and the United States. Canada, minister after minister frankly told me, was of significance only as a major source of development aid. And Canadians, I discovered, had exaggerated expectations that their support for Nelson Mandela and the African National Congress for all those years would translate into a flood of contracts from a grateful nation. In fact, we ruefully learned that those countries that had kept open their trade offices during the dark days of apartheid, when Canada had closed down its operations, and those companies that had continued doing business in South Africa when Canadian firms had pulled out, now garnered the lion's share of the available business.

Within these limits, however, there was much for me to do. I returned to an earlier love of my career, political and economic reporting, contributing to the work of the section head who was keeping Ottawa informed on the last months of the Mandela presidency. I worked closely with the commercial counsellor in lobbying senior officials and ministers in our fight for contracts for Canadian companies. I paid homage to my time in Bangladesh, when aid work helped give meaning to my life, by participating in our program of development assistance, visiting projects in Soweto and remote, desperately poor former home-lands. I pursued my long-time passion to learn as much as I could about local aboriginal peoples by exploring the living conditions, culture, and spirituality of the Bushmen or San of the Kalahari.

It was an interest that was shared only by a few anthropolo-gists, linguists, and art historians. The South Africans had other, more pressing priorities. When I mentioned my own aboriginal roots, usually in response to a polite enquiry on my family's origins, my interlocutors, white or black, would invariably laugh. "You mean there still are Red Indians around. I thought the cowboys killed them all off." Negative stereotypes about Canada's first peoples were as strong in South Africa as they were in down-town Toronto.

When I asked about their own aboriginal people, popularized in the famous 1980 movie *The Gods Must Be Crazy*, South Africans would usually become defensive.

"What is so special about them? There are only five or six thousand in shantytowns close to Namibia and Botswana where another one hundred thousand eke out besotted miserable lives. They deserve their fate. After all, they did serve as trackers for the South African army during the anti-apartheid struggle. They should feel lucky that we treat them so well, setting up a special government body to look after their interests, and even entertaining land-claim requests."

Marie-Jeanne and I decided to see for ourselves. A Canadian linguist who had made friends with an extended San family living close to a lodge specializing in ecological tourism accompanied us up to the high dry plateau south of the Namibian border. Our San hosts received us courteously, telling us that they spent half of the year at this spot, part of their ancient homeland, hunting for food and earning petty cash by making cheap souvenirs and selling them to tourists from the nearby lodge. The other half they spent in a settlement with two or three thousand other Bushmen. They recounted this as we sat drinking coffee.

The scene changed dramatically at the sound of an approaching bus. Our hosts hurriedly set aside their cups and stripped off all their clothes. "We look more authentic this way," one explained.

Sixty earnest German tourists were soon the unwitting participants in a very profitable charade. Grateful for a privileged look at the lives of the famous Bushmen, they happily took photographs. Our hosts studiously applied themselves to the making of bows and arrows, and carefully painted versions of traditional Bushman art on pieces of rock, all the while carrying out a busy commerce with the tourists. Twenty minutes later, the contented visitors were gone, off to continue their ecological experience by sampling gazelle and lion meat at a barbecue back at the lodge, and thrilled at having acquired Bushman artifacts that would eventually grace garage sales back home in Bonn or Bremen.

Our smiling hosts put their clothes back on and joined us, coffee cups in hand, to continue our visit.

Marie-Jeanne and I also met Nelson Mandela. He did not remember me, but I had been the silent note-taker at his bilateral meetings with Canada's prime minister at Commonwealth summits in Scotland and New Zealand when the two leaders discussed human rights in Nigeria. He had aged, I thought, as he came forward shakily, on legs damaged during his quarter-century of imprisonment, to receive a letter accrediting me as Canada's high commissioner to his country. There was no flash in the camera of the official photographer recording the scene – the president's eyes had been damaged by prolonged exposure to the glare of the sun off the rock walls of the stone quarry on Robin Island.

Marie-Jeanne and I discussed his struggle against apartheid as a white-gloved Afrikaans butler served tea in the same drawing room used by Mandela's white-supremacist predecessors. The polished British mahogany furniture, German grand piano, Indonesian silverware, and nineteenth-century Dutch paintings of rural South Africa were the artifacts of the minority that lost out in the century-long struggle for power and justice. South Africa's first black president, however, a member of Xhosa royalty and a universal hero, looked as at home in this transplanted European setting as he did in a purely African one.

In response to a question from Marie-Jeanne about conditions in the country of her birth, he graciously outlined what he was doing personally to promote peace in the Congo. He was as mentally alert as ever, quietly correcting an error that I made when trying to impress him by showing off my knowledge of obscure historical facts. I would later accompany him to Canada for an official visit and rush with his wife, Graça Machel, to assist him as he collapsed from exhaustion while delivering a speech in Toronto. He would retire the following year but would continue to make his mark on history as an elder statesman.

I had encountered more than my share of extraordinary individuals in the course of a long foreign-service career. Some were "ordinary" people quietly helping the less fortunate in their communities; others influenced the course of history. Nelson Mandela was in the latter category. Without him, majority rule in South Africa would have been delayed for years and the cost in lives lost would have been horrific. He likewise stood out morally through his lack of bitterness. I wondered if the young tortured Salvadoran woman who met Minister MacGuigan in my office and the priest preaching liberation theology in the high Andes of Peru so many years ago had been able to forgive. Sheikh Mujib of Bangladesh, who was unwilling to lend a hand to the millions of former opponents rotting in huge refugee camps, Fidel Castro of Cuba, who rationalized the human-rights abuses of his own people by saying the situation was worse elsewhere, and Tomás Borge of Nicaragua, who remained imprisoned psychologically after his release from his cell, were lesser leaders and human beings because they had not. Only Václav Havel and Lech Walesa, I thought, deserved to be in the same league as Mandela.

Meanwhile, my depression worsened. My nightmares intensified, intruding into the daylight hours with their messages of hopelessness. Life tasted of ashes. It was as if I were Harry Potter in *The Order of the Phoenix* having the everyday joys of living sucked from my being by the icy breath of an evil Dementor. Medication prescribed by a sympathetic local doctor did not help, at least initially. My nightmares were now in Technicolor rather than black and white, and I stumbled around the office in a daze, upsetting my co-workers. Christmas was especially difficult. Anne-Pascale and Laurent joined Marie-Jeanne, Alain, Stella, and me in Cape Town. They were happy, I think, to flee their strange dad and return to Canada when their holidays were over.

Why, I wondered, did people get depressed? Why was I sliding downwards? I could understand why I had become ill during my last two years with the prime minister: I had become a workaholic and paid the price. But why here in South Africa, where there was a normal workload and no pressure? Were the neurotransmitters of my brain wired to degenerate when I reached a certain age? Had the racism I had faced as a boy somehow damaged my psyche? Was it mid-life crisis, with its corrosive nostalgia for youth and adventures never to be relived? Was it mourning for a career in the fast lane that I no longer wanted but missed just the same? Was it the whiff of oncoming mortality and ensuing eternal oblivion? Intuitively, I knew that all of these reasons were to blame. My beloved grandmother, had she still been alive, would have reflected the attitudes of her generation and told me that I was a hypochondriac and to get a grip. I was, however, simply sick and getting sicker, even if my illness was mental and not physical.

In February 1999, matters came to a head. After a career punctuated by close calls around the world, my luck ran out. A criminal beat me viciously in a hotel-room robbery in Cape Town, tying my hands behind my back, breaking my nose and foot, and almost suffocating me with a gag. A flood of messages of support poured in from colleagues I had worked with over the years expressing their shock and revulsion. Prime Minister Chrétien also called, offering his sympathy and informing me that President Mandela had telephoned to offer his official regrets over what had happened. Mandela did not call me, and I wondered if this genuinely great world leader was actually not more comfortable in dealing with people in the abstract than in person.

I had little time to spare for speculation on the character of great men in history, for I plunged into a deep pit of post-traumatic shock that left me with an overwhelming desire to die. Doggedly, I forced myself to go to the office and carry on with my duties. Like the Ancient Mariner in Coleridge's poem, I recounted my story of confinement, near-death, and depression to my staff again and again until they started to avoid me. With their leader psychologically wounded, their morale plummeted. Other staff members were then victimized by criminals, including a driver who was shot in the leg, a clerk who was robbed at a cash machine, and a commercial officer whose house was emptied of its furniture. Petty rivalries between two of the secretaries then broke out into open quarrelling. The personnel took sides and the atmosphere in the mission became poisonous. Then, just as things could get no worse, I chanced across an anti-depressant medication that worked.

Australia and Recovery

I gradually restored order to the mission, but my heart was no longer in my posting. In April, the government proposed that we leave South Africa to make a new start in Australia and we accepted. At our cottage in Canada that summer, I started to write the memoirs of my boyhood and youth, focusing on life as a half-breed in a small central Ontario community in the immediate post-war years when overt racism was an accepted part of Canadian society. (Those memoirs became *Out of Muskoka*, published by Penumbra Press.) Without at first being conscious of my actions, the therapeutic magic of the pen started to kick in. Writing, as a form of self-discovery, was helping me to recover. And as I pulled myself together, I saw that I had another story to tell, now contained in this book, that of witness or bit-player to many of the seminal events affecting Canada's foreign relations in the latter third of the twentieth century.

In the fall, we departed once again for a southern-hemisphere spring. On first sight, Australia looked to me like South Africa without the criminal violence. Both had been colonized by the British, used the left lane of the road for driving, shared a love of rugby and cricket, and both were members of the Commonwealth. They also had huge uninhabited deserts, similar flora in many respects, and poisonous snakes, spiders, crocodiles and wild buffalos in abundance. And for those who care about such things, in both countries bathtub water ran clock-wise rather than counter-clockwise, as was the case in Canada. But here the similarities stopped. South Africa was a racially and socially unequal country; Australia was egalitarian. South Africa was the land of Mandela; Australia was the homeland of leaders who prided themselves in being mates to everyone. In South Africa, barefoot vendors and shantytowns were the norm for the great mass of the people; in Australia there were modern shopping malls and no poverty to speak of. South Africa was a defiant new Third World democracy demanding that the world take notice; Australia was a laid-back member of the First World.

Australia we loved on first sight and our affection for it grew with time. It was probably the country where Marie-Jeanne and I were the most comfortable. The people were friendly and unpretentious. The weather could not have been better, the coffee was superb, and the wines were a pleasant surprise. The place had an air of familiarity about it that dispelled any hint of culture shock. Like Canada, the country was a constitutional democracy, the land mass enormous, and the population sparse and concentrated in urban areas. Canada and Australia were true cousins who, for the most part, got along well together. They did not let distance stand in the way of people-to-people contacts: tourists, business people, university students, and backpackers surged back and forth across the distant borders.

The fact that we were in different neighbourhoods limited official contacts, but this was more than made up for by the warmth of the relationship between Canadian and Australian politicians and bureaucrats. In a unique arrangement, the two countries shared diplomatic missions and personnel in Cambodia and Barbados. We took turns carrying each other's diplomatic mail. We passed each other copies of our diplomatic correspondence and shared the most sensitive diplomatic secrets. At any one time, up to a dozen Australian public servants worked in Canadian government departments in Ottawa in exchange programs in which an equal number of Canadians filled their jobs in Canberra. When Australian prime minister John Howard called Jean Chrétien in the summer of 2000 seeking Canadian peacekeepers to assist Australia in East Timor, our prime minister immediately and positively responded. The Australians would have done the same to help us out of a jam, we were sure.

Australia's dark spot was its treatment of aboriginal peoples: its historic record was even more shameful than Canada's. As late as 1992, white Australians regarded their country as *terra nullius* – empty territory – before the arrival of the Europeans. In that year, under the landmark Mabo court decision, Australian Aborigines gained a legal claim to land. In Canada, on the other hand, Native rights were based on the Royal Proclamation of 1763, enshrined in our constitution of 1982, which recognized Indian tribes as nations. Canada had its residential-school tragedy, but in Australia, I discovered, children of mixed parentage had been routinely removed from their families as babies and sent to special schools to be turned into whites, never to see them again. And this practice – so poignantly captured in the Australian film *Rabbit-Proof Fence* – was still going on as late as the 1960s.

Enormous changes for the better had taken place over the years. What I found most unsettling, however, were the attitudes displayed by many Australians to Aborigines. In 1985, I had rejoiced when a change in legislation in Canada permitted my mother to regain the Native status she was stripped of when she married my father, a white man. It was a highlight of my life and a definition of my identity when I was granted recognition at that time as an aboriginal Canadian and was accepted as a member of my mother's First Nation. To return to the attitudes of Canada of the 1940s in Australia was a shock.

Aboriginal Australia will remain for me many things: the sacred art of Uluru; children frolicking in the water and men hunting kangaroos in a remote community in the heart of Northern Territory; Ethel Blondin, minister of state and a Canadian aboriginal leader from the Northwest Territories, discussing aboriginal rights over dinner in Adelaide with Lowita O'Donahue, an Aborigine leader and elder; Australians, hundreds of thousands strong, marching across the Sydney Harbour Bridge, appealing to their government to say it was sorry; and the director of the state museum in Hobart, Tasmania, telling me that she had returned to the community for proper burial at last the skeleton of an Aborigine woman that had been on display for generations.

The European Union and Adieu

"You can stay as high commissioner to Australia until you retire or return to Brussels this fall as ambassador to the European Union. My advice is that you go to Brussels: Marie-Jeanne should be near her Belgian relatives at this time of her life. You know Brussels from your previous postings there, you are one of our senior experts on European affairs, and the adjustment will not be difficult."

Prime Minister Chrétien was speaking to me on the telephone from Damascus, Syria, during an official visit to the Middle East. Marie-Jeanne and I were in Perth, capital of the Australian state of Western Australia, making our introductory visits to the governor. The call was so unexpected that I thought that the prime minister of Australia rather than the prime minister of Canada was on the line when I picked up the telephone.

I told the prime minister that I appreciated his thoughtfulness but that we would stay in Australia. We liked the people, the climate, the geography, and the work. He told me not to make a hasty decision but to discuss the matter with Marie-Jeanne and to call him back.

I had expected Marie-Jeanne to support my decision to stay put. She had developed a close circle of Australian friends and was being trained by the Australian National Gallery to become a volunteer guide. To my surprise, she said we should accept, pointing out that Alain was desperately unhappy at his Australian school, where he was treated as an outsider. Our two older children had excelled at the International School of Brussels a decade earlier; perhaps Alain would fit in better in a school where all the students were foreign, unlike his school in Canberra, where he stood out with his North American accent and lack of knowledge of cricket and Australian Rules football. Added advantages were that he would be able to live in a francophone environment and see his older sister and brother more often.

We thus made our third move in three years, arriving in Brussels in late August after visiting Saigon and New York City en route. In Vietnam, Alain fulfilled the dream of every eleven-year-old by being allowed to fire live ammunition from an AK-47 assault rifle and explore tunnels used by the Viet Cong in the war. In New York City, we toured the city, including the area of the World Trade Center, not imagining that in a little over a year the Twin Towers would be no more.

Brussels was, of course, familiar ground. I had met and married Marie-Jeanne there in the 1970s during my first posting to NATO. Anne-Pascale and Laurent had been born in the Belgian capital. I had served there again in the early 1990s. We had been back often in the interim during the final fatal illness of Marie-Jeanne's stepmother, Odette de Wynter. Odette's absence rendered our return difficult, reopening old wounds for Marie-Jeanne which would take a long time to heal.

We moved into the official residence at 145 Avenue des Dames Blanches in the suburb of Woluwe St. Pierre shortly after our arrival. With fifteen bedrooms and several acres of lawn and forest, the establishment was one of the largest and most elaborate in the inventory of the Canadian government – somewhat different from the Bartleman family home I had known as a child in Muskoka with its outdoor privy, uninsulated walls, and coal-oil lamps. Bought in the mid-1970s for a million dollars, its first official occupant was also one of Canada's greatest diplomats, Marcel Cadieux. At that time, it was thought that Canada's relations with the new Europe were about to blossom; a magnificent

residence was necessary to reflect the importance of the relationship and the quality of Canada's new head of post.

Foreign Minister Allan MacEachen, flinty Cape Breton Scot
that he was, had other ideas. He almost had an apoplectic fit when
he became foreign minister in 1974 and learned how much
Canada's new residence had cost. He gave orders for it to be sold
forthwith. Later, when I was in an administrative position in
Ottawa and sent as a member of the team to sell it, we found a
buyer, but the idea was quietly dropped by senior bureaucrats
since Mr. MacEachen had been shifted to another portfolio.
Further attempts to dispose of the property were mounted over
the years, but to no avail. "Baby Doc" Duvalier, the exiled Haitian
dictator, was even on the point of signing the purchase papers
when discreet pressure from the Belgian government, which did
not want him in Brussels, led Foreign Affairs to back down.

I had been a periodic visitor to Dames Blanches over the years,
even participating in a life-and-death drama in its dining room.
In 1985, I happened to be in Brussels. Jacques Gignac, Canada's
ambassador, and his wife invited me to dinner; Craig MacDonald,
an officer at the Canadian mission, and his wife were included.
Steak was on the menu and the ambassador was explaining a
complex issue while eating. Suddenly he fell quiet, his face
turned white, and he slumped forward. The rest of us sat in
stunned silence. I rose from my seat, crossed to where he was
sitting, and pounded him as hard as I could between the shoulder blades. The ambassador was choking and I had just lodged
the piece of steak even more firmly in the passageway to his lungs.

He was now at the point of death. Mrs. MacDonald took over,
pushing me out of the way before I could thump him again. She
put her arms around him from behind, clasped her hands in a
knot in the Heimlich manoeuvre and drove her clenched fists
into his solar plexus. A piece of steak popped out and landed on
the plate. The ambassador drew a long breath, grasped his knife
and fork in his hands, pushed aside the offending morsel, and cut

himself another slice of meat. He then carried on talking as if nothing had happened.

I was anxious to show this notorious residence to Marie-Jeanne and Alain, but initial impressions did not live up to expectations. A warm, humid, and fetid smell of dog urine overwhelmed us as we entered. The carpets, we discovered, were pockmarked by yellow splotches; even the silk drapes in the dining room were covered with urine up to two feet off the floor. The household staff were careful not to point the finger of blame at anyone, but mentioned that it was apparently a tradition for Canada to send dog-loving ambassadors to this residence. I had a momentary twinge of guilt when I thought back to some residences we had left in a somewhat similar state. Our dogs, however, had merely peed on the carpets, and all concerned pretended the stains were from sloppy guests who had spilled enormous quantities of coffee on the floor. Never had our domestic companions lifted their legs to urinate so high and so effectively, and I was filled with secret admiration for the prowess of the canines who had inhabited Dames Blanches. We warned Stella, our dog, who was showing an inordinate interest in the smells, to draw no conclusions, and quickly had the carpets cleaned and the drapes shortened.

In the summer of 2000, Europe was not at the top of Canada's list of foreign-policy priorities. Relations with the United States, Asia, and Latin America were being accorded greater attention by ministers and officials. The bitter legacy of the 1995 fish dispute with Spain and the European Union, in which Canada used force to get its way for a good cause, lingered on, affecting attitudes on both sides. Few Canadians knew the details of Europe's latest drive for integration and enlargement, and even fewer cared. When Canadians did think about Europe, it was usually in response to television coverage of instability and war in the Balkans or to complaints from spokespersons from Canada's farming sector who said that the Common Agricultural Policy was ruining world export markets. Adding insult to injury, the Europeans refused to allow Canadian wine imports despite the great improvement in the quality of our product in recent years and the annual export of over five hundred million dollars of European wines to Canada.

The Europeans, for their part, had little time to spare for Canada. With the end of the Cold War and the closure of our last NATO bases in 1992, we were no longer important to them in military and security terms. Our peacekeeping contributions to the Balkans were regarded as "nice" and "useful" but not essential; after all, Bangladesh and the Czech Republic provided as many troops as did Canada. Economically, Canada to Europe was just another mid-size industrialized nation, ranking somewhere between Taiwan and Singapore as a trading partner. Canada's image remained that of a supplier of raw materials, even though manufactured goods had long dominated Canadian export sales.

My goal as ambassador was, therefore, to do what I could to reforge the ties between Canada and its European allies that had been so badly neglected by both sides throughout the 1990s. I threw myself into my work with gusto, directing the work of my superb team of twelve officers, cultivating contacts with senior officials of the European Commission, European parliamentarians, the media, and the academic community, and making full use of Dames Blanches to attract influential Europeans to my dining-room table. In a return to the old days when I was at the prime minister's side during summit meetings as his advisor, I joined him twice a year in Ottawa and in various European capitals when he met the leaders of the new Europe to review our common agendas.

I could, however, hear the footsteps of the blind messenger of time stealthily creeping up behind me. The young foreign-service officer with his black hair and thirst for adventure who had joined the old Department of External Affairs at the height of the Cold War was no more. Thirty-five years, six continents, and nine postings later, seven of them as head of his own mission, he had been replaced by a somewhat battered, white-haired dinosaur, all too ready to waste the time of his officers by telling stories of life in years gone by. My young colleagues would rise respectfully from their seats when I entered their offices and give me the same polite attention I had accorded my ambassadors when I was their age – they were curious at meeting someone who had joined Foreign Affairs before most of them were born, who had served on every habitable continent, and who was still around in the new millennium. My diplomatic career had come full circle.

Epilogue

In January 2002, Marie-Jeanne, Alain, and I spent a week in Senegal. It was the first time we had set foot in Africa since our escape from South Africa to Australia following the mugging of 1999. I was anxious to see if I had put those events, irrationally associated with Africa, behind me.

It was a good visit. We saw a different Africa. Senegal may have been one of the world's poorest nations, but its people embodied a rich, confident, coherent fusion of francophone culture and language with indigenous African values. It was also safe – at least in Dakar, where we stayed. I also had the sense that the people had come to terms with the injustices of their colonial past. The South Africans, I realized, were making great strides under Mandela but still had a long way to go.

On a day's outing to Gorée island, a former notorious embarkation point for slaves and now a UNESCO heritage site, we saw Americans with tears in their eyes. Their ancestors had left this region hundreds of years ago in chains and now they, their descendants, were back, trying to come to terms with the harsh reality of their roots. Meanwhile, the locals gossiped, children frolicked in the sea, young men dove for coins tossed by middle-aged European tourists from the docks, hawkers sold crudely carved statuettes of African fertility gods, sunglasses, soft drinks, and colourful shirts, and property developers offered gentrified houses of former slave owners to members of the jet set. Life went on oblivious to the distress of American pilgrims trying to ascribe meaning to a massive historical injustice and to a former

Canadian high commissioner brooding on an obscure incident in a Cape Town hotel room. The time was overdue for me, I now knew, to bury the past and move on.

The telephone was ringing as we entered the house on our return to Brussels. The prime minister wanted me to be Ontario's next lieutenant-governor. With Marie-Jeanne's encouragement, I accepted. After being a diplomat for my country for so many years, I was being given an extraordinary chance to return home to be of service to the people closest to me. The causes I would embrace would include fighting racism, encouraging young aboriginal Canadians to stay in school, and joining the battle against the stigma associated with those suffering from mental illness. What's past, it seems, is really prologue.

OTHER TITLES FROM
DOUGLAS GIBSON BOOKS

PUBLISHED BY McCLELLAND & STEWART LTD.

DISTANCE *by* Jack Hodgins
A phone call to his ailing father's bedside in B.C. sets Sonny Aalto off on a
voyage to Australia and self-discovery. "A terrific read" *London Free Press*
"Without equivocation, the best novel of the year." *Vancouver Sun*
Fiction, 6 × 9, 383 pages, hardcover

BROKEN GROUND: A novel *by* Jack Hodgins
It's 1922 and the shadow of the First World War hangs over a struggling
Soldier's Settlement on Vancouver Island. This powerful novel with its
flashbacks to the trenches is "a richly, deeply human book – a joy to read."
W.J. Keith   *Fiction, 5⅜ × 8⅜, 368 pages, trade paperback*

THE MACKEN CHARM: A novel *by* Jack Hodgins
When the rowdy Mackens gather for a family funeral on Vancouver Island
in the 1950s, the result is "fine, funny, sad and readable, a great yarn, the
kind only an expert storyteller can produce." *Ottawa Citizen*
Fiction, 5⅜ × 8⅜, 320 pages, trade paperback

INNOCENT CITIES: A novel *by* Jack Hodgins
Victorian in time and place, this delightful new novel by the author of *The
Invention of the World* proves once again that "as a writer, Hodgins is unique
among his Canadian contemporaries." *Globe and Mail*
Fiction, 5⅜ × 8⅜, 416 pages, trade paperback

A PASSION FOR NARRATIVE: A Guide for Writing Fiction *by* Jack
Hodgins
"One excellent path from original to marketable manuscript. . . . It would take
a beginning writer years to work her way through all the goodies Hodgins
offers." *Globe and Mail* The Canadian classic guide to writing fiction.
Non-fiction / Writing guide, 5¼ × 8½, 216 pages,
updated with a new Afterword, trade paperback

THE SELECTED STORIES OF MAVIS GALLANT *by* Mavis Gallant
"A volume to hold and to treasure" said the *Globe and Mail* of the 52 mar-
vellous stories selected from Mavis Gallant's life's work. "It should be in
every reader's library."   *Fiction, 6⅛ × 9¼ , 900 pages, trade paperback*

LIVES OF MOTHERS AND DAUGHTERS: Growing Up With Alice Munro
by Sheila Munro
"The book will thrill anybody with a serious interest in Alice Munro."
Edmonton Journal "What Sheila Munro says about her mother's writing could be just as aptly applied to her own book; you trust her every word."
Montreal Gazette
        Biography/Memoir, 6 × 9, 60 snapshots, 240 pages, trade paperback

A PETER GZOWSKI READER *by* Peter Gzowski
The man who affected the reading habits of millions of Canadians gives us the work of a lifetime in this selection of his best writing, much of it never before published in book form.
        Anthology/Essays, 6 × 9, 228 pages, trade paperback

REMEMBERING PETER GZOWSKI
This lively and varied volume of tributes includes pieces from well-known friends like Robert Fulford, Alice Munro, and Shelagh Rogers, and from ordinary people touched by Peter Gzowski's life and work.
        Anthology, 5½ × 8½, 248 pages, including photographs, hardcover

RAVEN'S END: A novel of the Canadian Rockies *by* Ben Gadd
This astonishing book, snapped up by publishers around the world, is like a *Watership Down* set among a flock of ravens managing to survive in the Rockies. "A real classic." Andy Russell
        Fiction, 6 × 9, map, 5 drawings, 336 pages, trade paperback

THE GRIM PIG *by* Charles Gordon
The world of news is laid bare in this "very wicked, subversive book . . . it reveals more than most readers should know about how newspapers – or at least some newspapers – are still created. This is exceedingly clever satire, with a real bite." *Ottawa Citizen*
        Fiction, 6 × 9, 256 pages, trade paperback

AT THE COTTAGE: A Fearless Look at Canada's Summer Obsession *by* Charles Gordon *illustrated by* Graham Pilsworth
This perennial best-selling book of gentle humour is "a delightful reminder of why none of us addicted to cottage life will ever give it up." *Hamilton Spectator*   *Humour, 6 × 9, 224 pages, illustrations, trade paperback*

THE CANADA TRIP *by* Charles Gordon
Charles Gordon and his wife drove from Ottawa to St. John's to Victoria and back. The result is "a very human, warm, funny book" (*Victoria Times Colonist*) that will set you planning your own trip.
        Travel/Humour, 6 × 9, 364 pages, 22 maps, trade paperback

CONFESSIONS OF AN IGLOO DWELLER *by* James Houston
The famous novelist and superb storyteller who brought Inuit art to the outside world recounts his Arctic adventures between 1948 and 1962. "Sheer entertainment, as fascinating as it is charming." *Kirkus Reviews*
Autobiography, 6 × 9, 320 pages, maps, drawings, trade paperback

HIDEAWAY: Life on the Queen Charlotte Islands *by* James Houston
This gentle book is a song of praise to the rainforest magic of Haida Gwaii, its history, its people, and the little green cottage the author loves. "James Houston finally writes about his own backyard." *National Post*
Memoir/Travel, 6 × 9, 272 pages, 40 b&w illustrations, map, trade paperback

WHO HAS SEEN THE WIND *by* W.O. Mitchell
First published in 1947, this wise and funny novel of a boy growing up on the prairie has sold over 750,000 copies in Canada, and established itself as a timeless popular favourite. Complete text edition.
Fiction, 5½ × 8½, 384 pages, trade paperback

HOW I SPENT MY SUMMER HOLIDAYS *by* W.O.Mitchell
A novel that rivals *Who Has Seen the Wind*. "Astonishing . . . Mitchell turns the pastoral myth of prairie boyhood inside out." *Toronto Star*
Fiction, 5½ × 8½, 276 pages, trade paperback

THREE CHEERS FOR ME: The Journals of Bartholomew Bandy, Volume One *by* Donald Jack
The classic comic novel about the First World War where our bumbling hero graduates from the trenches and somehow becomes an air ace. "Funny? Very." *New York Times*
Fiction/Humour, 5½ × 8½, 330 pages, trade paperback

THAT'S ME IN THE MIDDLE: The Journals of Bartholomew Bandy, Volume Two *by* Donald Jack
Canadian air ace Bandy fights at the front and behind the lines in the U.K., gallantly enduring the horrors of English plumbing. "A comical tour-de-force." *Montreal Gazette*
Fiction/Humour, 5½ × 8½, 348 pages, trade paperback

IT'S ME AGAIN: The Journals of Bartholomew Bandy, Volume Three *by* Donald Jack
Bart Bandy's back, landing behind enemy lines in France, causing havoc in Halifax, and trying to roll back the red Russian Revolution in Archangel. "Outrageously funny!" *Hamilton Spectator*
Fiction/Humour, 5½ × 8½, 420 pages, trade paperback

ME BANDY, YOU CISSIE: The Journals of Bartholomew Bandy, Volume Four *by* Donald Jack

It's 1920, and fresh from fighting Bolsheviks in Russia, Bartholomew Bandy is in New York trying to establish an airline, a movie career, and a romance with a tycoon's daughter. "The Bandy Papers deserve to be read in private, where insane giggling can go unnoticed." Jack Granatstein

Fiction/Humour, 5½ × 8½, 304 pages, trade paperback

ME TOO: The Journals of Bartholomew Bandy, Volume Five *by* Donald Jack

"Vote for Bandy" proves to be an irresistible slogan when our hero comes slouching home again, hurrah, and is so desperate for work that he stumbles his way into Parliament. "Read this book at your own peril."

Fiction/Humour, 5½ × 8½, 404 pages, trade paperback

THIS ONE'S ON ME: The Journals of Bartholomew Bandy, Volume Six *by* Donald Jack

It's 1924 and ex-MP Bandy is back in the Old Country, blundering into trouble everywhere, from boarding house bedrooms to No. 10 Downing Street. "One of Canada's finest comic creatures, bashful Bandy." *Toronto Star*

Fiction/Humour, 5½ × 8½, 434 pages, trade paperback

ME SO FAR: The Journals of Bartholomew Bandy, Volume Seven *by* Donald Jack

Bandy goes to India in the 1920s and as commander of the state of Jhamjarh's air force through derring-do foils the evil Russians, saves the British Raj, and becomes Sir Bartholomew.

Fiction/Humour, 5½ × 8½, 380 pages, trade paperback

HITLER VERSUS ME: The Journals of Bartholomew Bandy, Volume Eight *by* Donald Jack

The Second World War is raging so Bandy (complete with toupee) returns to action with the RCAF – in the air, in a number of bedrooms and in a Gestapo cell just before D-Day.

Fiction/Humour, 5½ × 8½, 340 pages, trade paperback

TEN LOST YEARS: Memories of Canadians Who Survived the Depression *by* Barry Broadfoot

Filled with unforgettable true stories, this uplifting classic of oral history, first published in 1973, is "a moving chronicle of human tragedy and moral triumph during the hardest of times." *Time*

Non-fiction, 5⅞ × 9, 442 pages, 24 pages of photographs, trade paperback

PADDLE TO THE AMAZON: The Ultimate 12,000-Mile Canoe Adventure
by Don Starkell *edited by* Charles Wilkins
From Winnipeg to the mouth of the Amazon by canoe! "This real-life adventure book . . . must be ranked among the classics of the literature of survival." *Montreal Gazette* "Fantastic." Bill Mason
Adventure, 6 × 9, 320 pages, maps, photos, trade paperback

PADDLE TO THE ARCTIC *by* Don Starkell
The author of *Paddle to the Amazon* "has produced another remarkable book" *Quill & Quire*. His 5,000-kilometre trek across the Arctic by kayak or dragging a sled is a "fabulous adventure story." *Halifax Daily News*
Adventure, 6 × 9, 320 pages, maps, photos, trade paperback

DISCOVERIES: Early Letters 1938-1975 *by* Robertson Davies
From letters to his young daughters to in-process accounts of his Deptford novels, this revealing book shows a young, ambitious writer slowly achieving fame.
Belles lettres, 6 × 9, 400 pages, facsimile letters, notes, index, hardcover

ACROSS THE BRIDGE: Stories *by* Mavis Gallant
These eleven stories, set mostly in Montreal or in Paris, were described as "Vintage Gallant – urbane, witty, absorbing." *Winnipeg Free Press* "We come away from it both thoughtful and enriched." *Globe and Mail*
Fiction, 6 × 9, 208 pages, trade paperback

JAKE AND THE KID: *by* W.O. Mitchell
W.O.'s most popular characters spring from the pages of this classic, which won the Stephen Leacock Award for Humour.
Fiction, 5½ × 8½, 211 pages, trade paperback

THE BLACK BONSPIEL OF WILLIE MACCRIMMON *by* W.O. Mitchell *illustrated by* Wesley W. Bates
A devil of a good tale about curling – W.O.Mitchell's most successful comic play now appears as a story, fully illustrated, for the first time, and it is "a true Canadian classic." *Western Report*
Fiction, 4⅝ × 7½, 144 pages with 10 wood engravings, hardcover

ROSES ARE DIFFICULT HERE *by* W.O.Mitchell
"Mitchell's newest novel is a classic, capturing the richness of the small town, and delving into moments that really count in the lives of its people . . ." *Windsor Star*
Fiction, 5½ × 8½, 328 pages, trade paperback